Acknowledgment

I AM INDEBTED to several institutions and individuals for help in completing this project, and I apologize in advance to those whom I may have omitted due to limited space or faulty memory. Research leaves from Hofstra University enabled me to advance this work. I received assistance and access to invaluable resources from the staffs at several libraries and special collections departments: the New York Public Library, Library of Congress, State Library of Pennsylvania, Huntington Library, British Library, British Museum, and Bibliothèque Nationale de France, as well as libraries at Hofstra University, Dickinson College, Messiah College, Iona College, Princeton University, and the Catholic University of America. In particular, I am indebted to Charlotte Henneberger for extraordinary and extraordinarily gracious assistance.

Readers of this book's afterword will quickly recognize that I could not have pursued its analysis of the 1972 film *Pope Joan* were it not for the generosity of the movie's screenwriter, John Briley, and assistant producer, Daniel Unger, who answered my inquiries and provided copies of the shooting script.

A portion of chapter 2 was published as the essay "'Ceste Nouvelle Papesse': Elizabeth I and the Specter of Pope Joan," in *Elizabeth I: Always Her Own Free Woman,* ed. Carole Levin, Jo Eldridge Carney, and Debra Barrett-Graves (Aldershot, England: Ashgate, 2003). An earlier version of chapter 5 appeared as "Gender, Disguise, and Usurpation: *The Female Prelate* and the Popish Successor," in *Modern Philology* 98.2 (© 2000 by The University of Chicago. All rights reserved). I am grateful to Ashgate and *Modern Philology* for permission to reproduce that material here.

I have benefited from insightful responses to presentations and papers from audiences at Hofstra University and participants in several Shakespeare Association of America seminars led by Lynn Enterline, Carole Levin, and

Christina Luckyj. Conversations with Lisa Merrill have helped me better understand how scholarly writing finds an audience. Jerome Delamater has graciously answered my queries regarding film studies, and several colleagues have advised me on translation challenges: George Greaney, Sabine Loucif, Ilaria Marchesi, and Gail Schwab. Others—Scott Harshbarger, John Klause, Kevin LaGrandeur, Sabina Sawhney, and Shari Zimmerman—have offered valuable comments on draft chapters; Lee Zimmerman has been especially generous in sharing his talents as a critical thinker and attentive reader, thus enabling me to make the writing in several chapters more clear and forceful. I am also deeply indebted to LeAnn Fields for the confidence she placed in this project.

I am especially grateful to my father, Charles, arguably the most poorly compensated research assistant in America. Finally, I offer loving thanks to Jean for her patient support and to Liam for giving me such good reasons to look at things afresh.

The Afterlife of Pope Joan

Deploying the Popess Legend
in Early Modern England

Craig M. Rustici

The University of Michigan Press
Ann Arbor

2009   2008   2007   2006   4   3   2   1

A CIP catalog record for this book is available from the British Library.

Library of Congress Cataloging-in-Publication Data

Rustici, Craig M., 1964–
The afterlife of Pope Joan : deploying the Popess legend in early
modern England / Craig M. Rustici.
p.   cm.
Includes bibliographical references and index.
ISBN-13: 978-0-472-11544-0 (cloth : alk. paper)
ISBN-10: 0-472-11544-8 (cloth : alk. paper)
1. Joan (Legendary Pope)   2. Church history—Middle Ages, 600–
1500.   3. Women—History—Middle Ages, 500–1500.   4. Popes—
Legends.   5. Catholic Church—England—History.   I. Title.
BX958.F2R87   2006
262'.13—dc22   2005026030

FOR MY FIRST TEACHERS,
CHARLES AND PATRICIA,
AND MY BEST COLLABORATOR,
JEAN.

Contents

Introduction

İɴ ᴛʜᴇ sɪxᴛᴇᴇɴᴛʜ century, worshippers in the vast medieval cathedral in Siena who cast their gaze far above the inlaid floor, higher even than the striped black and white marble columns supporting the Romanesque arches, could view a sculpture that was stunning, if not for its artistry, then for its subject. Among the roughly 170 terra-cotta busts depicting Roman pontiffs that adorned the cathedral's nave, they could have found one representing a woman: Pope Joan.

The Story behind the Statue

According to influential accounts, this woman, born in Germany and originally named Gilberta, fell in love with a young student, probably a monk, and, in order to accompany him on his travels, disguised herself as a man. Together they journeyed to Athens, where her disguise enabled her to study diverse sciences, and she became more learned than all her contemporaries. She continued on to Rome, where she led a virtuous life, teaching the liberal arts and counting great scholars among her students. She earned such widespread admiration that when Pope Leo IV died in 855 she was unanimously chosen to succeed him. For more than two years, she governed the Roman Catholic Church as Pope John VIII, administering the sacraments, ordaining priests, and consecrating churches. Eventually, as the story goes, she succumbed to lust, and seeking out her old lover or finding a new one among the Roman cardinals, she became pregnant. Not realizing that her child's birth was imminent, she set out in a procession from St. Peter's Basilica to the Lateran Palace. Along the way, beset by labor pangs, she collapsed and gave birth in the street. She died either in childbirth or at the hands of a Roman mob enraged over her deception. Due to her scandalous behavior, she is omitted from official lists of Roman pontiffs, and subsequent popes have refused to process past the site where her imposture was revealed.

Is the story true? Probably not. At any rate, for centuries those who have attempted to prove this legend's veracity have confronted a seemingly insurmountable obstacle: a four-hundred-year gap between the time of Joan's alleged pontificate and the earliest written references to it, reports that in several cases express uncertainty about their own factual foundation. Although to this day that obstacle remains, up through the twentieth century it has neither discouraged artists, playwrights, novelists, and filmmakers from retelling and refashioning Joan's story nor prevented a few ardent believers from trying again and again to prove that it is true.

How, then, did the story arise? Over the years, several speculative explanations have been advanced concerning, first, a weak, effeminate pope; second, a Roman "pornocracy"; and third, the ordination of beardless eunuchs. The weak-pope explanation involves Pope John VIII (reigning 872–82). When he accepted the election as patriarch of Constantinople of Photius (ca. 810–ca. 895), a candidate whom an earlier pope had excommunicated and who had written an attack on Roman dogma and ecclesiastical policies, John VIII staved off a decisive schism between the Western and Eastern branches of Christianity but also invited the sexist charge that he had stooped to "womanish" conciliation (Duffy, *Saints* 81–82). Perhaps, some have suggested, the popess legend took shape when such metaphorical charges were mistaken for literal claims about John VIII's sex (Thurston 13–14; Patrides 162–63; Pardoe and Pardoe 54).[1]

Such slippage from the metaphorical to the literal also informs another hypothesis concerning the legend's origins. In the tenth century, a so-called pornocracy, or "government of harlots" (*OED* 12: 136), seemed to rule Rome, as two generations of aristocratic women managed to make or break the careers of several popes, some of whom they reportedly also bedded. The first of these women was Theodora (died ca. 926), who along with her husband, the Roman senator Theophylact (died ca. 920), led the dominant aristocratic faction in Rome and advanced several men to the papacy, including John X (reigning 914–28), her alleged lover, and Sergius III (reigning 904–11), who reportedly fathered a son with her teenaged daughter Marozia (ca. 892–ca. 937). Later, assuming powers that her parents had exercised, Marozia orchestrated the deposing of John X and, after a brief interval, the elevation of her son John XI (reigning 931–36) to the papacy. Perhaps the popess legend arose when Marozia, the lover of one pope, the domineering mother of another, and effective power behind the papal throne, who during her lifetime bore the titles *patricia* (noblewoman) and senatrix, seemed to merit yet another title: popess (Pardoe and Pardoe 54–55; Thurston 14; Boureau, *Myth* 306; Kelly 122).[2]

A third conjecture regarding the legend's origins concerns a rumor, circulating amid renewed hostilities between the Latin and Eastern Churches, that a transvestite woman had governed Eastern Christianity as patriarch of Constantinople. In 1053 the patriarch Michael Cerularius (reigning 1043–54) revived Photius's attack on Roman practices and even took the extraordinarily provocative step of closing all the Latin churches in Constantinople (Duffy, *Saints* 91). Confronting Michael in a letter, Pope Leo IX (reigning 1048–54) complained about several Eastern practices including the ordination of eunuchs and, to underscore the folly of that custom, observed: "God forbid that we wish to believe what public opinion does not hesitate to claim has happened to the Church of Constantinople; namely that in promoting eunuchs indiscriminately against the First Law of the Council of Nicaea, it once raised a woman on to the seat of its pontiff" (qtd. in Pardoe and Pardoe 56).[3] Leo seems to have reasoned that in the Eastern Church, where clerics were forbidden to shave, a beardless woman could pass as a man only if she pretended to be a eunuch. Consequently, the ordination of eunuchs made Eastern Christianity vulnerable to still greater errors. Two late ninth-century Latin histories further detail the story that Leo attributes to "popular opinion."[4] Reportedly, an unnamed late eighth-century patriarch of Constantinople lusted after his niece so intensely that in order to keep her in his household, he disguised her as a eunuch and passed her off as his nephew. After the patriarch died, this "nephew" (also unnamed) was chosen to succeed him, and for nearly a year and a half she presided over the see of Constantinople. Her ecclesiastical career ended when a devil visited a nobleman in his sleep, proudly declared "I will disclose to you what I have done," and then divulged the patriarch's (or rather matriarch's) secret (Thurston 16; Pardoe and Pardoe 57). Notably, in this narrative, as in the popess legend, lust for a clergyman initially motivates the woman's cross-dressing. Further, this report conforms to historical records no better than does the popess legend. No texts by Eastern authors confirm this story, and the documented patriarchs who occupied the see of Constantinople from 715 to 815 all reigned at least twice as long as this female patriarch reportedly did (Thurston 10, 15–17; Patrides 163; Pardoe and Pardoe 56–57). Although unsubstantiated, this rumor might have nonetheless given rise to the popess legend by provoking Eastern Christians to retaliate with a scandalous tale of their own; alternatively, oral transmission eventually might have transferred the female prelate's see from Constantinople to Rome.[5]

Without a ready means of determining how and when the popess legend entered oral culture, assessing the relative plausibility of such speculations remains difficult. Each of these episodes—John VIII's confrontation with Photius, the careers of Theodora and Marozia, and the putative reign of the female patriarch—occurred or are alleged to have occurred hundreds of years before the earliest written references to the popess. These references date from the late thirteenth century, when a cluster of Dominican and Franciscan authors inserted the popess into medieval chronicles. What, we might ask, prompted them to do so at that time? In the following section, I will explore two developments to which those authors might have been responding: first, conflict between their religious orders and the papacy; and, second, medieval women's importunate demands for greater opportunities to participate in religious life. First, however, I will examine these earliest written references to the popess and explore what they suggest about the legend's origins.

The Written Record

The earliest surviving written account of Joan's pontificate, a clear source for two subsequent thirteenth-century accounts, notably announces its own uncertainty. In his *Chronica universalis Mettensis* (ca. 1250), the Dominican Jean de Mailly recounts the career of an unnamed "female pope, who is not set down in the list of . . . bishops of Rome, because she was a woman who disguised herself as a man" and eventually (in 1099) became "by her character and talents" pope. The alliterative Latin phrase "Petre, Pater Patrum, Papisse Prodito Partum" (O Peter, Father of Fathers, betray the childbearing of the woman pope), he adds, marked the popess's grave (qtd. in Pardoe and Pardoe 16–17). Jean, however, implies he is unsure if the story he relates is true, as he opens his narrative with the Latin infinitive "Require," meaning "to be verified" or "to be inquired into" (qtd. in Boureau, *Myth* 107–10).

Soon after, in the *Chronica minor* (ca. 1265), an anonymous Franciscan friar of Erfurt seems to have drawn upon Jean's chronicle.[6] Describing the career of a "pseudopope" who was in fact a cross-dressed woman, this author echoes Jean by reporting the popess's seemingly good character and presenting a nearly identical six-word alliterative phrase concerning the disclosure of her pregnancy.[7] Importantly, like Jean, the Franciscan of Erfurt acknowledges obscurity or uncertainty regarding the foundation and details of his narrative, as he cites simply "the Romans" as his source and notes that the popess's "name and year are unknown" (Pardoe and Pardoe 16–18; Boureau, *Myth* 140).

At about the same time, but writing in a very different genre, the Dominican inquisitor and preacher Etienne de Bourbon composed a popess narrative also rooted in Jean's account. Like Jean, he reports that an unnamed woman, disguised as a man, rose from the rank of curial secretary to cardinal and then (around 1100) to pope. Etienne further echoes Jean as he asserts that she gave birth in public and was then dragged behind a horse "for half a league" and stoned to death. Moreover, according to Etienne, a six-word, alliterative phrase, closely resembling Jean's, marked her grave.[8] Although Etienne vaguely cites "the chronicles" as the source of his brief popess narrative, his debt to Jean is clear, especially since the prologue to the longer text in which that narrative appears, Etienne's *Tractatus de diversis materiis praedicabilibus* (A Treatise Concerning Diverse Materials for Preaching; ca. 1260), acknowledges Jean as a general source (Pardoe and Pardoe 16–17; Boureau, *Myth* 109, 118).

As his text's title suggests, Etienne was writing an expansive treatise on sermon topics rather than an authoritative history. Consequently, his anecdotes recount events that, to modern ears, seem quite improbable but may have functioned as compelling material for medieval homilies. He relates, for example, a story he had heard about "a certain rustic" who irreverently placed a consecrated host in his beehive only to find that within the hive the pious bees had crafted a little church to house the host and had begun singing "in their own manner certain wonderful melodies like hymns" ("Medieval Sermon Stories" 19). Etienne, who uses his account of the popess's election and fall as an exemplum to illustrate the need for the Holy Spirit's gift of Counsel, as well as the "detestable end" to which "such bold audacity leads," seems to have been more concerned with the story's didactic force than with its verifiable, historical accuracy (qtd. in Boureau, *Myth* 118). Indeed, none of the three earliest surviving accounts of the popess grounds its report in a specific, older source (extant or lost) composed closer to the time of Joan's alleged pontificate. In a sense, then, they all originate with Jean's wary infinitive: "to be verified."

Like those three earlier narratives, the most influential thirteenth-century account of the she-pope, which appears in the *Chronicon pontificum et imperatorum* (Chronicle of Popes and Emperors) by the Dominican Martinus Polonus (Martin Strebski of Troppou, died 1278), reveals little about its sources. Deriving prestige and credibility from Martinus's ties to the Roman hierarchy—before being appointed bishop of Gnesen he had served as chaplain and penitentiary (confessor) to several popes—the *Chronicon* account circulated so widely that it soon eclipsed the earlier thirteenth-century popess narratives. In 1312, for example, the Dominican historian Tolomeo

(Bartholomew) of Lucca (ca. 1227–ca. 1327), who was a friend and confessor of Thomas Aquinas, reported: "All whom I surveyed except Martinus, relate that Benedict III was after Leo IV. However, Martinus Polonus counts John Anglicus VIII," the she-pope (qtd. in Pardoe and Pardoe 21–22). As the omission of any reference to Jean de Mailly or Etienne de Bourbon from Tolomeo's remark implies, by the early fourteenth century their accounts of the popess had slipped into obscurity. The *Chronicon* account, however, met a very different fate. Martinus's chronicle proved so popular that the number of extant manuscript copies exceeds 425, more than the number of surviving manuscripts of Bede's widely read *Historia ecclesiastica* and Geoffrey of Monmouth's *Historia regum Britanniae* combined. Moreover, medieval translations into Czech, French, German, Italian, Spanish, and English made Martinus's chronicle available to a relatively wide readership (Embree 2). Not surprisingly, then, details that the *Chronicon* account introduced concerning the popess's name, birthplace, and lover, as well as the ninth-century date of her pontificate, became part of important later Pope Joan narratives by the humanist Giovanni Boccaccio (1313–75), the papal historian Platina (Bartolomeo Sacchi, 1421–81), and the Protestant polemicist John Bale (1495–1563).

Notwithstanding its reach and authority, however, the *Chronicon* narrative, which situates Joan's pontificate immediately after that of Pope Leo IV (reigning 847–55), also discloses its own uncertainty. Here is the full account:

After this Leo, John English born at Mainz [Maguntinus], sat [sedet, meaning "reigned"] two years, seven months, four days and died in Rome. The pontifical see was vacant for one month. This person, it is asserted [ut asseritur], was a woman, who in her youth, dressed in men's clothing, was taken to Athens by a certain lover. She became proficient in divers studies, no one could be found to equal her, so that later at Rome as reader [legens, meaning "lecturer"] of the trivium [grammar, logic, and rhetoric] she had important teachers as pupils and auditors. And as she was held in such great repute in the City [Rome], both with regard to her life and her erudition, she was unanimously elected pope. However, during her pontificate an intimate of hers [suum familiarem] caused her to become pregnant. Not knowing the time of parturition, taken with birth pangs whilst going between the Colosseum and the Church of St. Clement, she gave birth, and died in the same place and it is said [ut dicitur] she was buried there. And because the lord pope always turns aside from that way, it is believed by many [creditur a plerisque] that it is done in detestation of the fact [of the popess's scandalous career and exposure]. She was not put in the catalogue of the holy pontiffs on account of the deformity of the female sex in regard to this circumstance [reigning as pope]. (qtd. in Morris 87, 153)[9]

Passive constructions, which obscure the sources of the *Chronicon* narrative, frame this entry—"it is asserted," "it is believed," "it is said"—and the last of these implies oral transmission. Indeed, the radical disagreement about the date of Joan's pontificate (which began in 1099 or 1100, according to Jean de Mailly and Etienne de Bourbon, but in 854 or 855, according to Martinus Polonus) suggests somewhat vague oral origins. The popess legend, then, derives in large part from written accounts—at least one of which announces its own uncertainty ("to be verified")—composed as many as four hundred years after Joan's alleged career and drawing perhaps upon an earlier oral tradition.[10]

Although Martinus's career as a papal chaplain lent authority to the *Chronicon* narrative, that account might not have been the Dominican's own composition but rather an interpolation added shortly after his death. The account of the popess's career is absent from the earliest versions of Martinus's chronicle and markedly disrupts the structure the Dominican had developed for his text, appearing sometimes only in the margins of a page. On this basis, Rosemary Pardoe and Darroll Pardoe conclude that it was inserted into the *Chronicon* by another, later writer. Although more cautious, Alain Boureau too contends that the *Chronicon* account of the popess might have been an interpolation.[11] If so, it was added to Martinus's text quite early, so that by 1304 other writers were citing him as a source of the popess narrative.[12] Even if it is an interpolation, then, the *Chronicon* account attributed to Martinus remains a thirteenth-century invention.

Since at least the sixteenth century, however, writers have contended that reports of Joan's pontificate appear in texts composed several hundred years before the thirteenth-century Dominican and Franciscan chronicles. To assess these claims, we need to wrestle once again with the problem of interpolation. In the case of Martinus's *Chronicon,* the interval between the manuscript's original composition and the introduction of a Pope Joan interpolation was less than three decades; in other instances, however, that interval seems to have been much longer. The popess appears in a twelfth-century manuscript (Vaticanus latinus 3762) of the *Liber pontificalis,* a collection of papal biographies compiled first in the ninth century and augmented in later editions. However, the entry concerning Pope Joan—which matches the *Chronicon* account word for word—appears in the bottom margin of a page in handwriting that differs from that of the main text. Moreover, in the main text, the account of Pope Leo IV's career continues onto the next page, so that the marginal entry on Joan interrupts rather than follows that on Leo, the pope whose pontificate (according to this entry) immediately preceded hers. Modern scholars have concluded, therefore, that the *Chronicon* account was added to this manuscript in the fourteenth century, probably by the historian Landolfo Colonna (died 1331), who possessed the text at that time (Pardoe and Pardoe 12–14; Boureau, *Myth* 116; Patrides 157–58; Morris 71–72).[13] Whereas twenty-six years after Martinus composed the *Chronicon,* the popess narrative was accepted as part of it, only centuries after the composition of the *Liber pontificalis* did Joan's story appear in it, and then in just one manuscript copy.

The popess also appears in manuscripts of chronicles composed in the eleventh, twelfth, and early thirteenth centuries by the scholars Marianus Scotus (1028–82), Sigebert of Gembloux (ca. 1035–1112), Otto of Freising (ca. 1111–58), Godfrey of Viterbo (ca. 1120–ca. 1196), and Gervase of Tilbury (ca. 1150–ca. 1221). In each case, however, the reference to the popess is absent from the earliest surviving manuscripts of these texts, prompting modern scholars to dismiss these references as later interpolations. Such evidence, though, has not dissuaded the legend's true believers, who, in the sixteenth and seventeenth centuries and even occasionally in the twentieth, have contended that, rather than interpolations, the references to the popess in texts composed before 1250 are rare instances of passages that escaped a later Catholic campaign to expunge all textual traces of Pope Joan. The twentieth-century scholar Joan Morris, for example, has claimed that the absence of the popess from all but one manuscript of Godfrey's *Pantheon* "only shows how carefully any notice regarding Pope Joan was combed out" (83).

Further evidence that casts doubt on such claims and on the authenticity of references to the popess that appear in texts composed before 1250 can be found in several cases in either the text itself, its reception, or other works by the same author. According to Pardoe and Pardoe, Sigebert's discussion of Pope Joan, which begins with the rather cautious formulation "It is rumored" (*Fama est*), most often appears in the margins of the manuscripts that contain it, and "none of the chroniclers who used Sigebert as their source in the ensuing 150 years [after his chronicle's completion in 1111 or 1112] knew anything of the interpolation" (Pardoe and Pardoe 15; Morris 81). The reference to the popess in Otto's *Chronicon* appears only in sixteenth-century editions, which extend that text's catalog of popes to Leo X's accession in 1513; further, that reference consists of a single word, "foemina," following the name not of a ninth-century pope (nor even of an eleventh-century pontiff, as in the accounts by Jean de Mailly and Etienne de Bourton) but rather of the eighth-century John VII (reigning 705–7). Finally, although the clause "Joanna, the female pope is not counted" appears in one manuscript of Godfrey's *Pantheon,* all references to the popess are absent from the *Speculum regum,* another chronicle by Godfrey, which reports that Benedict III rather than Joan succeeded Leo IV (Pardoe and Pardoe 15). The available evidence suggests, then, that no one before Jean de Mailly committed the popess narrative to writing.

Even if the supposed eleventh- or twelfth-century references to the popess were authentic, as a written text the Pope Joan narrative remains principally a thirteenth-century invention. With the exception of the entry in the *Liber pontificalis* (whose appearance in a different hand, in the margin, and before the conclusion of the entry on Joan's supposed predecessor Leo IV strongly indicates that it is an interpolation), the pre-thirteenth-century references—the briefest of which is just one Latin word and the longest just twenty-seven—are far shorter and less elaborate than those attributed to Jean de Mailly, Etienne de Bourbon, or Martinus Polonus. Taken together, the supposed eleventh- or twelfth-century accounts of the popess provide only a bare skeleton for the Pope Joan narrative, reporting that a woman named Johanna or Johannes Anglicus succeeded Pope Leo IV and reigned as pontiff for nearly two and a half years until she became pregnant and gave birth between the Colosseum and the church of St. Clement. None of these accounts, which all assign Joan's pontificate to the ninth or eighth century, seems to have provided a source for Jean de Mailly's or Etienne de Bourbon's reports of an eleventh-century popess. Indeed, scholars have uncovered no earlier source, interpolated or not, for Jean's and Etienne's reports concerning Joan's death at the hands of "Roman justice" and burial half a league from the site of her parturition and beneath an inscribed stone marker, details that Jean therefore seems to have first recorded. Similarly, if we discount the obviously interpolated entry in the *Liber pontificalis,* which matches Martinus's account word for word, none of the eleventh- or twelfth-century chronicles anticipates Martinus's reports concerning Joan's birthplace, travels to Athens, and unequaled academic accomplishment, as well as the detour that subsequent papal processions reportedly followed to avoid the site of her parturition. Even if the thirteenth-century chroniclers did not invent the popess legend in its entirety, even if they inherited a bare skeleton from eleventh- or twelfth-century writers or (more likely) from oral tradition, as Martinus's "dicitur" implies, they apparently did invent many details through which the legend took flesh. As we shall see in the following chapters, early modern writers continued this process of inventing or textually elaborating the she-pope as they imagined Joan variously as a hermaphro-

dite, a sorceress, or the vengeful discarded mistress of an adulterous aristo-
crat.

Scholars have long suspected that the thirteenth-century Dominican and
Franciscan chroniclers who invented or at least greatly elaborated the Pope
Joan legend did so in order to annoy if not attack a papacy that often seemed
hostile to their religious orders. In the 1254 bull *Etsi animarum,* Pope Innocent IV (reigning 1243–54) restricted the liberties that members of these
orders had traditionally enjoyed to preach and hear confessions free from
local bishops' control. Although Innocent soon died, and his successor
Alexander IV (reigning 1254–61) annulled the bull, members of these orders
had nonetheless experienced a papal threat to their liberties. That same year,
masters of the University of Paris appealed to the pope to restrict the privileges that members of these orders enjoyed there (Moorman 126–27). Two
decades later, the Second Council of Lyons (1274) suppressed most mendicant orders (religious communities who rejected even the communal ownership of property and relied for their survival upon the laity's charity),
exempting the Franciscans and Dominicans (as well as the Carmelites and
Augustinians) but perhaps demonstrating to the surviving orders that they
might meet a similar fate. In this climate, Franciscan prophecies based on
the teachings of the Cistercian mystic Joachim of Fiore (ca. 1132–1202) and
predicting the reign of a false "pseudopope" gained popularity. Boureau suggests, therefore, that the Pope Joan legend derived, at least in part, from "a
Dominican and Franciscan construction of a spurious papacy."[14] In particular, he contends that when writing of a female "pseudopope" in his *Chronica
minor,* the Franciscan of Erfurt was expressing "a genuine fear that a
pseudopope might usurp the Holy See" (*Myth* 146–48, 174). Pardoe and Pardoe suspect that similar but more lighthearted motives prompted the chroniclers to fashion and circulate the popess legend "as an amusing way of get-
ting their own back" at popes such as Innocent IV and Boniface VIII
(reigning 1294–1303), who, like Innocent, restricted the rights of Dominicans and Franciscans to preach and hear confessions (Pardoe and Pardoe 59;
Moorman 202). We might infer, then, that by circulating tales of the popess,
the Dominican and Franciscan chroniclers suggested that imperious thirteenth-century popes were successors not only to Peter the Apostle but also
to Joan the She-Pope. They thus cast doubt on papal authority, inviting
readers to infer that since in the past Providence had allowed a woman to
mount St. Peter's Chair, it might now be allowing an unworthy man to
occupy the Holy See. Whatever the chroniclers' initial intentions might have
been, Protestants would later recognize the legend's darker implications and

seize upon it, in their most fiery polemics, to identify Catholic Rome with Antichrist.[15]

Although Pope Joan scholars have carefully attended to conflicts between popes and mendicant orders, they have largely overlooked another controversy that seems to bear upon Joan's entry into literary culture and especially to illuminate the gendering of the "pseudopope." During the thirteenth century, the Church attempted variously to accommodate or contain unprecedented demands for women's participation in the religious life. Originally male orders such as the Premonstratensian canons and Cistercian monks quickly felt overwhelmed by the number of nunneries that sought to affiliate with their foundations. Consequently, by the beginning of the thirteenth century, the General Chapter of Prémontré had already officially resolved to admit no more sisters (Southern 313–14).[16] For their part, the Cistercian monks at first simply ignored the existence of nuns who professed to follow their customs. In a sense, the sisters later returned the favor by disregarding the monks' 1228 prohibition against the founding of any additional Cistercian convents (Southern 317; Bynum 14). The large influx of women into religious institutions evidently encouraged a closer look at the roles women were actually playing within the Church, and male prelates often did not like what they found. While the order had ignored them, Cistercian convents had developed extraordinarily autonomous practices. In 1210 Pope Innocent III noted with dismay that abbesses bestowed blessings, heard their nuns' confessions, and preached from pulpits. Canon lawyers such as Bernard of Parma found it necessary to argue that regardless of past practices women could not teach or preach, handle sacred vessels, or grant absolution (Southern 315; Bynum 15). Women, however, resisted attempts to impose such restrictions. In 1243, for example, when the Cistercian abbess and sisters of Parc-Aux-Dames learned of plans to curb their liberties, they shouted at official visitors and walked out of their chapter house in protest (Southern 317). Thus the popess legend found its way into writing during a period sharply marked by conflicts over the place and power of women within ecclesiastical institutions.

The writing of the she-pope occurred, moreover, just as the restriction or suppression of women's preexisting roles within the medieval Church seems to have encouraged the development of alternative modes of religious life that offered women unprecedented freedom from the Church patriarchy. As Cistercians and Premonstratensians sought to slow the entrance of nuns and canonesses into their orders, a *Frauenbewegung,* or "women's movement," as German medievalists have termed it, took place, and its most intriguing and unprecedented manifestation was the beguines, members of lay sisterhoods devoted to religious life (McGinn 2–3). Under their own direction, these women formed intentional religious communities devoted to service, continence, personal austerity, and worship. Their "convents" or religious houses sought neither patrons nor papal authorization and functioned without irreversible vows, a definite "rule" or disciplinary code like those governing monastic communities, or a complex or hierarchical organization (Southern 321; Bynum 14). This movement spread through northern France, the Low Countries, Switzerland, and the Rhineland so that by 1320 ninety-seven beguine "convents" had been established in Cologne (Bynum 14; Southern 325). Although beguines initially enjoyed the support of some clerics, the movement's radical implications eventually became evident and intolerable. One bishop, Bruno of Olmütz, challenged the beguines' apparent piety as a pretense for evading subjection to priest or husband. Writing to the pope in 1273, he insisted, "I would have them married or thrust into an approved Order" (qtd. in Southern 329). Forty-five years later, the archbishop of Cologne, a center of the beguine movement, would institute just such a policy (Southern 330–31). In a tract presented at the Second Council of Lyons, Gilbert of Tournai accused the beguines of "cultivating novelties in their vernacular exegeses of Scripture" (Lichtmann 67). Later, the 1312 Council of Vienne charged that, "afflicted by a kind of madness," they "discuss the Holy Trinity and the divine essence, and express opinions on matters of faith and sacraments contrary to the catholic faith, deceiving many simple people." Since their relatively undisciplined organization fostered such reckless errors, the council decreed "that their way of life is to be permanently forbidden and altogether excluded from the Church of God" (qtd. in Southern 330). Thirteenth-century clerical writers who imagined the usurping pope as a woman may have been prompted, then, by anxieties regarding women's seemingly unmanageable demands to participate in religious life.[17]

Descent to Harlotry

Consider once again the Sienese bust of Pope Joan. Those who look for the popess in Siena Cathedral today will be disappointed. In 1600, after the French Catholic polemicist Florimond de Raemond (1540–1602) had complained of the bust to Pope Clement VIII (reigning 1592–1605), the Grand Duke of Tuscany ordered local craftsmen to remove it (Morris 138).[18] Those craftsmen reportedly altered the bust to represent Pope Zacharias and restored it to the cathedral's nave, effectively reenacting the cross-dressing—

the layering of one gender upon another—that was said to have enabled Joan's rise to the papacy. In his *Erreur populaire de la papesse Jane* (1587; enlarged in 1588 and 1594), Raemond had argued that no such popess ever existed and had campaigned specifically for the bust's removal (Tinsley, "Pope Joan" 391; Tinsley, *History* 72–73). That campaign and its consequences illustrate much about the early modern response to the Pope Joan legend.

Most important, the outcome of Raemond's campaign to expunge traces of the popess from the Cathedral of Siena points to my study's central claim: during the early modern period the popess legend repeatedly and variously frustrated writers' and artists' attempts to manipulate depictions of Pope Joan for polemical purposes. These frustrated attempts reveal not only the disruptiveness of transvestitism but also the period's conflicted constructions of feminine rule, anatomical sex, witchcraft, and atheism. In the Sienese case, like the authorities who in Michel Foucault's well-known account incited sexual discourse even as they seemed to repress it, those who sought to extirpate the bust set off a multinational discussion of it (Foucault 17–35). Before the publication of Raemond's tract, English Protestants seemed unaware of the Sienese statue. For example, in 1567, as John Jewel (1522–71) sought to demonstrate the legend's veracity, he claimed that a Roman sculpture of a woman in childbirth depicted Pope Joan, but he did not cite the less ambiguous image of the popess in Siena.[19] In contrast, two years after the publication of the 1594 edition of Raemond's *Erreur populaire,* Thomas Bell referred to the bust in *The Survey of Popery* (1596), as did the anonymous translator of a German treatise published in England three years later under the title *Historia de Donne Famose, or The Romaine Iubile* (Bell 192–93; *Historia* C4v). Moreover, in order to eradicate a modest indication of earlier belief in the popess's existence, Raemond and his allies created a compelling and far more damning demonstration of Catholics' willingness to destroy evidence. The "Protestant" in Alexander Cooke's 1610 *Pope Joane: A Dialogue between a Protestant and a Papist* draws just such a conclusion. After the "Papist" of the text's title has cited the bust's removal, his Protestant counterpart asserts: "Florimondus [Raemond] might do well to make request to the present Pope, that those books which write of Pope Joan may be burned; in hope, that the present Pope will as readily burn the books, as Clement the Eighth threw down that image. . . . And so, in time to come, when all evidences are embezzled [fraudulently destroyed or tampered with], and all monuments defaced, and made out of the way, it will be a plain case there was never any Pope Joan" (*OED* 5: 162; Cooke 19–20; Morris 142; Patrides 171).[20] As we shall see, Cooke's Protestant interlocutor, like other Protestant

controversialists, contended that the expurgating of texts, if not the whole-
sale book burnings that he mockingly proposes, was already under way and
in fact accounted for Joan's absence from important chronicles of medieval
Europe written before the thirteenth century. As Cooke's taunts suggest, in
some instances the logical or rhetorical difficulties that beset early modern
writers attempting to manage or exploit the popess legend were evident to
their polemical opponents. Taking my cue from Cooke's critique, in the
subsequent chapters I wish to elaborate the logical or rhetorical difficulties
inherent in such attempts.

The removal of the Sienese bust also suggests that, at least among political and ecclesiastical elites, attitudes toward the popess were shifting: representations of Pope Joan that had been tolerable in 1490 (when, accounting
records confirm, the busts were already adorning the cathedral) were no
longer tolerable in 1600 (Morris 138; Lusini 2: 150). The bust's removal thus
illuminates why here I focus my analysis on texts and images produced in the
sixteenth and seventeenth centuries. Whereas important earlier studies, such
as Alain Boureau's *The Myth of Pope Joan,* have addressed seven centuries of
European writing on the popess, I concentrate on how the legend was retold
and deployed during the two centuries in which its truth and import were
most hotly debated and in which the stakes of that debate were highest.

As we shall see in greater detail in the first chapter, when Catholics began,
somewhat belatedly, to rebut Protestant contentions that Pope Joan's career
not only demonstrated Roman depravity but also invalidated the pope's
claim to have inherited the authority of St. Peter through an unbroken succession from the apostles, they sparked a polemical exchange that produced
between 1548 and 1700 at least forty pamphlets devoted exclusively to the
popess and many more translations, new editions, and reprints. Boureau
points out that English writers contributed substantially to that exchange,
and although Boureau locates that contribution primarily in the sixteenth
century, in England the fourteen-year period between 1675 and 1689 produced five popess publications: a monologic version of Cooke's dialogue,
two new Pope Joan pamphlets, and two editions of a Pope Joan play
(Boureau, *Myth* 250).[21] Further, since a sometimes vocal, recusant Catholic
minority survived in England during the reigns of Protestant monarchs, the
English contribution to that polemical exchange included expressions of
Catholics' disbelief, as well as Protestants' eager embrace of the scandalous
popess narrative. Moreover, the prospect that a Catholic claimant (whether
Mary Tudor; Mary, Queen of Scots; or her great-grandson James Stuart,
later King James II) might accede to the throne troubled English Protestants
for much of these two centuries and consequently intensified interest in a

legend that appeared to demonstrate the corruption of Catholic mores and institutions. As I hope to show, in their number, variety, and passion, early modern English texts addressing the popess represent their period in vivid and telling ways.

The radical shift in attitudes suggested by the removal of the Sienese bust shapes the way that Joan is portrayed in late medieval and early modern texts and images. Before sixteenth-century Protestants such as Bale began denouncing Joan as a "harlot" and servant of Antichrist, and before their Catholic contemporaries dismissed her as a fiction, several fourteenth- and fifteenth-century writers portrayed her far more generously as a redeemable, if misguided, soul or, even more surprisingly, as a saintly woman (Bale, *Pageant* 105v; Morris 153; Pardoe and Pardoe 17). For example, although in his *De mulieribus claris* (1362) Giovanni Boccaccio bluntly condemns the "wicked fraud" Joan perpetrated as a female pontiff, he praises her earlier "virtuous and saintly" conduct as a transvestite scholar in Rome. In contrast to Protestants such as Bale who would later revile Joan as a whore, Boccaccio claims that after the death of her first lover (for whom she adopted her disguise) and before her election to the papacy Joan led a "remarkably virtuous" private life. In Boccaccio's view, accepting the papal tiara marked the turning point from notable virtue to shameful vice, as well as the moment when God "abandoned that unduly audacious woman to herself" (*Concerning* 230–32). In his dialogue *Le Champion des Dames* (1440–42), the French churchman, diplomat, and poet Martin le Franc (1410–61) echoes Boccaccio and in some ways goes further than him. Answering the charges that "Lourt Entendement" (Dull Understanding) levels against Pope Joan, the titular Champion of Ladies (named "Franc Vouloir," meaning perhaps "strong willed" or "good faith") contends that the cleric who seduced a youthful Joan was truly responsible for her cross-dressing. Like Boccaccio, Martin characterizes some of Joan's actions as "saintly" (sainctement):

> Moreover, there can be shown to you
> Many a preface [for the Mass] that [she] dictated,
> Well ordered and in saintly fashion,
> Where in matters of faith she did not hesitate.
> (qtd. in Boureau, *Myth* 156; stanza 502)

Further, Martin, who supported the view that a general council rather than the pope possessed supreme ecclesiastical authority, seized the opportunity to defend Joan's conduct as pope by attacking that of her successors. Turning the scant evidence of her pontificate to his advantage, the Champion asserts that no written records report that Joan abused power like Boniface VIII (reigning 1294–1303), "governed / in simony or heresy" like Nicholas III (reigning 1277–80), or denied the power of councils like Eugenius IV (reigning 1431–47) (S. Taylor 268–69; DuBruck 78; stanzas 504–5). Whereas Boccaccio contends that God was too "merciful to His people" to allow Joan's pontificate to continue very long, Martin suggests that the she-pope did far less harm than several putatively legitimate pontiffs.[22]

Other texts focused on Joan's repentance and redemption. For example, *Ein schön Spiel von Frau Jutten* (*The Play of Lady Jutta*, 1480–85), a drama by the Thuringian priest and imperial notary Dietrich Schernberg, offers a sympathetic portrait of Joan (Jutta) the sinner, presenting her initially as the victim of a demonic conspiracy and ultimately as the recipient of heavenly mercy. The play opens with a conference in hell concerning how to tempt Jutta into acting upon her sinful desire to disguise herself as a man and travel to the University of Paris with "a learned scribe" (ll. 68–84). The devils sent to "secretly ensnare her" employ brazen lies, swearing that she "shall never be betrayed / either now or at any time," that they would "hate to mislead" her and would never advise "anything that would bring . . . disgrace" upon her (ll. 92, 132, 135, 159–60). Whereas Boccaccio asserts that Joan's imposture was disclosed because she "lacked the astuteness to hide" her pregnancy and, "being closer to the time of birth than she thought," set out on a sacred procession (*Concerning* 232), Schernberg attributes her exposure to direct demonic intervention. When a senator implores the popess to exorcise the spirit possessing his son, Jutta is astute enough to fear the demon. Consequently, she first dispatches her cardinals, claiming, "I am not yet proficient at this" (l. 714). After the defiant demon warns the popess that "I will stay in here / until you yourself come forward" (ll. 734–35), Jutta exorcises the spirit herself. In retaliation, the demon reveals Jutta's pregnancy to all those assembled in the hall, declaring, "That's what she gets for expelling me, / otherwise I would have left her in peace" (ll. 767–68). We might imagine that Jutta felt compelled to perform the exorcism because refusing to act might have aroused suspicions. Even so, as Schernberg dramatizes it, the popess's exposure results not from stupidity or recklessness but rather from Jutta's successful performance of a pastoral function and relieving of a distressed soul. Drawing perhaps upon the Swiss priest and canon lawyer Felix Hemmerli's (or Hemmerlin's) claim that "for the remission of her sins" Joan chose to give birth during her ill-fated procession, Schernberg suggests that Jutta participates in her redemption (Pardoe and Pardoe 28).[23] When the angel Gabriel announces Jutta's impending death and punishment, he offers her a choice:

Do you now wish to perish
And be subjected to hell's eternal pain
(this is in your power to decide)
or would you rather be covered
with the temporal disgrace of the world
in your heavy fetters? (ll. 885–90)

Through his parenthetical clause, Gabriel insists that she has the power to choose redemption. Jutta, who had originally been seduced by the prospect of "great glory," "renown," and "honor" free from "any shame," abandons the ambitions that prompted her cross-dressing and opts for "worldly disgrace" (ll. 142, 145, 146, 235, 903). For Schernberg, then, the popess's parturition and exposure suggest at once both her fall and humiliation and her repentance and promised redemption. In the play's closing moments the audience sees that promise fulfilled, as Christ addresses Jutta as "my beloved daughter," welcomes her into his "heavenly kingdom," and promises that she "shall abide with me in eternal bliss" (ll. 1689, 1691, 1702).

Other fourteenth- and fifteenth-century writers addressed what might have awaited Joan after her deposition, sometimes imagining a remarkable rehabilitation for her soul and reputation. Admittedly, the poet and Carmelite monk Baptista Mantuanus (1447–1516) envisioned Joan hanging from a gibbet in hell. A 1375 guidebook to Rome, however, set a different tone by reporting that the popess's body was interred "among the virtuous" at St. Peter's Basilica (Pardoe and Pardoe 27–28; R. W. 14). A fourteenth-century page inserted into a manuscript of Martinus Polonus's *Chronicon* proposes an even more triumphant denouement in which Joan survives for many years after her deposition, performing penance and watching her son rise to the see of Ostia. After her death, Joan's son inters her remains in the cathedral there. This account closes with the ultimate endorsement of Joan's character, as posthumous miracles attest to her merit: "Cuius meritis Deus usque in hodier[n]um diem plurima operatur miracula" (On account of whose merits God performs very many miracles up to this present day) (qtd. in Morris 87–88, 155; Pardoe and Pardoe 27). Here, the woman whose "rash presumptuousness," in Etienne de Bourbon's estimation, led to "so vile an end" seems ready for canonization (Pardoe and Pardoe 17).

As the following chapters demonstrate, the entangling of the popess narrative in Reformation controversies left little room in sixteenth- and seventeenth-century texts for such flattering accounts of Joan's life or afterlife. We can see that entangling with particular clarity by focusing, in the following section, not on the texts themselves but on the images that illustrate those texts. Doing so will reveal how Reformation controversies prompted changes in representations of the popess and how such representations were manipulated for polemical purposes.

Picturing Joan's Fall

In June 1538 the bishop of Worcester, Hugh Latimer (ca. 1485–1555), wrote to the privy councilor Thomas Cromwell (ca. 1485–1540) recommending that "our great Sibyll," along with "her older sister of Walsingham, her younger sister of Ipswich, with their other two sisters of Doncaster and Penrice," should be publicly burned in "a jolly muster" at Smithfield (Duffy, *Stripping* 404; Dickinson 65; Warner, *Alone* 295). The sisters to whom Latimer refers were statues of the Virgin Mary that had formerly been venerated by pilgrims in shrines scattered across England but at that time were held at Chelsea in the custody of royal officials who destroyed them later that year. Latimer's diction seems to mock those who conflated such objects with the person they represented and who consequently imagined that such statues could perform miracles and, on rare occasions, move. However, as Michael Camille has noted, the manner of destruction Latimer proposes, incineration at the conventional site of criminal executions and heretic burnings, treats those statues as animate beings rather than as stock and stone (224). Certainly, Latimer's letter suggests the importance attributed to images, particularly those of religious subjects, in the early modern period, whether by Reformers who feared idolatry's hold upon the people or by Catholics who imagined that the Virgin might take vengeance on those who would dare desecrate her statues (Lipsius 8–9). Although Pope Joan was not credited with exciting idolatrous veneration or effecting divinely sanctioned miracles, the Reformation did change her visual representation, as it did the Virgin's: it discouraged portraits of the popess at the height of her powers and instead encouraged images that, far more than their late medieval counterparts, emphasized her downfall and degradation.[24] Moreover, as we shall see, in at least one case, a visual representation of the popess participated in the critique of Catholic Marian devotion that led to Latimer's call for a "jolly muster" at Smithfield.

The illustrations in two widely circulated texts that recount Joan's career figured in early modern debates regarding the veracity of the popess legend and, as we shall see, imply very different consequences of Joan's pregnancy and parturition. While attempting to prove that Joan's legendary pontificate truly occurred, two English tracts, *Historia de Donne Famose, or The Roman*

Iubile (1599) and *Pope Joan: or, An Account Collected Out of the Romish Authors* (1689), devote little attention to the words of Boccaccio's chapter on the popess in *De mulieribus claris* and instead focus on how through "picture and spectacle" several illustrated editions of that text "describeth" the popess "in her Travail" with "Cardinals and Bishoppes, standing by, like Midwiues or Nurses" (*Historia* C3v; R. W. 7).[25] Again attending more to images than to words, these tracts identify a second illustrated text, Hartmann Schedel's 1493 *Liber chronicarum* (often cited as the *Nuremberg Chronicle*), that pictures the popess this time as a "woman pontifically crowned" who in place of "her triple Crosier and thrise crossed scepter" holds "an Infant in her armes" (*Historia* D4r; R. W. 15).[26] The illustrations described in these English tracts established two dominant motifs in images of Pope Joan: the popess in childbirth and the popess and child.

   A third, contrasting but common motif presented the popess enthroned. Boureau has examined an instance of this motif that appears on tarot cards commissioned around 1450 in Milan for the Visconti and Sforza families. The popess did eventually become a standard trump card in tarot decks; however, in the late fifteenth and early sixteenth centuries a woodcut in the printed volume *De claris mulieribus* (1497), by the Augustinian friar Jacopo Filippo Foresti of Bergamo, doubtless disseminated the image of the popess enthroned far more widely than did the unique and costly Visconti-Sforza cards, hand painted with extensive use of gold and silver (Moakley 20). As its title (a slight inversion of Boccaccio's) implies, Foresti's text adapts and builds upon Boccaccio's work on famous women. The images that adorn the individual biographical sketches in Foresti's volume seem to represent classes or categories of women rather than individuals: the same woodcut depicting an amazon, for example, illustrates the entries for Semiramis, Penthesilea, and Camilla; another depicting a monarch illustrates entries for Tamyris, Artemisia, Mariam of Jewry, and Joanna of Sicily; yet another depicting a martyr illustrates biographies of Thecla, Eugenia, and Barbara. The depiction of Joan, however, is unique (fig. 1). Gazing to her right, she sits in a chair of state, wearing a cope and the papal triple tiara. Her left hand holds an open book facing outward to the viewer, signifying perhaps the intellectual accomplishment that enabled her rise to the papacy. Her right hand is raised, with the thumb and first two fingers extended and with the remaining two fingers resting on her palm, as in the *benedictio latina,* a conventional gesture of speech and blessing (Barasch 18–19, 35). The image resembles the portrait of a stern, seated, and crowned popess on the Visconti-Sforza tarot card and implies a widespread medieval attitude toward the popess legend, namely, sufficient tolerance or at least ambivalence to allow depictions of

Fig. 1. Pope Joan, engraving from Jacopo Filippo Foresti of Bergamo's *De claris mulieribus* (Ferrera, 1497). By permission of Rare Books Division, Department of Rare Books and Special Collections, Princeton University Library.

Joan at the height of her success. Boureau's comment on the tarot image could also describe the Foresti illustration: "Nothing about her suggests derision or inversion" (*Myth* 171).

Because Boccaccio's *De mulieribus claris* was reproduced repeatedly in manuscript or print during the fifteenth and sixteenth centuries, the illustrations of its chapter on Pope Joan record a change in the legend's reception. Boureau has suggested that the illuminated miniatures of the popess in childbirth that appear in two early fifteenth-century manuscripts (French translations of Boccaccio's *De mulieribus claris* and his closely related *De casibus virorum illustrium*, 1353–74) clearly denounce Joan and thus lack the "ambivalence, grave or joyous," of portraits of the popess enthroned like the image on the Visconti-Sforza tarot card or, one might add, the Foresti illustration (Boureau, *Myth* 208).[27] To be sure, these illuminations depict Joan not at the height of her fortunes but rather at the moment of reversal. Even so, they invest her with far more composure and dignity than do the woodcuts in subsequent, printed editions of *De mulieribus claris.* Indeed, comparing these illuminations to woodcuts in printed editions of Boccaccio's text reveals that the hardening of attitudes that Boureau detects in the illuminations grew more intense over the course of the fifteenth century, a period of heightened religious turmoil concerning, as we shall see, rival pretenders to the papal throne, the debunking of popes' claims to legitimate temporal authority, and the rise of a rebel Hussite church.

The most obvious contrast between the images in manuscript and print editions concerns Joan's posture. In fact, Brigitte Buettner has observed that posture and costuming are the principal elements by which illuminations within the manuscript translation of *De mulieribus claris* (*Des cleres et nobles femmes*) differentiate the heroines, who all seem to have been stenciled from the same "carton" or pattern, so that all of them, both maidens and matrons, appear, for example, with the "still-thick silhouette" that Boureau links to Joan's pregnancy and fall (Buettner 60; Boureau, *Myth* 208). The early fifteenth-century illuminations depict Joan standing, even as her newborn infant emerges from beneath her ecclesiastical robes; she appears unsteady perhaps but not toppled (fig. 2). In contrast, the woodcuts in the editions published in Ulm in 1473 and in Protestant Bern in 1539 (fig. 3) depict Joan supine; her body, like her deception and ecclesiastical career, has collapsed. Joan's somewhat surprising upright posture in the miniatures seems especially significant since, according to Buettner, in the illuminations that illustrate *Des cleres et nobles femmes* recumbent figures are almost "always and only an indication of death" (65). The only exception that Buettner cites, a miniature depicting Nero's would-be assassin Epicharis beaten by torturers and about to strangle herself to end her suffering, seems to depart from the pattern only slightly. Thus, in the iconographic context of the manuscript and in keeping with the account the miniature illustrates, Joan's erect posture suggests that she survives childbirth and unmasking.

Further, as deployed in early sixteenth-century antipapal iconography, a supine posture like the one Joan assumes in the Ulm and Bern woodcuts suggests complete defeat and repudiation by God. Such an image appears, for example, on the title-page woodcut of Walter Lynne's *The Beginning and Endynge of All Popery, or Popishe Kyngedome* (1548, 1588) beneath the text of 2 Thessalonians 2:8–9, which promises that the Lord shall consume and destroy the wicked (fig. 4). That promise seems fulfilled in the woodcut,

Fig. 2. Pope Joan, illumination from Giovanni Boccaccio's *Des cleres et
nobles femmes* (Manuscript 12420, Bibliothèque Nationale de France).
By permission of Bibliothèque Nationale, Paris.

which depicts a pope knocked backward by the power of the Holy Spirit,
represented by a dove and a shaft of light. He appears sprawled across the
back of the richly adorned mule that has collapsed beneath him. As in the
Pope Joan woodcuts, the pontiff has been laid low during an ecclesiastical
procession and in the presence of cardinals and bishops. John N. King has
traced Lynne's imagery back to a 1535 German treatise that Lynne was trans-
lating and to a medieval tradition of personifying pride as a toppled rider, a
motif linked to stories of Paul's fall on the road to Damascus (King, *Tudor*
166–67; Hall 253). Although the Boccaccio illustrations consistently depict a
procession on foot, the tradition of the toppled rider may have prompted
Jean de Mailly and Etieene de Bourbon to report that Joan gave birth while
riding or mounting a horse (Thurston 4; Pardoe and Pardoe 17).

Fig. 3. Pope Joan, engraving from *Ioannis Boccatii de certaldo insigne opvs De claris mulieribus* . . . (Berne, 1539). By permission of Rare Books Division, Department of Rare Books and Special Collections, Princeton University Library.

The woodcuts imply a more profound fall and humiliation than that suggested in the illumination not only through Joan's posture but also through her facial expressions, the arrangement of her hands, and the gestures of the crowd surrounding her. Whereas in the miniatures, Joan's countenance seems surprisingly placid, in the woodcuts, she looks pained: in the later, more refined and detailed Bern illustration a line of dots descends from her right eye as if suggesting tears, and her mouth appears twisted as if in discomfort or despair. In the illuminations her hands too imply composure. In *Des cleres et nobles femmes,* as in the Foresti illustration, her right hand forms the *benedictio latina,* as if dispensing a blessing; evidently, the popess depicted here is so self-possessed that she can continue playing her pontifical role even as the newborn bursts forth from beneath her robes. In contrast, in the Bern woodcut her left hand is clenched in a fist, and the fingers of her right are twisted as if in pain. Even the infant seems more vulnerable in the woodcuts. In the illuminations, he emerges exuberantly from his standing mother, arms extended as if to greet the world or at least to break his fall. In

Fig. 4. Title page from Walter Lynne's *The Beginning and Endynge of All Popery, or Popishe Kyngedome* (London, 1548). By Permission of the British Library, shelfmark C.25.c.16(2).

the Bern woodcut, he lies on his back, mirroring his supine mother, his hands pushing up the hem of her robes as if struggling for air. Near him rests the debris of Joan's fall: a religious image, evidently carried in the procession, lies discarded on the ground. In the illuminations, those who recognize what has happened to Joan mostly seem to react with surprise, often raising their hands, palms outward. On the woodcut's left margin, however, two spectators (one hiding behind a pillar and dressed perhaps as a jester) greet Joan's fall with finger-pointing derision. The popess clearly suffers more indignities in the woodcuts than in the earlier illuminations.

That difference reflects religious developments that took place after the completion of the French manuscripts around 1403 and before the publication of the first print edition of *De mulieribus claris* in 1473, developments that challenged the authority of the pope and the unity of Christendom. The

Council of Basle, initially convened by Pope Martin V, pressed claims of general councils' supremacy over the pope so far that in 1437 Martin's successor, Eugenius IV, ordered its dissolution; the council defied the papal command and retaliated by declaring Eugenius deposed (Duffy, *Saints* 130–31). The "Donation of Constantine," a document in which the emperor Constantine the Great (ca. 288–337) appeared to grant broad temporal as well as spiritual powers to the pope, came under close scrutiny, and in texts composed in 1440 and 1455 the humanist scholar Lorenzo Valla and the bishop of Chichester, Reginald Pecock (Pecocke), exposed the "Donation" as a forgery.[28] Earlier in the century, arguing against papal supremacy, Jan Hus (Huss) (ca. 1369–1415) contended that "the most unlettered layman, or a female, or a heretic and antichrist, may be pope" and, as one such instance, cited "pope Joanna," whose true name, he claimed, was Agnes (Huss 62, 126–27). After Hus's execution for heresy in 1415, adherents of his views established a heretical republic at Tabor in southern Bohemia and repelled several crusading armies sent to extirpate them. Thus, although early in the fifteenth century the Church repaired the Great Schism (1378–1415), which had produced rival popes in Avignon and Rome, it soon faced new crises and divisions.

Boureau has emphasized the novelty and significance of the Hussite revolution, which even before the Reformation produced a heretical church operating in an autonomous territory, and he has argued that Rome's confrontation with that church produced the earliest recorded Catholic assertion that the popess narrative was not credible. The Hussites fashioned a vernacular liturgy; abolished auricular confession; rejected the veneration of saints and images; and denied the existence of purgatory and the need for altars, vestments, sacred vessels, or consecrated church buildings. Some groups even elected their own bishop. Compared to a similar, earlier heretical movement, the thirteenth-century Albigensians, the Hussites controlled more territory, pursued greater political ambitions, and achieved more long-lasting success, so that even after the defeat of the most extreme Hussite faction, the kingdom established by the 1485 Peace of Kutna Hora maintained Hus's principal doctrines. Most importantly for Boureau, the Hussites established both a state and a religion. "In 1411 Jan Hus was still an ordinary heretic," he notes, but "in 1451 he had become the posthumous head of another church, operating in another territory" (Boureau, *Myth* 223, 226; Kaminsky 163–70, 193–98, 212–215, 338, 385).

According to Boureau, this development began to change the way that Catholics thought and wrote about Joan. In 1451, Enea Silvio de Piccolomini (1405–64), bishop of Siena and later Pope Pius II, traveled to Bohemia on an embassy from Frederick, king of Germany and later Holy Roman Emperor. In a letter he reported a debate between himself and leaders of the Hussite republic of Tabor. Arguing against the infallibility of the apostolic see and echoing Hus, the Taborites cited the "manifest error in Agnes" (Hus's "pope Joanna"), the "woman, whom the Roman see honored as a man and placed at the summit of the apostolate." Piccolomini countered their point in two ways. First, as earlier writers had done, he denied the story's significance: "But in that case, there was no error, either of faith or of law, but ignorance of a fact." Second, he questioned its credibility: "And the story is not certain" (neque certa historia est . . . quam Agnetem . . . nescio) (qtd. in Boureau, *Myth* 221–22). For Boureau, this statement, uttered in the face of the Hussite challenge, marked a significant change. Ecclesiastical discourse was, as he puts it, losing "its power to coopt or neutralize." It was no longer enough to argue, as the Dominican St. Antoninus Pierozzi of Florence (1389–1459) had earlier that century, that even if the popess story were true, "it bears no prejudice for salvation, for the Church in those times was not deprived of its head, which is Christ; . . . and the ultimate effects of the sacraments that she [the popess] conferred were not lacking to those who accepted them devoutly from her" (qtd. in Boureau, *Myth* 155). Church loyalists could no longer approach scandalous figures such as the popess as incautiously as the Franciscan Jean Roques had, when, arguing for the necessity of an ecclesiastical hierarchy headed by the pope, he cited Joan's pontificate to illustrate the disorder that would result if there were no pope. The debate at Tabor thus marks the beginning of the end of Joan's "Catholic career" (Boureau, *Myth* 155, 162–64, 223, 229).

The process that began with Piccolomini's 1451 expression of uncertainty regarding the popess narrative did not culminate in a systematic Catholic refutation of the legend until 1562. Not surprisingly, then, images of the popess enthroned continued to appear in, for example, a later fifteenth-century manuscript of *Des cleres et nobles femmes* (Bibliothèque Nationale, Paris, 599) and Foresti's 1497 *De claris mulieribus*. Nonetheless, the shift in attitude that Boureau links to the 1451 debate likely underlies the contrast between early fifteenth-century manuscript illuminations and later print illustrations of Boccaccio's Pope Joan chapter.

The Mediatrix and the Meretrix

With at least one notable exception, images of the popess and child follow the pattern evident in the Boccaccio illustrations and imply a far more critical view of Joan after the Reformation than before it. In the woodcut from Schedel's chronicle (fig. 5), produced by the Nuremberg artists Michael Wolgemut and Wilhelm Pleydenwurff, Joan, like her immediate predecessors and successors, wears the papal tiara; however, that headdress appears above a face that, compared to those in the other papal portraits on that page, seems extraordinarily youthful and unwrinkled (Schedel CLXIXv; Wilson, *Making* 43). Unlike those other pontiffs, Joan does not carry a crosier; instead, she cradles an infant in her arms. Her eyes look downward and to the left to meet the infant's gaze. Unlike depictions of the popess in childbirth, this image, which seems to use the infant to signify Joan's gender and transgression, does not depict her fortunes at the moment of reversal. Instead, it breaks with the conventional narratives, in which the beginning of Joan's motherhood marks the end of her pontificate, to portray her as simultaneously pope and mother. Schedel's text reports that, after giving birth, Joan died on the spot. According to Jean de Mailly and Ettienne de Bourbon, an angry mob stoned her to death, and according to Boccaccio, the cardinals whom Joan had deceived cast her into a dungeon where she died in lamentation (Pardoe and Pardoe 16–17, Boccaccio, *Concerning* 232–33). None of these scenarios seems to allow for the tender and contented maternal moment envisioned in the Schedel illustration.[29] By picturing such a moment, this image seems to convey the surprisingly tolerant medieval view of the popess also evident, as we have seen, in texts by Martin le Franc and Dietrich Schernberg. In contrast, a woodcut in Johann Wolf's 1600 *Lectionum memorabilium et reconditarum* (Memorable and Hidden Lessons), illustrating verses on the popess by Baptista Mantuanus, emphasizes Joan's downfall and degradation (Wolf 1: 230). In this image (fig. 6), Joan appears once again wearing the tiara and papal robes and cradling her infant; this time, however, she resides in hell, hanging from a gibbet, menaced by demons, and strung up beside the cardinal who impregnated her. Rather than a contented maternal moment, this image, illustrating Wolf's decidedly Protestant account of Church history, portrays an anguished infernal eternity.

In a departure from the pattern that we have been observing, the image of the popess and child on the title page of *Johanna papissa* (1616 and 1619), a Latin translation of Alexander Cooke's English dialogue *Pope Joane* (1610), suggests nothing of Joan's downfall; instead, it implies an analogy between the popess and the Virgin Mary, a woman whose veneration, as Latimer's call for a "jolly muster" at Smithfield demonstrates, Protestants sometimes condemned as idolatrous. That woodcut (fig. 7), which bears a label identifying the *Nuremberg Chronicle* as its source ("Haec figura est desumpta ex

Fig. 5. Pope Joan, engraving from Hartmann Schedel's *Liber chroni-carum* (Nuremberg, 1493). By permission of the Rare Books Division, The New York Public Library, Astor, Lenox and Tilden Foundations.

Chronicis Nuremberge editis Anno 1493"), differs from Schedel's in subtle ways that concern the popess's costume. Here again, a youthful woman, perhaps in this case with an even more pronounced smile, looks down upon the babe cradled in her arms. Her garments, however, seem simpler than the multilayered robes suggested by the many folds visible in the Schedel illustration. Most notably, rather than a pope's triple tiara, she wears a crown. Such changes suggest that this popess image functions within a critique not only of the papacy but also of Catholic veneration of the Virgin Mary. Scholars have conjectured that medieval viewers mistook the image of Madonna and Child for that of popess and child, giving rise to reports that an effigy of Joan and her unfortunate newborn marked the location of her disclosure on the Roman Via Dei Querceti, the so-called *vicus papisse,* or "street of the popess" (Boureau, *Myth* 90, D'Onofrio 232–33). The removal of Joan's tiara and the simplification of her garments on the Cooke title page

Fig. 6. Pope Joan, engraving from Johann Wolf's *Lectionum memora-bilium et reconditarium centenarii XVI* (Lavingae, 1600). By permission of the Rare Books Division, The New York Public Library, Astor, Lenox and Tilden Foundations.

invite an inverse mistaking of Joan's image for that of the Virgin crowned Queen of Heaven.[30]

For Protestant polemicists, the resemblance between Madonna and popess was not merely iconographic, since, as they saw it, Catholic writers and artists had fashioned Mary into a feminine usurper of properly masculine authority. Although in its most extreme formulation the Protestant complaint that Catholics had transformed one of God's creatures into a goddess seems extravagant, so too do some late medieval expressions of Marian devotion (Floyd 139; Crashaw, *Iesvites* 36). For example, on an additional leaf inserted in his personal copy of the *Nuremberg Chronicle,* Hartman Schedel (1440–1514) penned a poem entitled "Adivem—Virginem—Mariam" (To the Divine Virgin Mary) celebrating Mary as "the most beautiful among the ethereal nymphs" and comparing her to Diana the Huntress (Wilson, *Mak-*

ing 210–11). Similarly, the Dominican preacher Gabriel Barletta (died after 1480) recounts the story of a man who met Mary after Jesus's ascension but before her assumption into heaven. Overwhelmed by this encounter, he fell to the ground and exclaimed, "If I were not grounded in the faith I would not believe in any other god but she, because such a clear radiance proceeds from her" (qtd. in Ellington 109). In a 1607 sermon, the English Protestant William Crashaw (1572–1626) quotes another Catholic writer, the Italian Jesuit Orazio Torsellino (1545–99), who flirts with portraying Mary as divine, as he claims that God "hath made his Mother fellowe and partaker of his diuine Power and Maiestie." The Englishman includes the Jesuit's qualifying parenthetical clause "as farre as it is lawefull" but dismisses it as "idle" or impious (Crashaw, *Sermon* 68). As further evidence that papists deify the Virgin, Crashaw cites "our ladies psalter," a sixteenth-century text "wherein euery one of the 150. psalmes are in whole or in part turned from *Dominus* to *Domina,* that is from God or Christ, to our Lady," so that, as if concurring with Torsellino, this new psalter declares, "The Lord said vnto our Lady, Sit thou mother at my right hand" (Crashaw, *Iesvites* 102–3; Crashaw, *Sermon* 64).

As Catholics exalted the Virgin, some seemed to credit her with redemptive powers that belonged to Christ alone. In a wide-ranging 1614 tract, Andrew Willet (1562–1621) argues that by honoring the Virgin with devotional titles such as "ladder of heaven" or "gate of Paradise," Catholics "in a manner . . . make her our redeemer" (519). Even more blasphemous, in Willet's eyes, are prayers that beseech the Virgin to "wash away our sinnes" through her intercession, so that "being redeemed by thee, we may be able to climbe to the seat of eternall glory" (Willet 523). Medieval preachers and mystics set the stage for such prayers by emphasizing Mary's participation in Christ's suffering at Calvary. In a sermon on the Passion, Jean Gerson (1363–1429), chancellor of the University of Paris, imagines Mary addressing God and asserting that she shares the pain of the son whose flesh is one with hers: "As of old, sin passed by woman to man, thus the grief of man returns to me, a woman; and by it I purchase and buy back the sin of Eve. And I am willing to suffer, since this pleases God. I consent that I be in some small way a partner and cause of redemption for the human race" (qtd. in Ellington 79). Commenting on this sermon, Donna Spivey Ellington observes that Gerson was too careful a theologian to cast Mary as "Co-Redemptrix"; however, by imagining that she purchases the sin of Eve and, through willing suffering, acts as a "partner of redemption," Gerson risks blurring the distinction, which Willet draws sharply, between recognizing Mary as a "holie vessel, and instrumentall cause" of salvation and mistaking her for a "meri-

Fig. 7. Title page from Alexander Cooke's *Johanna papissa toti orbi manifestata . . .* (Oppenheim, 1619). By permission of the Rare Books Division, The New York Public Library, Astor, Lenox and Tilden Foundations.

torious efficient cause thereof" (Willet 519). According to the mystic Bridget of Sweden (1301–73), canonized just eighteen years after her death, Christ himself suggested a redemptive partnership between mother and son when, appearing in a vision, he declared, "And therefore I can well say that my Mother and I have saved man as it were with one heart, I by suffering in my heart and flesh, she in the sorrow and love of her heart" (qtd. in Ellington 91). On another occasion Bridget, who called the Virgin "salvatrix," attributed much the same assertion to Mary: "As Adam and Eve sold the world for one apple, so my Son and I have redeemed the world as it were with one heart" (qtd. in Graef 1: 309). In Crashaw's view, by continuing to embrace such misguided expressions of Marian devotion, the "Romish" Church acted as a new "mysticall" Babylon and, like the "olde and *literall Babylon*" denounced in Jeremiah 51:9, refused to be healed (Crashaw, *Sermon* 1–3, 67–68).

What Protestants regarded as Catholics' improper elevation of the Virgin rested on two principal foundations: her spiritual mediation—emphasized in several narratives concerning the popess—and her maternal authority—emphasized in images of the Madonna and Child. To some, Mary's role as mediatrix seemed to undermine divine sovereignty and to render her a usurper of authority that properly belonged either to her divine Son or to God the Father. Willet complains, for example, that prayers beseeching Mary's intercession often "giue her iurisdiction ouer her sonne": "*Iube natum;* commaund thy sonne . . . *Cogo Deum,* compel God to be mercifull to sinners" (519). Crashaw quotes and condemns the rationale that the Franciscan Minor Bernardine of Busti (died 1500) articulated for such prayers of intercession. "A man may appeal to the Virgin Mary not onely from a Tyrant, and from the Divell, but even from God himself," Bernardine asserts, since "God hath diuided his kingdom [with Mary]: For wheras God hath iustice and mercie; Hee hath reserued Iustice to himselfe to bee exercised in this world: and hath granted Mercie to his Mother." Incredulous, Crashaw asks, "hath God indeede diuided his kingdome? and diuided it with a creature, yea with a woman?" (Crashaw, *Sermon* 61). Mary's gender renders the proposition all the more unimaginable. By employing the metaphor of law courts, as Jean Gerson did in much the same context, and casting Mary as a superior court, a chancery of sorts, to which one might appeal divine judgments, Bernardine renders the Virgin, in Crashaw's words, "greater than God" (Crashaw, *Sermon* 62, 65; Ellington 118). It would seem, then, that medieval Catholicism produced more than one female usurper.

Beginning in the fourteenth century, the two usurpers meet in versions of the popess narrative in which the Virgin intervenes to enable Joan's redemption (Wright, *Medieval* 190). For example, an early fifteenth-century Catalan adaptation of Arnoldus of Liège's collection of exempla, the *Alphabetum narrationum* (*Alphabet of Tales*), reports that as the popess's fateful procession reached an image of the Virgin, she offered Joan a choice between eternal damnation and immediate, painful humiliation; Joan's decision secured both her redemption and her infamy (Boureau, *Myth* 123). In the Pope Joan morality play *Ein schön Spiel von Frau Jutten,* Schernberg elaborates the topic of Marian intercession. According to the play's sixteenth-century Protestant editor Hieronymus Tilesius, *Frau Jutten* demonstrates how Mary's role as mediatrix diminishes Christ's as savior. Nonetheless, as if anticipating the objections that would lead Protestants to insist that Christ alone was their mediator, Schernberg handles the question of mediation rather delicately (Hotchkiss, "Dietrich" 198; Wright, *Medieval* 16–18; Wright, "Joseph" 161, 163–64; Pelikan 154–55). Whereas in the Catalan narrative Mary seems to act upon her own initiative, in *Frau Jutten* Christ involves her in Jutta's (Joan's) fate, complaining to his mother of the popess's iniquity and announcing his intention to damn her. When Christ initially seems unmoved by her entreaties on Jutta's behalf, the Virgin acts to dispel any jealous resentment that might motivate Christ's unresponsiveness. She urges her son, "do not be distressed / if she directs her tears and cries to me," and insists that she takes up Joan's cause "for the sake of your own honor"(ll. 1474–75, 1483). As she continues, Mary addresses Christ respectfully as "my Creator and Lord" and acknowledges that he gave her the authority to intercede for sinners and could conceivably "remove" it (ll. 1503–10, 1537). Even so, as if helping to make Crashaw's case, Schernberg's Mary does term herself "a Shield of Salvation" and insists:

> I am indeed the one
> who should banish sin
> and show forth mercy. (ll. 1478–80, 1481)

Moreover, in the play's final passage, after praising Christ in a single line, the popess celebrates the Virgin at great length, declaring that "in her lies all our salvation" and

> That is why my head shall always bow to her,
> And my tongue shall never fall silent,
> But I will praise and adore her. (ll. 1712, 1719–21)

Schernberg's version of the popess legend thus demonstrates how devotion to the mediatrix could obscure the savior's glory.

Although Schernberg's Mary does address Christ as "my Lord" and acknowledges that he has empowered her to intercede, she more often calls him "dear child"; implores Christ to grant her request "for the sake of your mother's honor"; and even insists at one point, "Answer your mother now" (ll. 1473, 1483, 1497–98, 1527, 1538, 1557). She thus alludes to a second source of Marian authority: her status as mother of the divine. The Catholic author of the 1619 *The Widdowes Mite* (sometimes attributed to Sir Tobie Matthew) grounds the Virgin's maternal authority in scripture and flesh. He first cites Luke 2:51, which reports that even after the twelve-year-old Jesus was found pursuing his "Father's business" by discoursing with the learned in the Temple, he returned to Nazareth and was subject to Mary and Joseph ("erat sub-ditus illis"). For this author, the authority to govern the youthful Jesus derived more powerfully from fleshly ties than from a parental role and office. Since Joseph was merely Jesus's "supposed Father," but Mary was "all the parents of flesh and bloud that he had," she was "infinitly preferred before him, both in dignity" and in "obligation." "How much more was our Sauiour Christ to be accounted subiect to our B[lessed]. Lady, then to *S[t]. Ioseph,*" this writer asks, "and consequently how much greater was the superiority which she had ouer him, then *S[t]. Ioseph* had?" (*Widdowes* 36–37, 40). Clearly, this view of Christ's peculiar parentage disrupts the conventional familial hierarchy, investing wife and mother with more authority than husband and father. Writing in the same vein in a 1606 tract, Richard Chambers asserts more succinctly that Jesus was "subject vnto" Mary and "subject to Ioseph for her sake" (C5r). Although *The Widdowes Mite* limits Christ's subordination to Mary to the first thirty years of his life, "till he came to preach & publish himself," the prayers condemned by Willet imply that such subjection is ongoing: "*Iure matris impera filio,* commaund thy sonne by the right of a mother" (Willet 519; *Widdowes* 40–41). Moreover, Crashaw cites devotional verses that seem to infantalize Christ by addressing him as "youngling" in a "sporting speech fit to be spoken to a playing *childe.*" Such texts convince Crashaw that "the Christ of the Romish church is a childe inferiour to his mother and may deny her nothing" (*Iesvites* 61, 65, 67).

Protestants denounced images of the Madonna and Child because they seemed to represent that inferiority visually. As Frances E. Dolan has pointed out, the relative size of Mary and Jesus in these images seemed to misrepresent the relative power and authority of each (*Whores* 113). Crashaw fears that the "common people" who view pictures of the infant Jesus in his mother's arms will imagine that Mary's authority over her son matches the "power of ouerruling and commaunding the *Mother* hath over her *little childe*" (*Iesvites* 31). Such a conflation of physical and spiritual power seems to inform the blasphemous mockery that the Catholic John Floyd attributes to Protestant wags who assert that pictures of the Virgin with the almighty "*King* of the world in her armes" depict Mary as "*a kind wench, good at a dead lift*" (128). According to Crashaw, Catholics insist upon envisioning the relationship between Jesus and Mary in this distorted way. "Generally in all places where the mother and the sonne, the virgin Mary, and our *Lord Iesus* be pictured together in their churches," he contends hyperbolically, "she is always set forth as a woman and a mother, and he as a childe and infant."[31] In Crashaw's eyes, this insistent iconographic pattern perpetuates Christ's infantile subjection to the Virgin, prompting the frustrated question, "and yet must he now after 1606 yeres be an infant in his mothers armes?" "And yet now after 1600. yeares," he complains, "she must still be a commaunding mother, and must shew *her authority ouer him*" (*Iesvites* 36).

In response to what they saw as this derogation of Christ's sovereignty, Protestants attacked both the Virgin's moral character and her physical image. To dispute the claim, advanced by revered Catholic theologians such as Ambrose, Thomas Aquinas, and Bonaventure, that Mary never committed sin, both Martin Luther (1483–1546) and John Calvin (1509–64) attributed specific transgressions to her (Graef 2: 87–88, 279, 282; O'Meara 121, 132–34). For example, concerning the wedding at Cana (John 2), when Mary encourages Jesus to perform a miracle even before his "hour" had come, Calvin charges (as *The Widdowes Mite* accurately renders it), "*That she sinned by exceeding her boundes, and by intruding herselfe so fare, as that she might chance to haue obscured that glory of Christ thereby*" (*Widdowes* 82). In Protestants' eyes, by thus going beyond her proper human role and presuming to act as intermediary, Mary commits what would become the characteristic sin of Catholic Mariology (O'Meara 133). Although Calvin condemned Mary's behavior at Cana cautiously, observing that "she did not knowingly and willingly offend" (qtd. in O'Meara 134), according to *The Widdowes Mite*, Edmund Bunny exercised far less restraint in his 1598 *Christian Directorie*, as, "with a most blasphemous mouth," he accused the Virgin of "hauing committed no lesse then foure mortall sines, in the short tyme of our Sauiours passion" (*Widdowes* 83).

The virulence that seems to have marked Bunny's verbal attack on Mary's sanctity also characterized physical attacks on her image. John Stow's *A Survey of London* (1603), for example, details how a statue of the Virgin situated at the foot of a three-hundred-year-old cross in West Cheapside was repeatedly and elaborately vandalized. The statue's desecration, occurring in several episodes between 1581 and 1600, seemed to focus on iconographic elements important to Catholic Mariology. As if contesting Mary's status as Queen of Heaven, vandals "pluck[ed] off her crowne, and almost her head." As if attacking the veneration of the Virgin's milk as a sacred fluid that, like Christ's blood, could wash away sin, they stabbed her statue in the breast (Crashaw, *Iesvites* 55). "Her whole body also was haled [hauled or hoisted] with ropes, and left likely to fall," as if to travesty the Virgin's bodily assumption into Heaven and to render her a feeble deus ex machina. Beside the cross, someone "set vp a curious wrought tabernacle of gray Marble, and in the same an Alabaster Image of *Diana*," implying, through the juxtaposition of pagan and Christian virgins, the Protestant charge that papists make an idol and goddess of Mary (O'Meara 133).[32] In fact, the Elizabethan *Homilie against the Perill of Idolatrie* (1563–71) makes explicit the analogy implied by this juxtaposition, as it argues "that our [Christian] Images, and idoles of the [pagan] Gentiles bee all one." Commenting on the proliferation of Marian shrines and the practice of speaking of the woman venerated at each site as a separate and distinct person, this homilist complains: "When you heare of our Lady of Walsingham, our Lady of Ipswich, our Lady of Wilsdon, and such others: what is it but an imitation of the Gentiles idolatere? Diana Agrotera, Diana Coriphea, Diana Ephesia" (46–47). Most important, the West Cheapside vandals seemed to deny Mary the dignity and authority she acquired through her maternal superiority over the child Jesus, as they "robbed her of her son" and broke her arms "by which she staid him on her knees" (Stow 265–67). This iconoclastic violence, as Dolan has suggested, seems to imply a desire "to free Jesus and unmother Mary" (*Whores* 114).

Viewed in light of the Protestant critique of Catholic Mariology, the image of the popess and child that appears on the Cooke title page effects a similar, albeit nonviolent, desecration of Marian iconography. By replacing the papal tiara with a crown and simplifying Joan's garments, this image blurs the distinction between popess and Madonna, between meretrix and mediatrix, and heightens the resemblance between these two female usurpers who, to paraphrase Calvin, exceeded their bounds and intruded themselves too far. As Paul Whitfield White has pointed out, early in the English Reformation Henrician iconoclasts sought to demystify religious images by displacing them from a sacred context to a profane one—removing crosses from monasteries, for example, and displaying them in the marketplace (36–37). The Cooke title page effects a similar displacement, relocating the image of the serene, adoring royal mother and cherubic child from the context of Marian devotion into that of Johannine scandal. As the Catholic Floyd caricatures the Protestant critique of Mariology, he mockingly warns that Reformers might "giue vs a Pope *Mary* to be Anti-Christ, as they haue done a Pope *Joan*" (Floyd 150). Floyd warns in jest, but Cooke's title page does indeed announce the conflation of the Madonna and the popess. This conflation suggests the polemical context in which early modern representations of Pope Joan circulated.

The Resistant Legend

However subtly effective the iconography of the Cooke title page might have been, the following chapters will argue that Protestant attempts to deploy the Pope Joan legend often proved as unpredictable in their consequences or implications as Catholic attempts to suppress it. The first chapter examines the most elaborate and most frequently republished early modern English treatise devoted to Pope Joan, Cooke's *Pope Joane: A Dialogue,* in order to reveal the ways that Protestants, eager to demonstrate Roman corruption and challenge the pope's claims to unbroken succession from St. Peter, sought to establish the truth of the popess legend. Lacking convincing textual proof, such writers fashioned arguments starkly at odds with common Protestant assumptions regarding the unreliability of tradition and images. Citing Catholic religious ceremonies as evidence of Joan's pontificate, they bluntly disregarded Protestant skepticism about whether such ceremonies could convey clear meaning. Moreover, to explain Joan's absence from numerous important medieval chronicles, Protestant polemicists posited a systematic Catholic campaign to "geld" or expurgate texts, a prospect that implied vexing questions regarding textual criticism and canon formation, questions capable of shaking the foundations of the Reformers' simple, confident maxim, "sola scriptura."

In certain political contexts, however, even Protestants found the popess legend too hot to handle. As we shall see in the second chapter, whatever the difficulties entailed in attempting to prove that Joan's pontificate actually occurred, and however much the scandalous legend might have appealed to Protestant polemicists, Elizabethan printers were disinclined to publish texts devoted to the popess. Their reluctance reflected anxieties aroused when supreme political and ecclesiastical authority was vested in a woman. Answering Protestant references to Pope Joan, Catholic polemicists argued that Elizabeth I (1533–1603, reigning 1558–1603), who had assumed authority once reserved for the pope and claimed the title "Supreme Governor" of the Church of England, was, as Raemond put it, "ceste nouvelle Papesse" (101, 107). The queen lent support, perhaps unwittingly, to such charges by presiding in a nearly priestly manner over the Royal Maundy and the ceremony of the royal touch, rituals that originated in or resembled liturgy. Moreover, persistent rumors of Elizabeth's sexual misconduct and concealed pregnancies intensified the resemblance between her and the woman one early modern polemicist termed the "whore-pope" (Papa meretrice) (Bale, *Scriptorvm illustrium* 1: 117). Investigating the Elizabethan reception of the popess legend, then, illuminates how an unmarried female monarch disrupted sixteenth-century assumptions regarding authority and gender.

In contrast to those who lobbied for the removal of the Sienese bust, the Catholic polemicist Alan Cope (died 1578) sought not to eliminate evidence of past belief in the popess but rather to alter the legend's significance by sug-

gesting that Joan may have been a hermaphrodite or a medieval instance of
the sort of remarkable physiological change that sixteenth-century writers
and physicians such as Michel de Montaigne (1553–92) and Ambroise Paré
(ca. 1510–90) reported, namely spontaneous sexual transformation. Cope's
attempt to rehabilitate the popess in this way, however, failed, as those hostile to the legend disregarded his distinction between transvestitism and
anatomical ambiguity, and those eager to turn the legend against Rome
ridiculed his physiological hypothesis. The third chapter explores two questions raised by that hypothesis and its reception. Why would Cope think
that, compared to a transvestite popess, a hermaphrodite or transsexual pope
would bring less disrepute to the Holy See? In turn, at a time when
respectable writers were documenting cases of women transformed into
men, why did Cope's polemical opponents dismiss his conjectures as ludi-
crous? Answers lie in the equivocal way that early modern medical, legal, and
literary discourse portrayed hermaphroditism, presenting it at times as an
ideal integration of feminine and masculine principles but at others as a
grotesque deformity; these discourses thus both invited and undermined
Cope's attempt to rehabilitate Joan. Further, by mocking Cope's hypothesis
rather than challenging its disputable assumptions concerning physiology
and canon law, his opponents avoided confronting early modern fears of
effeminacy and gender instability. This episode thus illuminates the complex
way the early modern period constructed not only gender but also anatomical sex.

Oddly, the same controversialist who characterized Joan as the "whore-
pope" asserted that by writing a book on sorcery she had earned a place
among the illustrious writers of Great Britain. Although such a report might
at first appear as an oblique attack on learned and literary women, my fourth
chapter argues that John Bale's entry on Joan in *Illustrivm maioris Britanniae
scriptorum . . . summarium* (1548), his encyclopedic collection of English literary biographies, instead advances a critique of medieval Catholic textual
culture and the monastic institutions that fostered and sustained it. Bale's
contribution to that critique, however, assumes the validity of early modern
witchcraft lore, validity that in subsequent decades fewer and fewer readers
were likely to concede, as skepticism concerning such lore grew. At least one
genre within Catholic textual culture, devotional books that assigned indul-
gences to particular prayers, resembled the sort of conjuring book that, Bale
suggests, Joan composed in that they promised those who recited their texts
properly that they would gain great benefits: remission of purgatorial punishment, safe childbirth, or even knowledge of the exact date of one's death.
Joan's conjuring book thus hyperbolically figures the errors and evils of

Catholics' belief in salvific prayer. Moreover, by elaborating the established popess narrative to emphasize how Joan's character and career were shaped by monks and monasteries, Bale crafted a literary biography for Joan that could address his ambivalence concerning monastic institutions. In the 1530s, through polemical drama, Bale had promoted the Henrician dissolution of English monasteries; by 1548, however, he had come to regret one of the dissolution's consequences: the destruction of monastic libraries and the reckless scattering of their contents. The sorcerous literary activities that Bale attributed to Joan suggest that some contents of those libraries and some aspects of the medieval literary culture preserved in them were profoundly flawed, better off lost. However, since Bale's account of those activities and his accompanying reports of sorcerer popes invest belief in early modern witchcraft lore, the rhetorical impact of that suggestion was quite likely modest or at least short-lived. Growing skepticism concerning such lore would soon erode the credibility of Bale's claims and the effectiveness of his attempt to reshape the popess legend to exemplify the iniquity of Catholic book culture.

Whereas the presence of an unmarried woman in a position of supreme political and ecclesiastical authority discouraged Elizabethan printers from bringing out Pope Joan publications, a century later fears of the influence exercised by Catholic queens consort and of the prospect that Charles II's Catholic brother might succeed him on the throne seem to have prompted a string of such publications, including two editions of Elkanah Settle's *The Female Prelate* (1680), the earliest extant English play dramatizing the popess legend. As it adopts and alters traditional popess materials, that play, the subject of my final chapter, draws upon Joan's cross-dressing, sexual conduct, and manipulation of papist institutions to critique Catholic theology, spirituality, and church polity. In an instance of what Marjorie Garber has termed the "transvestite effect," a cross-dresser's destabilizing of gender boundaries stands in for the (less readily acknowledged) blurring of the boundary between anti-Catholicism and impiety, as the play's dramatization of ecclesiastical threats to civil authorities ranges beyond Settle's apparent intention and interrogates religious belief itself. Once again, in proving resistant to polemical manipulation, the popess legend suggests the instability of the rhetorical constructions that organized early modern ways of seeing the world.

1 *Debating Joan*

IMAGES, CEREMONY, AND
THE GELDED TEXT

Writing in 1697 and looking back on more than a century of debate concerning the Pope Joan legend, the skeptical French Huguenot philosopher Pierre Bayle (1647–1706) observed: "I believe that some traditions, which are advantageous to the Popes, and supported by as strong reasons as those are which support this [popess] story, would seem worthy [of] the utmost contempt to those who dispute most ardently for it. So certain is it, that the same things appear to us true or false, according as they favour our own, or the opposite party" (Bayle 4: 732–33; Tinsley, "Sozzini's Ghost" 609). By alluding to Reformers' distrust of tradition and pointing to inconsistencies in what anti-Catholic writers embraced as convincing evidence, Bayle identifies a central difficulty for Protestant polemicists. The arguments they deployed to prove that Joan's pontificate had occurred often conflicted with common Protestant assumptions concerning the unreliability of tradition and images, the obscurity of ceremonies, and the certainty of written texts.

Reformers certainly found the popess legend useful and, to borrow Bayle's term, "advantageous." For John Jewel, Joan's "naughty" exploits illustrated popery's moral corruption, and, as we shall see, for John Bale and John Foxe (1516–87), they confirmed the equation between the Church of Rome and the Whore of Babylon (Jewel, *Apology* 52; Rev. 17–18; Bale, *Scriptorvm illustrium* 1:116–17; Bale, *Pageant* 55v–56v; Foxe 2: 7). John Calvin contended that Joan's pontificate undermined papal claims to unbroken apostolic succession from St. Peter, since it would be impossible for subsequent popes to "leap over Popess Joan" (qtd. in Tinsley, "Pope Joan" 388), and Alexander Cooke (1564–1632) went further, suggesting that the popess episode cast doubt on Catholicism's entire sacramental system. "For, it may be well enough," Cooke contends, "that the priests of this present age are descended from those who were ordained by her." In that case, the sacraments administered by such priests would be empty and ineffective: "For, unless the popish priests be priested by a lawful bishop, their priesthood is not worth a rush; unless you lay-papists be absolved by a lawful priest, your absolution is nought worth; and, unless the words of consecration be uttered by a lawful priest, intent upon his business, there follows no substantial change in the creatures of bread and wine" (*Pope* 108). One can understand, then, why Protestant polemicists wished to argue that the stories concerning Joan were true.

Actually, for more than a decade, such polemicists did not need to argue about the legend's veracity at all, since their assertions passed unchallenged. Although in the fourteenth and fifteenth centuries, Pope Joan figured in debates, not until the sixteenth century did the legend itself become a subject of debate. The philosopher William of Ockham (ca. 1280–ca. 1349), for example, cited the popess in two tracts addressing the Franciscan order's disputes with Pope John XXII (reigning 1316–34) to demonstrate that a false pope, someone unable or unworthy to exercise true papal authority, could occupy the Chair of St. Peter. Although Ockham does not cite Joan by name, as he refers to the woman who "was venerated as pope by the universal Church for two years, seven months, and three days," he echoes Martinus Polonus's report concerning the length of Joan's pontificate almost exactly and thus points to Martinus's "Johannes Anglicus" as the person in question (qtd. in Pardoe and Pardoe 35–36; Boureau, *Myth* 153–55).[1] Joan also figured in controversies surrounding the Great Schism of the West (1378–1417), the ecclesiastical crisis that erupted when two, and later three, rivals were hailed by different constituencies as the rightful pontiff. Both Jean Gerson, who in order to resolve the crisis asserted the authority of church councils over the pope, and Jean Roques (Jean de Rocha), who defended papal supremacy, cited Joan in their arguments (Boureau, *Myth* 161–62). Further, according to Peter of Mladonovice's eyewitness account, during the heresy trial of John Hus conducted at the Council of Constance (which was convened to end the Great Schism), Hus's accusers did not challenge his claim that the Church "had been without a head for two years and five months" while a popess occupied St. Peter's Chair (Petr 212).[2] As I note in the earlier discussion of Pope Joan illustrations, even St. Antoninus Pierozzi of Florence, evidently concerned about how the popess narrative might figure in ecclesiastical controversies, contested its import but not its veracity (Boureau, *Myth* 155). With the modest exception of Enea Silvio de Piccolomini's cautious assertion " the story is not certain," the content of the popess narrative seems to have passed unquestioned until the sixteenth century (qtd. in Boureau, *Myth* 221–22).

In fact, not until 1562, more than a dozen years after Bale and Calvin incorporated Joan into their polemics, did a Catholic author set out for the first time to disprove the popess's existence. Commissioned by the Roman Curia to update the *Liber de vita Christi ac omnium pontificum* (*Lives of the Popes*) (1479) by Platina, the Augustinian friar Onofrio Panvinio (1530–68) took the opportunity to assess Platina's problematic entry on Pope Joan. Platina's text had circulated widely, appearing in forty-three Latin editions before 1600. Moreover, although Platina's early career was stormy, marked by charges of heresy and of conspiring to assassinate Pope Paul II, his later appointment as prefect of the Vatican Library lent authority to the papal biographies that he composed at the suggestion of Sixtus IV. Panvinio's efforts, then, were well placed (Boureau, *Myth* 22; Hay 147–48; Tinsley, "Pope Joan" 386–87).

In just three pages, Panvinio outlines the arguments against the veracity of the popess legend, arguments that subsequent Catholic writers would repeat and elaborate. He notes the tentativeness of Platina's report, which concludes, "This story is vulgarly told, but by very uncertain and obscure authors" (Platina 1: 225). He examines the documentary evidence, interrogates the least credible details, and speculates about the legend's true origins (Boureau, *Myth* 246–47). In doing so, he set off a flurry of publications. In 1584 the Austrian Jesuit Georg Scherer (1539–1605) published the first volume solely devoted to refuting the popess legend. Three years later, Florimond de Raemond published his own book-length refutation. Within a year, Protestants had begun publishing their responses. Between 1548 and 1700 the polemical exchange between Protestants and Catholics produced at least forty pamphlets devoted exclusively to the popess. Adding in reprints, new editions, translations, and lost publications cited in surviving texts would, Alain Boureau estimates, increase the number by a factor of at least four, producing "an average of one work per year for a century and a half" (*Myth* 251). Counting discussions of Pope Joan that constitute only one part of a more broadly focused text would swell that number even further. A century after Panvinio set this exchange in motion, the Calvinist pastor David Blondel (1591–1655) set the stage for its conclusion by, in effect, crossing party lines and composing a Protestant repudiation of the popess legend (published in French in 1647 and 1649, Dutch in 1650, and Latin in 1657). Blondel did not settle the matter; indeed, as recently as 1985 a book attempting to substantiate the legend (Joan Morris's *Pope John VIII: An English Woman*) appeared in print. However, Blondel's work did demonstrate that skepticism regarding the legend could derive from something other than sectarian bias. As recognition of that fact spread, the pamphlet wars cooled, and the pace of Pope Joan publications slowed.

The most elaborate and most frequently republished English contribution to this early modern exchange was *Pope Joane: A Dialogue between a Protestant and a Papist,* a text that we touched upon when discussing the images of the popess and child. Its author, the Anglican vicar Alexander Cooke, published at least three other polemical tracts, one in multiple editions, prompting Anthony à Wood (1632–95) to report that he was "hated" by all the Roman Catholics "who had read his works" (qtd. in *Dictionary* 4: 1001). Cooke's 128-page treatise on the popess was published in London in 1610 and again in 1625; translated into Latin and published at Oppenheim in 1616 and 1619; adapted into French in 1633; and transformed into a monologic tract and published again in 1675, 1740, and 1785 as *A Present for a Papist: or The Life and Death of Pope Joan.* It incorporates arguments advanced in less detail by earlier English writers such as John Jewel, Thomas Bell, John Mayo (died 1629), and Andrew Willet. Examining this widely circulated text, well grounded in the first fifty years of debate regarding the popess narrative, reveals the difficulties that Protestants confronted. Lacking compelling textual proof of Joan's career, they sought evidence from sources they conventionally approached with deep distrust: Catholic traditions, images, and ceremonies.

"If Your Stories Be True"

In addition to interrogating the evidence (textual or otherwise) for Joan's pontificate, Catholic writers also cited seemingly confused or implausible elements within the conventional popess narrative: the uncertain national or ethnic origin, for example, of a figure who, according to Martinus Polonus's highly influential thirteenth-century account, was named Johannes Anglicus (John English or John the Englishman) but born at Mainz on the Rhine. Catholics also questioned the likelihood that ninth-century Athens, where Joan reportedly achieved unequaled proficiency in various sciences, was in fact a great center of learning and, most important, the prospect that Joan could have disguised her true sex for so many years. Cooke's treatment of this last issue exemplifies a recurrent pattern in his handling of evidence. To confirm that a woman might succeed at an imposture such as Joan's, Cooke first cites the evidently effeminizing clerical practice of shaving: "For men by shaving may make themselves look like women" (*Pope* 73). However, since not only facial hair but also "countenance," "voice," and "actions" might betray a woman's sex, for further support Cooke falls back upon the unsteady foundation of Catholic hagiography, a structure that he has challenged earlier in his dialogue. Addressing his "Papist" counterpart, the Protestant interlocutor in Cooke's text contends that Joan's imposture could certainly pass undetected "if your stories be true, that divers women have lived longer among men, in men's apparel unknown, than Dame Joan lived in the Popedom" (*Pope* 73). To make much the same point, Jewel and Mayo cite a varied set of examples, including the ancient Greek women Lasthenia and Axiothea, who reportedly disguised themselves as men in order to study with Plato, and in his Restoration adaptation of Cooke's dialogue Humphrey Shuttleworth points to, among others, an unnamed Englishwoman who "in our late Civil wars . . . was sixteen years a Soldier" (Jewel, *Defence* 651; Mayo 41; Shuttleworth 97). In contrast, the "divers" crossdressed women whom Cooke cites are all Catholic saints, namely Marina, Eugenia, Pelagia, Euphrosyne ("Euphrusina"), and Margaret ("Margareta"), who each reportedly lived for several years disguised as a monk or hermit and whose stories belong to a set of roughly twenty transvestite saint narratives that, John Anson contends, originated in the monastic communities of sixth-century Egypt (12–13). As pieces of evidence within Cooke's argument, these narratives pose at least two sets of problems.

First, details in some of these saints' lives suggest that the transvestite disguise is less effective than Cooke's allusion implies. Forewarned by a dream concerning a female idol, the bishop Helenus recognizes the true gender and identity of the youth who presents himself as "Eugenius" and seeks admission to a monastery (Anson 22; Frantzen 463). Even so, declaring "Justly you call yourself Eugenius, for you are behaving like a man," Helenus endorses Eugenia's disguise, which successfully deceives those not enlightened by prophetic visions. More significantly perhaps, cross-dressing evidently fails to obscure completely Euphrosyne's erotic charms, since after she enters the monastery disguised as the eunuch Esmeraldus (or Smaragdus in Aelfric's version), her beauty so excites the other monks' desires that, in order to eliminate perilous temptations, the abbot restricts the new arrival to an isolated cell (Anson 16; Frantzen 464). If Joan's feminine beauty had proven as difficult to suppress as Euphrosyne's, or if she had suffered such isolation, her ecclesiastical career would have ended before it began.

Cooke's conditional clause "if your stories be true" points to a second, greater difficulty. Several elements within the transvestite saint narratives have prompted modern scholars to suggest that these tales borrow motifs and situations from ancient pagan fiction, modifying them to glorify not, as in the pagan narratives, the marriage of hero and heroine but rather "the union between Christ and the Church, or Christ and the individual soul" (Pavlovskis 138–39). In light of such borrowings, the transvestite saint narratives seem, as Anson puts it, to "move in a world of pure erotic romance" (11). Three of these tales include the folklorists' Potiphar's wife motif, which draws its name from an episode in the biblical story of Joseph (Genesis 39) and is also present in the biography of St. Macarius, who founded the Egyptian monastic community that seems to have produced these accounts (Anson 18). Thus, as monks, Marina, Eugenia, and Margaret are falsely accused of impregnating or violating a local woman, only to have the accusation discredited when, at trial or after death, their true sex is revealed. Two of these narratives also feature unlikely reunions between the saintly women and the family members they have left behind, as the disguised Marina is brought before her father, a prefect, to answer charges of impregnating a maiden, and the abbot of Euphrosyne's monastery, unaware of her true sex and identity, directs her to offer spiritual counsel to her father, who mourns his daughter's disappearance. Eugenia's tale also includes miraculous deliverance as she escapes Roman attempts to execute her through drowning, burning, and starvation before ultimately suffering martyrdom at the point of a gladiator's sword (Anson 11, 15–16, 21, 25, 29–32). The foiled executions, improbable reunions, and Potiphar's wife motif suggest fantastic fiction rather than documented fact, and Cooke's tentative conditional clause does little to dispel that impression.

Moreover, Cooke's allusion to transvestite saints fails to meet the evidentiary standard that he sets for hagiography earlier in the dialogue. While critiquing religious artwork, Cooke's "Protestant" disparages representations of other saints (namely George, Christopher, Catharine of Alexandria, and Hippolytus), whose lives seem to belong to the world of romance, as he complains that "in all antiquity, there is no mention of such saints" (*Pope* 20). Later, however, when he cites the transvestite saints, Cooke does little to provide the ancient documentation that he appears to demand here. In the body of his text, he vaguely asserts that "Marina, *they say,* lived all her life among monks" (*Pope* 73, my emphasis). His marginal annotation cites Johannes Ravisius Textor's 1532 *Officina;* Textor in turn cites the late fifteenth-century scholar Raffaelo Maffei (Raphael Volaterranus, 1451–1522). A second annotation in the margins of Cooke's text cites as a further source the fourteenth-century hagiographer Petrus de Natalibus. None of these constitutes the ancient authority that Cooke earlier demands for the lives of

St. Christopher and St. George. Here, then, Cooke's "Protestant" seems to illustrate Bayle's point, accepting weak evidence that if it were "advantageous to the Popes . . . would seem worthy of the utmost contempt."

The audience that Cooke imagines for his text and the purposes that he assigns to it make him content here to demonstrate merely that the popess narrative is no less believable than accepted Catholic traditions. Cooke addresses the dialogue's preface "To the Popish, or Catholick Reader" and thus suggests that he envisions an audience much like the "Papist" interlocutor whose objections he sets out to debunk. Although the dialogue's subtitle credits it with "manifestly proving, that a woman called Joane, was Pope of Rome," in his dedicatory epistle (to the Anglican archbishop of York) Cooke seems to subordinate that proof to another end. Lamenting that apostate Protestants have "of late" converted to the Church of Rome, he announces his "purpose . . . to lay open" Catholics' "impudency" and "dishonesty" in "denying known truths," vices that are most apparent, he contends, as writers disputing the popess legend "are driven to feign, to forge, to cog [cheat or deceive], to play the fools" (*Pope* 9–10). Exposing inconsistencies in positions taken by Catholic Johannoclasts (to borrow a term Boureau has coined) might advance Cooke's stated purpose but still fall short of proving Joan's existence for an audience that is more heterogeneous than the one he envisions. Consider an additional hagiographic example. To answer the "Papist" interlocutor's charge that discrepancies among different versions of the popess narrative "prove it a fable," Cooke's "Protestant" cites the abundant discrepancies among different versions of the popular legend of St. Ursula and the Eleven Thousand Virgins.[3] Cooke's interlocutors agree that chronicles assign the popess different given names (Agnes or Gilberta), different papal designations (John VII or John VIII), different dates for her accession to the papacy (853, 854, 857, or 858), and different durations for her pontificate (*Pope* 77–80). With similar inconsistency, hagiographies, according to Cooke's "Protestant," characterize St. Ursula as a Cornish or Scottish princess; daughter of Maurus or Dionotus; betrothed to Aetherius, Holofernes, or Conanus; and martyred in the third, fifth, or ninth centuries. "The difference among writers, about a circumstance," he concludes, "doth not weaken any man's argument touching the substance. If it do, . . . blot out for shame, St. Ursula and her fellows" (*Pope* 82–83). Although the Roman controversialist Cesare Baronius (1538–1607) had already rejected some elements of the St. Ursula legend as fabulous, a Catholic reader might have been reluctant to sacrifice Ursula in order to discredit Joan (*Catholic Encyclopedia* 15: 226; Tout 34–35). A skeptical Protestant, however, could have felt free to "blot out" both. Therefore, once Protestants such as Blondel and Bayle applied the same skepticism to the popess legend as to other traditions, many of Cooke's arguments became outmoded.[4]

Illegible Images

Although, very early in the dialogue, Cooke's "Protestant" cites more than twenty Catholic authors who report Joan's pontificate, before examining those accounts in any detail he discusses the papal busts in Siena and another marble image of Joan that allegedly stood in Rome, monuments, he suggests, that could corroborate "book-proof" (*Pope* 21). By thus comparing images and texts (or, put differently, pictorial and verbal texts), he seems to adopt the Catholic view, often traced to Pope Gregory I, that "images be the Laymens Bookes, and that pictures are the Scripture of . . . simple people" (*Certaine* pt. 2, 72; Phillips 90).[5] Soon enough, however, Cooke's typically Protestant iconoclasm surfaces and undermines the evidentiary value of the images that he cites.

Concerning the marble image of the popess in Rome, Cooke's "Papist" interlocutor objects, "For neither was it like a woman lying in child bed, nor was the boy, which was engraven by her, like a child in the swaddling clouts, but like one of some years" (*Pope* 15). Since, as we have seen in the earlier discussion of illustrations, most narratives suggest that Joan suffered death or imprisonment immediately after her parturition, such an image of mother and toddler, Cooke's "Papist" asserts, does not seem to depict the popess. The "Protestant's" counterargument sows more doubt than it dispels. "This your exception is to no purpose;" he contends, "for that age was a brainless and a witless age" with precious little "skill in engraving, carving, and painting." Although Cooke initially gestures toward a relatively narrow, historicist claim about artistic backwardness of a dark age, as the dialogue continues his "Protestant" questions the representational adequacy of images more broadly. Turning to a "better time than that of Pope Joan," he quotes Enea Silvio de Piccolomini, who remarked: "If thou observe the engraven or painted images, which were made two or three-hundred years ago [in the twelfth or thirteenth century], thou shalt find, that they are faced more like monsters, and hobgoblins, than men" (Cooke, *Pope* 15). Both interlocutors agree that, to overcome such inadequacies, artists often use captions to clarify what their images depict. The marble image in Rome, however, lacked such an illuminating caption.

Similar doubts about representational adequacy inform much Reformation discourse concerning idolatry and iconoclasm. As Lord Protector

Edward Seymour (ca. 1506–52), for example, defends iconoclasm in a 1547 letter to Stephen Gardiner (ca. 1493–1555), bishop of Winchester and later Mary Tudor's lord chancellor, he questions whether images can perform the function that religious conservatives assign to them. Echoing the Catholic position in order to disparage it, he observes: "We cannot but see that images may be counted marvelous books, to whom we have kneeled, whom we have kissed. . . . Indeed images be great letters; yet as big as they be, we have seen many which have read them amiss" (qtd. in Phillips 91). Moreover, Seymour contends, his correspondence with Gardiner confirms his point. Gardiner had written to the royal authorities to complain about the destruction of religious images in Portsmouth and to argue that such iconoclasm threatened not only religion but civil authority as well, since the king too communicated through images (standards, banners, and coats of arms) that should be revered. The king's great seal, for example, relied upon images, of St. George on horseback and the king seated in majesty, to command even illiterate subjects' respect for royal documents (S. Gardiner 274). Seymour asserts that Gardiner thus proved his point about widespread misreading of images, since the mounted figure on the great seal represents the king rather than St. George (Phillips 92). By voicing skepticism about images, then, Cooke articulates a common Protestant position. In doing so, however, he diminishes the value of monuments as proof of Joan's pontificate. If artists could not be counted upon to produce images that recognizably represent the popess, then what could the images that they did produce prove?

Moreover, the problems iconoclasts attributed to images extended beyond artists' technical skill and addressed their knowledge of the subject and their perilous flights of fancy. As the Protestant Thomas Bilson (ca. 1546–1616) observed concerning depictions of Christ, "the forme is nothing but the skill and draught of the craftsman, proportioning a shape not like unto Christ whom he never sawe, but his owne fancie leadeth him." Even if artisans' skills are excellent, the images they fashion are "but the conceite of this maker," and in depictions of Christ that conceit cannot be literally and historically accurate (qtd. in Phillips 87). The Elizabethan *Homilie against Peril of Idolatrie* (1563–71) makes this point more bluntly, insisting that "no true image can be made of Christs body, for it is vnknowen now of what forme and countenance he was. . . . Wherefore, as soone as an image of Christ is made, by and by is a lie made of him. . . . Which also is true of the images of any saints of antiquity, for that it is vnknowen of what forme and countenance they were" (*Certaine* pt. 2, 42). In this sense, the Sienese bust of Joan, crafted centuries after her alleged pontificate and evidently without knowledge of her actual appearance, is a "lie." Moreover, the artists who fashioned the roughly 170 busts situated high above the cathedral's nave were clearly not attempting to reproduce the countenances of their subjects. Among those busts a small number of faces repeat themselves over and over, and the labels fixed below the sculptures, rather than the details within them, serve to differentiate the images and identify which pope each bust portrays (Pardoe and Pardoe 35; Boureau, *Myth* 250). Of course, Cooke appeals to the bust to establish not Joan's precise appearance but rather her existence. His distrust of images' reliability, however, extends beyond small details of "forme and countenance."

Cooke's two interlocutors agree that the fancies of artists sometimes lead them to act without scriptural or documentary support and therefore to depict, for instance, Christ ascending to heaven on an eagle's back. Cooke's "Protestant" adds several more examples of false or unsubstantiated images: portraits of saints such as George and Christopher whose biographies rest upon legend rather than documentary evidence or of "the Virgin Mary treading on the serpent's head, which the scriptures foretold [Genesis 3:15], that Christ himself should do." Such examples persuade him to embrace and reiterate his Catholic opponent's warning "that, if we believe painters and carvers, we shall soon mar all" (*Pope* 20–21). This extremely broad assertion discredits even the Sienese bust, which both interlocutors agree represented the popess. Only if "book-proof concur[s] with painting and carving," Cooke's "Protestant" suggests, can we "give credit to painters and carvers." Images, then, so dependent on linguistic texts for corroboration, can do little or nothing to prove the truth of the popess legend. In the dialogue's dedicatory epistle, Cooke contends that Catholic writers who deny Joan's pontificate become "so intangled" in the subject "that it is with them, as with birds in the lime-twigs, which stick the faster in, by how much they flutter to get out" (*Pope* 10). In his discussion of painters' and carvers' images of the popess, however, Cooke, rather than his opponents, seems to be fluttering in vain.

Mysterious Rituals

Before examining the "book-proof" in detail, Cooke addresses papal rituals, another form of nonverbal evidence that proves to be fraught with much the same difficulty as the carvers' images of the popess. Alluding to a detail from Martinus Polonus's account of Joan's pontificate, Cooke's "Protestant" contends, "That your popes, when they go in procession, refuse to go through that street [where Pope Joan gave birth], in detestation of that fact, and go further about" (*Pope* 14). The modern historians Cesare D'Onofrio and Alain Boureau have confirmed that medieval popes did alter the route of the processions they undertook from the Lateran Palace to the Vatican. As the pope and his entourage traveled toward the Colosseum along what is now the Via San Giovanni in Laterano and approached the church of San Clemente, the ruins of an ancient gladiatorial school (the Ludus magnus) blocked their way, forcing them to turn to one side.[6] Until the mid–twelfth century, they veered left and proceeded a short distance along a narrow street before turning right onto the Via del Santi Quattro Coronati and continuing toward the Colosseum. In subsequent centuries, however, they turned the other way near San Clemente, veering right and then turning left onto what is now the Via Labicana, which they followed to the Colosseum. The narrow street that the later route avoided, the Via del Querceti, became known as the *vicus papisse* (the street of the popess), and the fresco of the Virgin and Child that adorned a chapel on that street was interpreted as an image of Joan and her infant (Boureau, *Myth* 90; D'Onofrio 212–40). As we saw in the introduction, Martinus, who reports that while processing from St. Peter's to the Lateran Joan gave birth in a narrow lane between the Colosseum and San Clemente, asserts that now popes always avoided that street and that many believed ("creditur a plerisque") they did so out of loathing for the popess's disgraceful deeds (Pardoe and Pardoe 11; Morris 153). Notably, Martinus stops short of endorsing this explanation for the alleged detour. Of course, as Catholics, including Cooke's "Papist" interlocutor, were quick to point out, the narrowness of the street, "unfit for so great a train," offers a sound, alternative explanation, particularly if one grants that the size of the procession may have grown over time (Cooke, *Pope* 14). Moreover, the timing of the "detour," beginning in the mid–twelfth century, suggests that, if it had anything to do with Pope Joan, the altered route was more likely a response to the popess legend, which would soon find its way into thirteenth-century chronicles, than to Joan's pontificate, which had allegedly occurred three centuries earlier.

As further evidence of Joan's pontificate, Cooke's "Protestant" cites another ritual, as he demands, "Was there not made of old, for fear of such like after-claps [subsequent surprises], a stool of easement, on which they [popes or popes elect] were set at their creation, for proof of their humanity [masculinity]?" (*Pope* 14). Here, Cooke refers to an object that still exists and a ceremony that, according to Boureau's exhaustive study, never took place. By "stool of easement" Cooke seems to mean one of an identical pair of marble chairs (sometimes described as porphyry) that once stood in the chapel of San Silvestro at the Lateran Palace and remain extant, one in the Vatican

Museum and one in the Louvre. A circular hole about twenty-one centime-
ters in diameter appears in the seat, connected to a roughly thirteen-cen-
timeter square opening that begins at the seat's front. That odd perforation
has prompted scholars to speculate that the chairs were originally birthing
stools; bathing chairs; or, as Cooke's reference to "easement" suggests, toi-
lets. These chairs were used in ceremonies celebrating the investiture of new
popes, but not in the way that Cooke and several other early modern writers
claim. Boureau has uncovered references to newly elected popes reclining in
the chairs in accounts of the accessions of Paschal II in 1099, Gregory XII in
1406, and Leo X in 1513 and in twelfth-century ordines, or service books,
spelling out the investiture ceremony (Boureau, *Myth* 13–17, 48, 53, 55). Neither these accounts nor the ordines, however, mention a procedure for proving the pope elect was male. That procedure first appears around 1290 as a
bit of hearsay in a chronicle by the Benedictine Geoffroy de Courlon. After
echoing Martinus Polonus's account of Joan's pontificate, Geoffroy adds, "It
is said that this is why the Romans established the custom of verifying the sex
of the elected [pope] through the opening in a stone throne" (Boureau, *Myth*
10). Evidently content to rely, indirectly at least, on a vague oral tradition,
Cooke quotes some sources, namely the Dominican mystic Robert d'Uzès
(died 1296) and the fifteenth-century English traveler William Brewyn, who
like Geoffroy attribute their reports to hearsay: "it is said" (dicitur) or "I have
heard" (audivi) (Cooke, *Pope* 17–18; Boureau, *Myth* 21). In contrast to
Cooke, the fifteenth-century Florentine humanist Jacopo d'Angelo of
Scarperia, writing a long, detailed description of Pope Gregory XII's investiture, dismisses the rumor of a verification ritual as a "senseless fable" spread
by the "common people" (Boureau, *Myth* 16). Although that fable circulated
so widely that it even found its way into François Rabelais's *Gargantua et
Pantagruel* (1552), Boureau, who has found no report of the verification ritual that can be traced to an eyewitness, concludes, "The rite never existed
. . . [or] at least none of the many and detailed normative texts that outline
the formalities of papal coronation mentions it" (Rabelais 336, 627; Boureau,
Myth 11, 33–34).[7]

In Cooke's dialogue, debate concerning the pierced chairs centers on their
function and meaning within the investiture ritual and illustrates what
Protestants considered a fundamental flaw in Catholic ceremonies: the
obscurity of their meanings. Many of the same concerns that underlay the
Protestant distrust of images also informed reformers' critique of Roman
ceremonies. As John Jewel complains in his *Apology of the Church of England*
(1562) that Catholics "have brought the sacraments of Christ to be used now
as a stage play and a solemn sight; to the end that men's eyes should be fed

with nothing else but with mad gazings and foolish gauds," he implies that Roman rituals, like the work of painters and carvers, offer primarily visual gratification (35–36). Thomas Becon (1512–67) anticipates both Jewel's theatrical metaphor and his emphasis on the visual, as he characterizes the "scenical and stage-like supper" of the Mass as "none other thing than a dumb fable or play, full of trifling and hickscorner-like [theatrical and perhaps irreligious] gestures" (378).[8] Importantly, this comparison to a dumb show foregrounds the Mass's putative lack of any meaningful verbal component. As Huston Diehl has noted, that lack, rather than the mere presence of visual or dramatic elements, prompted English Calvinists to condemn the Mass as preposterous and harmful (104). The Elizabethan *Book of Common Prayer* (1559) illustrates Diehl's point, as it insists somewhat defensively that the Church of England has preserved only those ceremonies that "be neither dark nor dumb" (20). Echoing charges made by Calvin and William Tyndale, Becon explains that the lack of a meaningful verbal component produces the Catholic Mass's darkness or obscurity: "As touching Christ and his death, the hearers hear nothing at all, that by this means they might lift up and confirm their faith toward God. That massing priest mumbleth all things secretly and in a strange tongue; so that the congregation is nothing edified, nor hath any profit at all" (378).[9] In place of comprehensible, edifying speech, the priest offers histrionic gestures.

As Jonas Barish has put it, according to this Calvinist perspective, "traditional liturgy was designed to mystify rather than elucidate. What was merely seen could never be more than an enigmatic tableau until properly glossed and explicated" (163). Such glossing and explication are not part of the investiture rituals that Cooke's interlocutors discuss. Felix Hemmerli (or Hemmerlin, ca 1388–ca. 1460) did add an audible and verbal (albeit Latin) component to the verification ritual as he reported that after the clerics conducting a manual examination had confirmed that the pope elect was male, they exclaimed, "Testiculos habet" (He has testicles). "At this," Hemmerli continues, "the priest and the people responded 'Deo gratias'"(Thanks be to God) (qtd. in Boureau, *Myth* 21–22). Cooke's dialogue, however, lacks any reference to this exchange. The omission of such edifying speech enables Cooke's Catholic interlocutor to propose alternative explanations for the meaning of seating the pope elect in the pierced chairs. Accepting his Protestant counterpart's suggestion that these chairs were associated with bodily relief or "easement," and citing Catholic authorities such as Raemond and Robert Bellarmine (1542–1621), Cooke's "Papist" proposes that the ceremony may have signified that the pope elect "is not God, but Man; inasmuch as he stands in need of a close-stool [seat holding a chamber pot] as well as others," or it may have represented how he "is raised from base estate to supreme honor" (*Pope* 18–19). In fact, both the twelfth-century service books and Jacopo D'Angelo's account of the 1406 investiture of Pope Gregory XII report that a different chair, a "stercoria," or "seat of mire," located at the portico of the Basilica of St. John Lateran (rather than in the chapel of San Silvestro, where the pierced marble chairs stood), functioned in the way that Cooke's "Papist" describes, reminding the pope that he "arises out of clay and dung" (*stercus*) (Boureau, *Myth* 16, 92). The diction that Cooke's "Protestant" employs as he challenges these alternative interpretations draws attention to the enigmatic character of Catholic ritual: "Besides, methinks they should not have intended such a mystery by such a ceremony, because they set him therein before he was in his *Pontificalibus;* for till he be mitered . . . there should be no great fear of forgetting himself" (*Pope* 19). In the early modern usage employed here, the term *mystery,* with all its connotations of secrecy, obscurity, and incomprehensibility, denotes "meaning" (*OED* 10: 173).[10] Like images, then, ceremonies, whose meanings remained obscure without verbal explication, could offer little proof that Joan's pontificate had truly occurred.

Gelded Texts

Concerning "book-proof," which the inadequacies of evidence drawn from images and ceremonies made all the more important, Cooke's dedicatory epistle confidently asserts that in the dialogue "the report of Pope Joan . . . is proved by a cloud of witnesses" (*Pope* 10). The diction and biblical allusion employed in this statement, however, point to difficulties regarding such proof. Hebrews 11 and 12, in which the phrase "cloud of witnesses" appears (with "cloud" denoting a dense crowd), concerns not documentary evidence but rather faith, which Paul here defines as "the substance of things hoped for, the evidence of things not seen" (Heb. 11:1, 12:1); indeed, as Paul reviews the working of faith in biblical history, he cites at least one incident, the framing of worlds, that no human could have witnessed. Similarly, none of the "witnesses" that Cooke cites had any direct knowledge of Joan's pontificate. The absence of eyewitness accounts of Joan's career, or at least reports from her supposed contemporaries, constituted a formidable obstacle for controversialists who, like Cooke, set out to prove the veracity of the popess legend.[11] In particular, the absence of an entry on Joan in the *Liber pontificalis* (Book of Popes), a collection of papal biographies stretching in early medieval editions from St. Peter to Nicholas I (reigning 858–67), one of Joan's alleged successors, seemed problematic and prompted Cooke's "Protestant" to challenge the "great reputation" of Anastasius Bibliothecarius (ca. 810–79), the librarian of the Roman Church to whom the *Liber* was then attributed (Cooke, *Pope* 48–52; Pardoe and Pardoe 12–14).[12] As Cooke's "Papist" puts it, "no-body, within four hundred years after, mentions her popedom; and, is it possible, that all writers should so conspire together, that the truth thereof could never be certainly known, till four hundred years after?" (*Pope* 64). He thus anticipates the skepticism of modern scholars who note the long interval between the thirteenth-century composition of the earliest extant written accounts of the popess (in Jean de Mailly's *Chronica universalis Mettensis,* ca. 1260; Etienne de Bourbon's *Tractatus de diversis materiis praedicabilibus,* ca. 1261; and Mattinus Polonus's *Chronicon pontificum et imperatorum,* ca. 1280) and the start of her alleged pontificate in 1099, 1100, or, as reported in the most influential early account, 855.

Although, as we shall see, Cooke's "Protestant" contends that the interval between event and report was far shorter than his opponent claims, he dismisses the significance of even a four-hundred-year gap, insisting, "do not you papists commend unto us ma[n]y stories, as true, for which you can bring us no proof out of any writer who lived within four hundred years after?" (*Pope* 64). Here, as he does when he appeals to Catholic hagiography to establish the plausibility of Joan's transvestite disguise, Cooke's "Protestant" adopts rather low standards, suggesting that the popess legend is as credible as are poorly documented Catholic traditions. Moreover, the examples that he cites to support his claim do little to raise these standards. Catholics' much maligned fascination with religious images informs most of these examples, namely, reports that St. Luke painted portraits of the Virgin Mary; that Christ's contemporary and disciple Nicodemus sculpted a miraculous statue capable of "wonderful things" and depicting Christ crucified (the revered Volto Santo crucifix displayed at the Lucca Cathedral); that by wiping his face on a handkerchief Christ imprinted the cloth with a visible image of his features; and that at a council at Antioch the apostles encouraged the faithful to "make the image of our Saviour Christ, both God and Man, and the images of his servants" (Cooke, *Pope* 65; Kristof 170). It seems unlikely that the precedent of an alleged apostolic directive to fashion religious icons would enhance the credibility of the popess narrative for anyone who believed, as the Elizabethan *Homilie against Peril of Idolatrie* insisted, that images of Christ (which cannot express his divine nature) and images of the saints (which cannot express their "soules, the most excellent partes of them") are "not onely defects, but also lies," forbidden "by GODS word"

(*Certaine* pt. 2, 42). Such examples fail to render the four-hundred-year gap between event and report inconsequential.

As I have noted, Cooke's "Protestant" does not rely entirely on the analogy to Catholic traditions but also contests the gap itself. He contends that long before the thirteenth-century reports, Joan's story appeared in chronicles by the Benedictines Marianus Scotus and Sigebert of Gembloux.[13] The debate that Cooke composes for his interlocutors concerning these texts points to a central issue for Protestants adhering to their principle "sola scriptura." If, as one of the Thirty-nine Articles of the Religion of the Church of England (1571) declares, "Holy scripture," alone and without the aid of church traditions, "containeth all things necessary for salvation" (qtd. in Schaff 3: 490), then salvation depends upon establishing the authenticity and integrity of foundational texts—and so too does verifying the references to Joan in early chronicles. Cooke's Catholic contends (and modern scholars have confirmed) that although Joan's story appears in sixteenth-century "printed copies" of Marianus's *Chronicon* and Sigebert's *Chronographia,* it is absent from "the most ancient hand-written originals" (*Pope* 38, 40).[14] Moreover, as I note in the introduction, the references to the popess that do appear in late medieval manuscripts of these texts seem to date from the fourteenth century and are often written in the margins, as if added after the main text was completed (Boureau, *Myth* 116, 317; Pardoe and Pardoe 14–15). The interlocutors' discussion of inconsistencies among manuscript and print editions of these texts generates predictable conjectures. Perhaps those determined to "make the Pope odious" had "chopped this tale into" later manuscripts or printed volumes (*Pope* 39). Alternatively, those following what Cooke's "Protestant" presents as a standard Catholic policy, "that such things should be altered or put out, which tend to the discredit of the clergy," may have tampered with the early manuscripts, "rasing" or "cutting out" material that "touch[ed] at the quick" Rome's "ecclesiastical state" (*Pope* 42–43). These competing explanations suggest that, even if one sets aside problems of interpretation and translation, textual variants might render even "book-proof"—the needed corroboration for less reliable evidence drawn from images and ceremonies—uncertain.

Cooke's "Protestant" contends that textual discrepancies like those found in copies of these chronicles are common and of little consequence, insisting to his "Papist" counterpart, "I presume you are not so ignorant, but you know, that words, sentences, and memorable accidents have, sometimes by negligence, sometimes by willfulness, been left out of copies?" To support his point, he rather surprisingly cites examples from the Christian gospels

(Mark 13:32, Luke 22:43–44, John 8), verses that, he contends, are missing from some manuscripts but accepted as scriptural by both Catholics and Protestants. Elaborating on his reference to "willfulness" and citing as a source the cardinal and controversialist Robert Bellarmine, he explains that by the fourth century one of these passages had been "blotted out" of many Greek and Latin manuscripts "by the enemies of God's truth" and that by the fifth century another had been "rased" out of "many copies" by "some simple catholicks, fearing" that, with its reference to an angel's "strengthening" Christ as he contemplated his imminent crucifixion (Luke 22:43), "it made for the Arians," who espoused the heresy that Christ was created by God and was hence neither equal to nor coeternal with the Father (*Pope* 42–43).[15] Although here Cooke's "Protestant" cites verses that reportedly were no longer controversial, earlier in the dialogue he suggests that scriptural variants figure in more recent disputes, as he cites a Catholic bishop who, to advance his reading of John 21:22, a verse "about which you know there hath been hot contention," appealed to a variant that he claimed to have seen in "an ancient hand-written original kept at Aix in Germany" (*Pope* 36–37). Later, when he reunites his interlocutors in another dialogue, this time concerning *The Abatement of Popish Brags, Pretending Scripture to Be Theirs* (1625), Cooke reveals that Catholics and Protestants even dispute the canonicity of entire scriptural books. When in that later text the Catholic interlocutor cites Tobit 12:9—"For alms doth deliver from death, and shall purge away all sin"—to support justification through good works, the "Protestant" dismisses that point by observing, "The book is Apocrypha," and thus, according to the Anglican Thirty-nine Articles, good to "reade for example of lyfe and instruction" but not to "establishe any doctrene" (Cooke, *Abatement* 21; Schaff 3: 490–91). Defending Protestant doctrine, then, depends upon establishing both a scriptural canon and the authenticity of texts within it.

With his seemingly casual reference to biblical variants, Cooke's "Protestant" points to questions regarding whether the authenticity of scriptural texts could be established as certainly as Protestants' reliance on "scripture alone" would seem to require. Recognizing the centrality of such questions in early modern religious debates and arguing in his *Dialogue Concerning Heresies* (1529) that the principle "sola scriptura" paradoxically renders the church indispensable, Sir Thomas More (1478–1535) reminds his readers of the apocryphal gospels and observes, "There were many that wrote the gospel. And yet hath the chyrche by secrete instinct of god rejected [th]e remenaunt & chosen out these foure for the sure vndoubted trewe" (181). In his *Institutes of the Christian Religion* (1536), Calvin rehearses the questions that Catholic controversialists such as More put to Reformers, as he prepares to answer them: "For thus, with great contempt of the Holy Spirit, they inquire, Who can assure us that God is the author of them [biblical texts]? Who can with certainty affirm, that they have been preserved safe and uncorrupted to the present age? Who can persuade us that this book ought to be received with reverence, and that expunged from the sacred number, unless all these things were regulated by the decisions of the Church?" (1: 86). Here, Calvin considers questions regarding both the contents of the canon (which "book[s] ought to be received with reverence") and the authenticity of the texts included within it ("have [they] been preserved safe and uncorrupted to the present age"). Calvin's initial response to such questions was doubtless too simple for opponents such as More and too simple, perhaps, to convey how sixteenth-century Protestants struggled to arrive at a canon: "This is just as if any one should inquire, How shall we learn to distinguish light from darkness, white from black, sweet from bitter? For the Scripture exhibits as clear evidence of its truth, as white and black things do of their colour, or sweet and bitter things of their taste." (*Institutes* 1: 87).[16] In contrast, such easy clarity seems to have eluded Martin Luther. Although he expresses dissatisfaction with some biblical books, reporting that he hates Esther and II Maccabees due to their "heathenism," and dismissing the Letter of St. James as an "epistle of straw," and although in 1546 the Council of Trent explicitly listed the contents of the Catholic canon, Luther and his successors stopped short of defining their scriptural canon in the 1530 Augsburg Confession and 1577 Formula of Concord (Bainton 6–7; Hotchkiss and Price 21). As Cooke attempted to dismiss questions regarding medieval chronicles, then, he introduced troubling, central questions regarding Protestantism's textual foundation.

Although other Protestants who engaged in the debate concerning Joan's existence did not necessarily draw attention to variants in scriptural manuscripts, the long interval between event and report did prompt some to posit a Catholic cover-up that might include not only removing the papal bust in Siena but also expurgating problematic texts. The metaphor that one of Cooke's successors used to describe such expurgation further reveals how the notion that Catholics had been altering texts, cutting out authentic material or "chopping" in false, unsettled the foundations of Protestantism. Concerning the absence of the popess narrative from some seemingly early manuscripts of Sigebert's *Chronographia,* "R. W.," the author of the 1689 *Pope Joan: or, An Account Collected out of the Romish Authors,* observes, "It is known how *Romanists* can and have Gelded Books, after they have printed second Copies" (3). The recurrent early modern use of this metaphor of censorship as castration and its underlying logic have been explored by Gary Taylor. Like a body, a book (or codex) possesses bilateral symmetry: "When we open a book, the opening displays two pages, symmetrically aligned. Moreover, a codex can be mutilated at any point by tearing out a page. And because a page is written on both sides, such mutilations always excise not one part of the text but two. In other words, mutilating a codex resembles mutilating a human male by removal of his two symmetrical bilateral testicles" (90).[17] Thanks to feminist inquiries into the intersection of phallocentrism and logocentrism, the gendering of texts as male in this metaphor comes as no surprise. In a further parallel, castration and expurgation, which, as Taylor points out, are effected through similar means, also accomplish much the same objective: preventing reproduction. Of course, the expunged passages would be missing from any subsequent handwritten or printed copy of a mutilated text. The metaphor, however, seems to imply something more; it concerns the immaterial reproduction of ideas rather than simply the physical reproduction of the book as object. Geldings, after all, do not reproduce geldings. "To say that a text has been castrated," Taylor contends, "is to imply that the text, in its natural original form, is a bilateral repository of male seed" (91). Alluding to the biblical parable of the sower (Matt. 13; Mark 4; Luke 8), Taylor identifies the seed with good teachings; indeed, as Luke explains, "The seed is the word of God" (Luke 8:11). The reader or hearer, then, corresponds to the soil or womb waiting to be seeded or inseminated, and the expunged text, like the amputated testes, is imagined as a lost essential element that would have enabled the reproduction and growth of good teachings. Alluding to the use of castration to achieve selective breeding and adopting the perspective of those hostile to censorship, Taylor explains that "textual castration was an attempt to cut off the life-giving seed, to prevent true texts from impregnating souls—and thereby to enable illegitimate suitors to father bastard doctrines" (91).

As the relevance of the parable of the sower suggests, the gelding metaphor proves especially suggestive within discussions of religious or theological texts and, in fact, appeared repeatedly in early modern Protestant polemics. In that context, the metaphor drew upon established patterns of association, since, in Reformers' eyes, Catholic ecclesiasts encouraged or effected several forms of literal or figurative castration. For example, a papal injunction against women's singing in public encouraged the use of castrati in church choirs. After Pope Sixtus V issued a bull directing the inclusion of four eunuchs in the choir of St. Peter's, the practice became more widespread, so that by 1640 eunuchs sang in all the main church choirs of Italy (Jenkins 1877–78; Scholz 274–76; G. Taylor 39). More important, both

Luther and Calvin charged that the requirement of clerical celibacy effectively demanded that Catholic priests, like the ancient self-castrating devotees of the goddess Cybele, "unman themselves" (Luther 36: 114; Calvin, *Commentaries* 338; G. Taylor 14, 78–79). "Romanists," then, were no strangers to literal or metaphorical castration.

Far from being isolated events, instances of "textual castration," to borrow Taylor's phrase, appeared to be part of a systematic campaign guided by the Catholic indexes that prohibited some books and directed the expurgation of others (Benson 58; Hildersam 38). Protestant polemicists imagined differing scopes and consequences for that campaign. In a 1606 tract, William Crashaw initially suggested a relatively narrow scope—"they haue corrupted all the Authors of this last two hundred yeares"—but then broadened it, as he asserted that they had "razed the records of higher antiquitie [earlier date] reaching vp to some that liued 500. and 800. years ago, taking out words and whole sentences, adding to, and altering at their pleasure in some one booke foure or fiue hundred places," and producing texts "gelded, and clipped, and chopped" beyond recognition (*Romish Forgeries* E3v). Others claimed that the campaign extended to the works of the early Church Fathers and even of the third-century theologian Origen (ca. 185–ca. 254; Hildersam 38–39; Benson 58; Fulke, *Two Treatises* pt. 2: 250). At times, Protestants suggested that these Catholic efforts were futile since, as Arthur Hildersam (1563–1632) put it, "they haue knowne well, that we haue many printed and written copies to control them by," that is, with which to compare and check expurgated texts (38).[18] R. W.'s claim that "Romanists" gelded books "*after* they have printed second Copies" seems to imply as much (3, my emphasis). Just one page after claiming that gelded texts can be "controlled," however, Hildersam asserts that such gelding had produced profound obscurity: "There is not certainty euen of the most legitimate bookes of the best Fathers; for, heretiques haue gelded and corrupted them, and foisted into them their owne errours" (39). These writers do not seem to contemplate the prospect that Calvin imagines Catholics raising: that scripture might not "have been preserved safe and uncorrupted." However, if "Romanists" were such shameless gelders of texts, and if even a millennium earlier "simple catholicks" had cut verses from copies of scripture in order to gain an advantage in doctrinal controversies, could one be certain that the scripture had remained "safe and uncorrupted"? Calvin insisted that the authenticity of scripture was as evident as the difference between white and black, sweet and bitter, but would the deletion or omission of a scriptural word or sentence be so obvious? Even if Hildersam does not imagine that textual castration obscures the scripture, by suggesting that it casts doubt on the writings of the Church Fathers, representatives of the uncorrupted primitive church and "good helpes for the vnderstanding of the Scriptures" (Hildersam 38), he credits it with weighty consequences.

As Cooke sees it, the popess episode poses a fundamental challenge to Catholicism, causing the ninth-century church to "hop headless" (to borrow his colorful phrase) for more than two years; invalidating the sacramental system; breaching apostolic succession; and thus rendering the Roman Church a mere pretense since, he contends, "it is no true church, which cannot" provide "without any breach" and "in plain authentical writing, the lawful, orderly, intire . . . succession of bishops" (*Pope* 107).[19] Cooke's reference to scriptural variants and altered manuscripts, however, poses a challenge for Protestantism that, if more modest, is similar in important respects. By breaking the apostolic succession, Joan's pontificate denies Catholics a legitimate pope (*papa* in Latin) or "Holy Father"; in turn, the sorts of textual issues raised in Cooke's dialogue cast doubt on Protestants' access to the metaphorical fathers whom they valued. Although, as we have seen, Anglicans contended that "Holy scripture containeth all things necessary for salvation," they also claimed further support for their doctrine and practices (Schaff 3: 490). In his *Apology of the Church of England,* Jewel declares, "We are come, as near as we possibly could, to the church of the apostles and of the old catholic bishops and fathers, which church we know hath hitherto been sound and perfect" (121). Through such claims, Anglicans could answer opponents' charges that all their beliefs and practices "be but new and yesterday's work" and assert that on the contrary they had "returned to the apostles and old catholic fathers" (Jewel, *Apology* 17, 83). For Hildersam, however, the sorts of textual problems that Cooke cites render "the most legitimate bookes of the best Fathers" uncertain and unreliable. As he evokes the castration metaphor, Hildersam's contemporary George Benson (ca. 1569–ca. 1647) elides the distinction between text and author and thus casts the issue in sharp relief. Catholics, he contends, have set out to "geld and purge the Fathers of all such sentences as might make against the Church of Rome" (58). Gelded fathers cannot perform the function assigned to them; they cannot reproduce good teachings and confirm the legitimacy of Protestants who aspire to be heirs to the "sound and perfect" primitive church.

Here, we see a more developed instance of the pattern we glimpsed in the removal of the Sienese papal bust and will encounter again in subsequent chapters: the Pope Joan legend complicates attempts to manipulate it for polemical purposes. Using the popess controversy to "lay open" the allegedly shameful way that Catholics support their claims in interdenominational disputes prompts Cooke to rely upon evidence that, to borrow Bayle's formulation, were it "advantageous to the Popes . . . would seem worthy [of] the utmost contempt," as he appears to credit images and ceremonies with an authority that his Protestant convictions disallow. Moreover, attempting to fill a gap in the documentary evidence (by claiming that Marianus Scotus and Sigebert of Gembloux reported Joan's pontificate) prompts him to introduce questions regarding textual variants and expurgation that, in turn, suggest the Protestants' simple maxim "sola scriptura" obscures the complex issues concerning textual criticism and canon formation with which it is necessarily entangled. Inconsistencies in the positions that Cooke adopts thus undermine his efforts to "lay open the shame" that should attach to Catholics' "handling of points in controversy," for his own polemical tactics sometimes seem to entail, as he claims of Catholics, "play[ing] the fool." In the next chapter, we will explore how the risk of articulating inconsistent positions regarding another matter—feminine rule—deterred the Protestant subjects of Elizabeth I, the "Supreme Governor" of the Church of England, from entering the popess controversy as boldly and elaborately as Cooke later did.

2 *Comparing Joan*

THE WHORE OF BABYLON
AND THE VIRGIN QUEEN

In MARCH 1592, at the Rose Theatre, Lord Strange's Men dramatized the career of Pope Joan. Unfortunately, no copy of the play they performed, which the impresario Philip Henslowe (ca. 1550–1616) recorded in his diary as "poope Jone," has survived (Henslowe 22; Patrides 169; Pardoe and Pardoe 84). At first glance, this might appear to be all there is to say about this tantalizingly lost drama. However, the absence of an extant printed edition fits into a pattern that is itself significant. No copy of "poope Jone" survives because, most simply, none was published, even though Henslowe's notes suggest that the play was a commercial success, evidently performed more than once and generating receipts comparable to those of better-known and subsequently published plays such as Robert Greene's *Friar Bacon and Friar Bungay*.[1] If, as both James Shapiro and Leeds Barroll have suggested, Elizabethan authorities responsible for censorship manifested more concern for printed than for performed texts, some sensitivity to the play's content may have prevented its publication (J. Shapiro 429–30; Barroll 444–52; Siebert 63).[2] In fact, Elizabethan printers seem to have been reluctant to bring out texts devoted wholly to the popess: scholars have uncovered only two published in England during the queen's reign. The title of the first, John Mayo's *The Popes Parliament . . . Whereunto Is Annexed an Anatomie of Pope Joane* (1591), inaccurately implies that its appendix alone concerns the popess. The second, a 1599 translation of a German tract, rather cautiously uses only two initials ("T. B.") on its final page to identify its author or translator; moreover, its title, *Historia de Donne Famose, or The Romane Iubile which Happened in the Yeare 855* (1599), stops short of mentioning Joan by name and instead alludes to her only indirectly by citing the year when her pontificate reportedly began.[3] In contrast to their predecessors, Stuart printers brought out at least six texts concerning the popess between 1610 and 1689, often assigning them frank titles such as *The History of Pope Joan and the Whores of Rome* (1687) and in several cases publishing multiple editions.[4] Furthermore, since none of these Stuart texts was published during the Interregnum, the antiecclesiastical sentiments of Commonwealth and Protectorate governments do not account for this contrast between sixteenth- and seventeenth-century publishing practices. A possible explanation does appear, however, in the work of the French Catholic controversialist Florimond de Raemond.

Within a 1594 monograph devoted to disproving the existence of the medieval popess, Raemond assigns two chapters to England's queen. He charges that Elizabeth has seized papal authority and has called herself ruler of the English Church ("se dict chef d[e] l'Eglise"). Consequently, he characterizes her as "ceste nouvelle Papesse"; indeed, he contends, Elizabeth is the only popess who is not merely an empty phantasm conjured up by Reformers (Raemond 101, 107; Tinsley, "Pope Joan" 381; Tinsley, *History* 77). Writing nearly a decade later, the exiled English Catholic Robert Persons follows the lead of his French coreligionist and observes less elaborately that talk of female prelates "is more against the protestants, then vs. For that their Church admitteth for laufull and supreame head therof eyther man or woman: Which our Church doth not" (390). Raemond's argument, thus echoed by Persons, helps us to see how likely comparisons between Pope Joan and Queen Elizabeth might have discouraged Elizabethan printers from bringing out texts devoted to the popess.[5] In this chapter, I propose to explore the foundation for Raemond's analogy and to demonstrate how a further, interrelated analogy between Pope Joan and the Whore of Babylon rendered the popess legend an awkward polemical instrument for Elizabethan Protestants.

Joan at the Rose

Of course, my suggestion that some form of censorship or self-censorship might have blocked the publication of the lost play assumes that the portrait of Pope Joan staged at the Rose Theatre was so unflattering that comparisons between the play's protagonist and England's queen would have troubled Elizabeth and her adherents. The evolution of the popess legend during the sixteenth century supports that assumption. Admittedly, by cross-dressing in order to secure greater social influence, or at least freedom of movement, Joan anticipates the actions of several appealing and resourceful heroines in Elizabethan drama. Nonetheless, I suspect that the protagonist of the 1592 play shared more traits with Shakespeare's "high-minded strumpet" La

Pucelle (*1H6* 1.5.12) than with the virtuous Portia or "heavenly" Rosallind (*AYL* 1.2.280). As we have seen, by the mid–sixteenth century, the ambivalent or flattering view of Joan evident in some medieval accounts had disappeared. Even in a text devoted to expounding the "nobility and preeminence" of women (*Declamatio de nobilitate et praecellentia foeminei sexus,* 1532), Henricus Cornelius Agrippa suggests that Joan's "egregious imposture" (*egregia impostura*), like Delilah's victory over Samson, brings more disgrace than glory to her sex (Agrippa 66; Hotchkiss, "Legend" 499). By 1592 a Protestant account of the popess's shameful career had been widely disseminated in England through John Foxe's *Acts and Monuments* (1563), a text that, according to a 1571 order, was to be installed and available to read in each of the kingdom's cathedral churches (Foxe 2: 7; Morley 147). Further, John Mayo's *The Popes Parliament,* published just a year before the Rose Theatre performance, offers particular insight into the legend's reception in late sixteenth-century England, as it both conveys a Protestant view of the popess and imagines a Catholic reaction to her. In Mayo's fanciful narrative, a statue depicting Joan's "filthinesse and abhomination" so disturbs Pope Gregory XIV that he breaks off a solemn procession; runs back to his papal palace; and declares that all English Catholics, whose homeland gave birth to the vile popess, should be cast out of Rome (1, 17). Since my research has uncovered no sixteenth- or seventeenth-century English text that counters such representations and portrays Joan admirably, I doubt that the 1592 play did so.

On the other hand, a play depicting Joan as a corrupt villainess would seem at home among the others performed by Lord Strange's Men in March 1592. According to Henslowe's notes, the play produced most frequently (six times) at the Rose that month was "harey the vj," possibly part of Shakespeare's tetralogy. Even if the history play cited in Henslowe's diary was not Shakespeare's, another Elizabethan playwright drawing upon the same historical materials may well have produced a similar drama. Perhaps, then, the popess shared the Rose Theatre stage with "haughty prelate[s]" such as Shakespeare's bishop of Winchester and with another cross-dressing, Catholic woman, Joan of Arc. Although the two Joans differed in many ways, Shakespeare's La Pucelle resembles the popess in several respects. As if reenacting Pope Joan's audacity and licentiousness, Shakespeare's Joan of Arc announces her determination to "exceed my sex" and later claims to have bedded several different French aristocrats (*1H6* 1.2.90, 5.4.59–85). She also conjures fiends (*1H6* 5.3) and thus establishes a further parallel between herself and the popess, who reportedly not only rose to St. Peter's Chair "under the Devil's direction" but also wrote a "Booke of *Necromancie*" (Pardoe and Pardoe 16–17, 34; Boureau, *Myth* 118; Bale, *Scriptorvm illustrium* 2: 122; Wolf 1: 239; *Historia* C2v). Similarly, the portrait of an overreaching Catholic cleric practicing sorcery in *Friar Bacon and Friar Bungay* would have complemented a theatrical representation of a popess thus associated with devils and necromancy. Additionally, a corrupt popess counseled by demons would have had much in common with the treacherous, unprincipled Catholics portrayed in *The Spanish Tragedy* and *The Jew of Malta* (performed three and two times that month, respectively). In fact, the latter play's lecherous friars and opening allusion to Machiavellian popes (prologue 10–13) would have made it another apt companion piece for a scurrilous portrait of Joan. Moreover, if, as Lawrence Manley has argued, Lord Strange's Men seem to have "courted controversy by being unusually defiant of authority," the uncomfortable parallels between queen and popess might not have deterred them from portraying Joan. The Lord Mayor of London complained in a November 1589 letter to the queen's chief minister, Lord Burghley (William Cecil, 1520–98), for example, that when he "required" Lord Strange's Men "in her Maiesties name to forbere playinge" they "in very Contemptuous manner departing from me, went to the Crosse keys and played that afternoon, to the greate offence of the better sorte that knewe they were prohibited by order from your L[ordship]" (Manley 254–55; E. K. Chambers 4: 305).[6] A scurrilous portrait of the popess, then, would have accorded with sixteenth-century English references to Pope Joan, the Rose Theatre repertoire, and the evident audacity of Lord Strange's Men.[7]

Supreme Governor

Both Anglican Church polity and certain royal practices lent credibility to Raemond's troubling contention that Elizabeth rather than Joan was the true popess. For one thing, the Frenchman's claim that Elizabeth named herself ruler of the Church alludes to a controversy that confronted the queen as soon as she acceded to the throne. The Calvinist Anthony Gilby, who no doubt shared very few of Raemond's views, agreed that royal supremacy over the Church effectively made English monarchs popes by another name. Writing at the time of Elizabeth's accession, Gilby charges that Henry VIII (1491–1547, reigning 1509–47) emulated "the Romish Antichrist" by imposing "the king's book and the king's proceedings, the king's homelies in the churches where God's word should only have been preached" (qtd. in Cross 118–19). The ecclesiastical title that both Henry

VIII and Edward VI (1537–53, reigning 1547–53) adopted, "Supreme Head" of the Church of England, encouraged comparisons such as Gilby's since, as Robert Persons's remark concerning female supremacy implies, popes claimed that title for themselves. Elizabeth recognized that her role in the Anglican Church could excite controversy. Consequently, she set aside the title that her father and brother had employed and instead, through the 1559 Act of Supremacy, pronounced herself "Supreme Governor" (Cross 22–29, 126–31).

Gender concerns reportedly did not trigger Elizabeth's decision; nonetheless, the revised title could shield a queen regnant from certain, likely rhetorical attacks. Although Elizabeth believed, as John Jewel reports in a 1559 letter to Heinrich Bullinger, that the title of head of the Church was "due to Christ alone, and cannot belong to any human being soever," some bishops contended that the queen's gender rather than her humanity disqualified her (qtd. in C. Levin, *"Heart"* 14; Cross 138; Strype, vol. 1, pt. 2, 406–7). The body-politic metaphor implied in the title "head" could serve as a potent weapon for those arguing that position. John Knox (ca. 1514–72), for example, writing just a year before Parliament passed the Act of Supremacy, uses the body-politic metaphor to portray the monstrousness of feminine rule, as he asks: "For who would not judge that body to be a monster where there was no head eminent above the rest, but that the eyes were in the hands, the tongue and mouth beneath in the belly, and the ears in the feet? . . . And no less monstrous is the body of that commonwealth where a woman beareth empire" (56). Although Elizabeth's revised title could not quell all objections to her "power to command," it could help to deflect the charge that she had transformed the Church into the sort of a metaphorical monster that Knox describes.

Even the cautious Elizabeth sometimes engaged in practices, such as the Royal Maundy and touching to cure the King's Evil (scrofula), that seemed to infringe on the ecclesiastical domain. As Marc Bloch has observed, by the sixteenth century the ceremony of the royal touch had become "a veritable liturgical service," in which the monarch, "assisted by his [or her] chaplain, almost played the part of officiant"—in fact, the ritual was included in the 1633 *Book of Common Prayer.* Moreover, the widespread notion that the sovereign's healing powers resulted from the anointing at coronation recalled medieval claims that the royal unction invested a monarch with an almost priestly status (Bloch 112, 122, 130, 139).[8] During Elizabeth's reign, the healing ceremony most often took place in St. Stephen's Chapel in the palace at Westminster. While the sick approached and knelt before the queen, her chaplain read Mark 16:14–20. As the queen touched the diseased areas on the body of each afflicted person, the chaplain repeated the verse, "they shall lay hands on the sick, and they shall recover" (Mark 14:18), suggesting that Elizabeth had taken up the wonder-working task of the earliest Christian believers. While touching the afflicted, she made the sign of the cross over the scrofulous areas, a gesture that provoked objections from some of her Protestant subjects. Next, the chaplain read the richly metaphoric account of the incarnation and of the ministry of John the Baptist in John 1:1–14 while the sick filed past the queen, who presented each with a gold coin, appropriately enough, an angel. Deborah Willis contends that this scriptural passage "links the Queen to John the Baptist, bearing witness to the light, while the gold coin represents the 'new light' itself." To conclude, Elizabeth knelt, and she, rather than her chaplain, led the assembly in prayers, including the kyrie, a part of the Anglican communion service. This ceremony inspired the queen's surgeon William Clowes (ca. 1540–1604) to portray Elizabeth as a unique conduit of divine grace. He reported that "our most Sacred and Renowned Prince" healed the afflicted "through the gift and power of Almightie God" and claimed "that (for the certaine cure of this most miserable Malady) when all Arts and Sciences doe faile, Her highness is the only Daystarre, peerless and without companion" (qtd. in Willis 148, 154; Bloch 53, 191, 208; C. Levin, *"Heart"* 31; *Book of Common Prayer* 249).[9]

Like the royal touch, the Royal Maundy seemed to cast the queen in a clerical role. This ceremony was rooted in Christ's instructions to his apostles at the Last Supper. After washing the feet of each apostle, according to John's gospel, Christ explained, "For I have given you an example, that you should do as I have done to you" (John 13:15). The ritual imitation of this action, the Mandatum, had become part of the Holy Thursday liturgy by the seventh century, and by the eleventh century popes had begun washing the feet of twelve archdeacons at Mass on that day. Edward II (1284–1327, reigning 1307–27) was the first English monarch to emulate this liturgical practice. During Elizabeth's reign, the ceremony, conducted in a royal hall on Maundy (Holy) Thursday, began with song, prayers, and a gospel reading. Then the queen, evidently using holy water, washed and kissed the feet of several poor women, their number equaling the queen's age. As in the ritual of the royal touch, she made the sign of the cross on the bodies of her subjects, which, according to the Spanish ambassador Guzman de Silva, provoked "the sorrow of many persons who witnessed it and of others who would not attend the ceremony" (qtd. in C. Levin, *"Heart"* 35). Before the women departed, the queen presented each with gifts of cloth, food, wine, and money.[10] As if to demonstrate Elizabeth's ecclesiastical supremacy and to intensify the liturgical character of the proceedings, a chaplain and at least one bishop (the almoner) attended and assisted the queen on these occasions (C. Levin, *"Heart"* 33–34).

As De Silva's remark suggests, by conducting these ceremonies Elizabeth invited disapproval. Both practices incorporated vestiges of Roman rites, most notably the signing of the cross—in fact, Elizabeth reportedly acknowledged as much. De Silva claimed that when he praised the queen for performing the Maundy and particularly for "the devotion with which she made the crosses on the feet of the poor women," she answered, "Many people think we are Turks or Moors here, whereas we only differ from other Catholics in things of small importance" (qtd. in C. Levin, *"Heart"* 35). More significantly for our current discussion, the queen's participation in these ceremonies did not easily fit within the constraints that men such as the archbishop of York, Nicholas Heath, sought to impose on Elizabeth's ecclesiastical role. "Her highness, beyinge a woman by birthe and nature, is not qualyfied by God's worde to feed the flock of Chryst," he contended during 1559 debates in the House of Lords. "A woman, in the degrees of Chryst's churche, is not called to be an apostel, or evangelst, nor to be a shepherd, neyther a doctor or preacher" (qtd. in Strype vol. 1, pt. 2, 406–7; C. Levin, *"Heart"* 14). For those who agreed with Heath, a woman who performed a ritual lifted from the Holy Thursday liturgy, laid on healing hands, and led a chapel congregation in the praying of the kyrie most likely seemed to manifest an impudence reminiscent of the legendary popess. Admittedly, Mary Tudor (1516–58, reigning 1553–58) had conducted these ceremonies in much the same form; however, since she did not claim supreme ecclesiastical authority, she was immune from some of the attacks that could be leveled against her Protestant half-sister. Further, the nearly magical character of the royal touch intensified the potential resemblance between Elizabeth and Pope Joan, the alleged author of a "Booke of *Necromancie.*" This feature of the royal touch troubled early modern observers. James I (1566–1625, reigning in England 1603–25), for example, initially challenged the practice by asserting that "the age of miracles" was "past" (Harrison, *Jacobean* 31). Such concerns evidently prompted Reginald Scot (ca. 1538–99) to defend the ceremony in his 1584 *The Discoverie of Witchcraft*. While acknowledging that some attribute the healing effects of the royal touch to "the efficacie of words," Scot insists that "God will not be offended" by Elizabeth's actions "for hir majeste onelie useth godlie and divine praier, with some almes, and refereth the cure to God and to the physician" (172). However pious her actions might have been, by presiding over ceremonies that appeared to imitate liturgy and, in the case of the royal touch, to assign what Clowes termed "artificiall" powers to the monarch, the Supreme Governor of the English

Church provided a foundation for Raemond's troubling analogy between queen and popess.[11]

"So Vyle a Woman"

In some sixteenth- and seventeenth-century representations, Elizabeth I resembles not only Pope Joan but also what Protestants regarded as another feminine embodiment of Catholic corruption: the Whore of Babylon.[12] In fact, due to a conventional analogy between Pope Joan and the Whore, any resemblance to the Babylonian strumpet in turn intensified Elizabeth's resemblance to the popess. The Whore thus functioned as a middle term connecting Elizabeth and Pope Joan. The analogy between popess and Whore appeared during Elizabeth's reign in the passing references to Pope Joan that English printers published, even as they eschewed texts that focused on the popess. No doubt, tales of Joan's disastrous sexual indiscretion, along with the papacy's claims to supremacy, inspired writers to equate the popess with the Biblical "MOTHER OF HARLOTS . . . which reigneth over the kings of the earth" (Rev. 17:5, 18). At the beginning of Elizabeth's reign, the influential polemicist and playwright John Bale established a precedent that John Foxe later bluntly followed as he introduced his account of Joan's pontificate by declaring, "And here next comes the whore of Babylon . . . rightly in her true colors" (Bale, *Scriptorvm illustrium* 116–17; Foxe 2: 7; Hotchkiss, "Legend" 501–2).[13]

Claire McEachern has identified an instance in which the Whore's "true colors" disturbingly paralleled Elizabeth's royal iconography. According to McEachern, such parallels may have prompted the radical revision of an illustration of the Whore that appeared in *A Concent of Scripture,* an exegetical tract that the Protestant Hugh Broughton (1549–1612) dedicated to the queen (McEachern 53–57). The Whore depicted in the first edition (ca. 1588) of this text wears the costume and adopts the posture of a courtly lady (fig. 8). The Flemish engraver Jacobus (or Jodocus) Hondius dresses her in an elaborate gown with full sleeves and bejeweled farthingale. A square jewel and double string of pearls adorn her neck. Another jewel dangles from her waist, and a crescent-moon ornament decorates her hair. She bears a regal scepter in her left hand; as one might expect, the biblical cup full of the "filthiness of her fornication" occupies her right hand (Rev. 17:4). As befits an elegant lady, she rides her seven-headed beast sidesaddle. A few years later, a different engraver produced a strikingly different illustration for the second edition (ca. 1590) of Broughton's text.[14] Although Revelation 17 portrays the Whore as an emphatically feminine seductress, the new engraver, William Rogers, recasts her as an amazon dressed in a suit of armor and sitting astride her beast (fig. 9). This refashioned harlot lacks her predecessor's farthingale, scepter, and crescent hair ornament; moreover, no jewels hang from her neck or waist. We, in turn, lack definitive evidence concerning the motives for Rogers's revision. We know, however, that as engraver of the 1589 *Eliza Triumphans* portrait commemorating the Armada victory (fig. 10), Rogers was familiar enough with reproductions of the royal image to recognize that Hondius's Whore wears regalia that befit England's Gloriana. Like Hondius's harlot, Rogers's 1589 "Eliza" wears a square neck jewel and two strands of pearls; another jewel rests near the top of her full, richly ornamented skirt. To signify the queen's triumph over foreign aggression, on this occasion an olive branch replaces the scepter in her right hand.[15] Most surprisingly, perhaps, the crescent hair ornament in Hondius's illustration appropriates the moon imagery that became associated in the mid-1580s with the virginal Elizabeth (Berry 126, 183–84). In light of such disturbing appropriations, Rogers was evidently prudent enough to depart from Hondius's precedent and to establish an unambiguous contrast between his portraits of an amazonian "BABYLON THE GREAT" (Rev. 17:5) and of an elegant Eliza Triumphans (McEachern 53–57).

The queen's detractors, however, behaved far less decorously. Although admirers such as Sir Walter Raleigh (ca. 1554–1618) and Sir Edmund Spenser (ca. 1552–99) cultivated the image of Elizabeth as the Virgin Queen, those hostile to Gloriana created competing and sharply contrasting, whorish portraits of her. For much of her life, reports of Elizabeth's alleged sexual misconduct circulated among both foreigners and English subjects. No doubt, her mother's execution for adultery and incest, along with the official declaration of Elizabeth's illegitimacy, encouraged these rumors, which first appeared while she was a teenager. At that time, the young princess became caught up in a scandal concerning the recklessly ambitious Lord Admiral Thomas Seymour, who was ultimately arrested and executed for treason. Witnesses reported that Seymour, brother to Henry VIII's third wife and husband to the king's widow Catherine Parr, hoped eventually to marry Elizabeth and treated her with unseemly familiarity within the princess's bedchamber. According to the testimony of Elizabeth's steward, these improprieties prompted Catherine Parr to expel the princess from her household. Elizabeth herself reported learning of rumors that she was pregnant with Seymour's child. As Sheila Cavanagh has noted, according to early modern conceptions of consanguinity, sexual relations between Elizabeth and a man who was both her half-brother's uncle and her stepmother's hus-

The State of Rome for crucifying our Lorde.

Babylon & mother of filthy fornicatio

The empire Romania, the vsurping Vicar, & belly god cleargy, Satans Throne. Ap. 8 . 9 . 1 . 12 . 13 . 17.

Fig. 8. Jocobus Hondius, "The State of Rome," engraving in Hugh Broughton's *A Concent of Scripture* (London, ca. 1588). By permission of the Rare Books Division, The New York Public Library, Astor, Lenox and Tilden Foundations.

band would have been not only adulterous but also incestuous. The accusations concerning Elizabeth and Seymour thus suggested that the princess had inherited her mother's vices (Cavanagh 10–14, 16–19; C. Levin, *"Heart"* 6–7). She seemed, then, destined for iniquity.

Ultimately, Elizabeth survived the investigation of the Seymour episode with her place in the line of succession intact; nonetheless, rumors of fornication and secret pregnancies followed her to the throne. Drawing upon sources such as diplomatic correspondence and court records, Carole Levin has cited at least fifteen references to such rumors, which clearly surfaced during each decade of Elizabeth's reign. Moreover, several of the reports of Elizabeth's sexual misconduct fostered a resemblance between the queen and the scriptural Whore of Babylon. In 1589, for example, a parson was accused

Fig. 9. William Rogers, "The Empire of Rome," engraving in Hugh
Broughton's *A Concent of Scripture* (London, ca. 1590). By permission
of the Henry E. Huntington Library and Art Gallery.

of proclaiming "openly in church . . . that the Queen's Majesty was an arrant
whore," and ten years later a laborer declared that Elizabeth was "Antechrist"
itself (C. Levin, *"Heart"* 83; C. Levin, "'We'" 90). Moreover, one of the
most elaborate and lurid of the surviving reports appears to echo several
details from Revelation 17–18. In 1600 William Knyght, an Englishman traveling in Germany, encountered Hugh Broughton. A dozen years after dedi-
cating *A Concent of Scripture* to the queen and presenting her with a copy of
that text, Broughton had become bitterly dissatisfied with Elizabeth and
with her seeming indifference toward his labors. He charged that "she was an
atheist, and a maintainer of atheism," and he went on to recount the experiences of an unfortunate midwife summoned to a secret chamber within a
Hampstead palace where she attended a woman in childbirth (Elizabeth).
After delivering an infant girl, the midwife

Fig. 10. William Rogers, *Eliza Triumphans,* engraving (1589). Copyright of the British Museum (inventory number 1901-4-17-35).

was brought to another chamber where was a very great fire of coals, into which she was commanded to cast the child, and so it was burnt. This midwife was rewarded with a handful of gold, and at her departure, one came to her with a cup of wine, and said, Thou whore, drink before thou goest from hence, and she drank, and was sent back to her house, where within six days after she died of poison, but revealed this before her death. (*Calendar of State Papers* 23–24; C. Levin, *"Heart"* 84)

The epithet "whore," here assigned to the hapless midwife, seems more likely to befit the mother eager to conceal her pregnancy at any cost; it might even call to mind the archetypal "mother of harlots" portrayed in Revelation and in the engravings that illustrated several of Broughton's texts.[16] The noxious cup, associated with the birth of bastards and handed to a woman addressed as "whore," recalls the Babylonian strumpet's "golden cup," from which "the inhabitants of the earth have been made drunk with the wine of her fornication" (Rev 17:2, 4). Similarly, the blood money paid to the midwife parallels the rich wares with which the biblical harlot procures the allegiance of "the merchants of the earth" (Rev. 18:11–17). Moreover, the incineration of the innocent infant (a motif that appears in at least three of the accounts of Elizabeth's rumored pregnancies) recalls not only the Whore's thirst for "the blood of the saints, and . . . martyrs" but also one of the most notorious and controversial atrocities perpetrated by English Catholics, the alleged servants of Babylon: the 1556 burning of a condemned heretic's newborn son (Rev 17:2, 4). According to John Foxe, while suffering martyrdom at the stake, a Guernsey woman named Perotine Massey gave birth. Although an onlooker rescued the infant from the flames, the provost ordered that the babe should be cast back into the fire where, as Foxe puts it, "baptized in his own blood," he "was both born and died a martyr." In Foxe's *Acts and Monuments* a woodcut depicting the little martyr's birth amid the flames reproduces this "spectacle" of "Herodian cruelty" (8: 227–30).[17] Drawing perhaps upon this much-discussed incident, as well as upon Broughton's study of apocalyptic literature, the story of the poisoned midwife transforms Elizabeth from the "naughty woman" of scandalous gossip (C. Levin, *"Heart"* 76) to a participant in, if not source of, grotesque abominations including murder and infanticide.

Not surprisingly, Catholic polemicists in particular portrayed Elizabeth in ways that paralleled the Whore of Babylon. A Latin text that appeared in England in 1609 characterized the late queen as the daughter of Antichrist (meaning Henry VIII). Like the scriptural Whore, who draws her paramours, the "kings of the earth" (Rev. 17:2), from diverse lands, Elizabeth, according to this tract, had prostituted herself with men of different nations, "even with blackamoors" (Harrison, *Second* 143–44). Decades earlier, a conspirator in the Ridolfi Plot anticipated such accounts of the queen's depravity when he reportedly characterized her as "so vyle a Woman . . . that desyrethe nothinge but to fede her owne lewd fantasye" (C. Levin, *"Heart"* 78, 85) Hoping to inspire other English subjects to strike out against the queen, William Cardinal Allen formulated an especially elaborate portrait of Elizabethan decadence. "She hathe abused her bodie . . . by unspeakable and incredible variety of luste," he claims. As if inviting analogies to the Babylonian seductress, he goes on to charge that Elizabeth has "made her Courte as a trappe, by this damnable and detestable arte, to inta[n]gle in sinne and ouerthrowe the yonger sorte of nobilitye and gentlemen of the lande." Allen even equates the queen with a Biblical fornicatress, the false prophetess

Jezebel of Thyatira (Rev. 2:20). This analogy, like the Pope Joan legend, links a woman's sexual iniquity with her usurpation of religious authority (Allen, *Admonition* V, XIX). Thus, for those who questioned Elizabeth's ecclesiastical role and personal morality, the analogy Raemond drew between queen and popess most likely seemed quite reasonable.

Babylon and Faerie Land

Thomas Dekker's allegorical history play *The Whore of Babylon* (1607), which articulates perhaps the most sustained early modern comparison between Elizabeth and the Whore, further demonstrates that within imaginative portraits these two women could all too easily resemble each other. The play's prefatory Lectori announces Dekker's intention to set "the incomparable Heroical vertues of our late Queene" against "the inueterate malice . . . and continual blody stratagems, of that Purple whore of Roome" (*Dramatic* 2: 497). Nonetheless, the play's imagery and diction, which most often associate the Babylonian harlot and her forces with the threatening maternal body, come to belie the contrast that the Lectori articulates, as Titania, the Faerie Queene who in Dekker's appropriation of Spenserian allegory represents Elizabeth, also portrays herself in (sometimes menacing) maternal terms.[18]

Through the reports of diverse characters, Dekker (ca. 1570–1632) insistently portrays the titular Empresse of Babylon as fertile and maternal. In the play's opening lines, she claims to "Be fruitfull as the Vine in sonnes and daughters" and later in the same scene asserts that "a mothers holy loue" motivates her actions (1.1.4, 29). Even while launching an invasion fleet against Titania's faerie kingdom, the Empresse portrays herself as the (perhaps none-too-gentle) "mother of Nations" (4.3.31). Later, after the overthrow of Babylon's armada, a cardinal leading a delegation of political and religious officials informs the Empresse that "your children come / Vpon their knees to take a mothers doome." (5.6.120–21), and the seemingly omniscient allegorical character Time offers to display "this *Concubine* of Kinges / In her majesticke madnes with her sonnes" (5.6.77–78). Thus, both the Empresse's servants and her enemies confirm her maternal identity.

At first glance, portraying the Empresse as a fertile mother might seem to differentiate her from Dekker's "Queene of maides" (1.2.68); however, Titania, like the English queen whom she represents, does not completely eschew maternal roles. In fact, William Camden (1551–1623) reports in his annals of Elizabeth's reign that the queen portrayed herself as spouse to her kingdom and mother to her subjects (M. Axton 38–39). Moreover, in his 1608 pamphlet *The Wonderfull Yeare,* Dekker himself characterizes the late queen as "the Citizens mother" (*Plague* 12). The virginal Titania does differ from the Empresse in that she attempts to participate in generation and nurture indirectly and without the taint of sexuality and parturition.[19] Like her English counterpart, Titania engages in metaphorical marriages, which produce figurative offspring. Whereas Elizabeth I imagined wedding the kingdom, Titania chooses even more abstract spouses, as she declares:

> Deepe rooted is a state, and growes vp hie,
> When Prouidence, Zeale, and Integritie
> Husband it well: Theis fathers, twill be said,
> (One day) make me a grandame of a maid. (2.1.34–37)

Titania's metaphors preserve the contrast between herself and the Empresse, but at a price. The role she assumes here seems less attractive later, when, on the eve of a Babylonian invasion, her advisor Parthenophil characterizes zealous faerie grandmothers as both enfeebled and bloodthirsty:

> Old grandams that on crutches beare vp age
> Full nimbly buckled Armours on their sonnes,
> And when twas on, she clapt him on his backe,
> And spake thus, runne, my boye, fight till th'art dead.
> Thy bloud can neuer be more brauely shed. (5.2.215–20)

As if eager to see a young soldier share in the infirmity that her crutches signify, the hobbled matron seems to achieve eerie, new dexterity, as she "nimbly" prepares her grandson for battle. Moreover, her instructions to the "boye" focus disturbingly more on death than victory as the soldier's ultimate objective. In light of this passage, the role of "grandame" seems to offer the virgin queen little genuine opportunity to nurture her subjects.

Images of the threatening maternal body appear most strikingly when Dekker describes the Babylonian and faerie fleets and compares their ships to wombs. Echoing a very different passage in Shakespeare's *A Midsummer Night's Dream* (2.1.128–32), a faerie scout who has seen the enemy's armada reports:

> . . . the windes haue got the sailes with childe,
> With such big bellies, all the linnen's gone
> To finde them linnen, and in *Babylon*
> That ther's not one ragge left. (5.2.17–20)

This voracious appetite for fabric befits a fleet that, according to the Empresse's proclamation, "is ordayned to swallow vp the kingdome of *Faiery*" (4.3.37). The odd choice of linen (rather than canvas) for sailcloth also points to the ships' mission. Through biblical associations between linen and burial shrouds (Matt. 27:59; Mark 15:46; Luke 24:12; John 19:40), this detail links the armada's material constituents to the objective that the faerie lord Florimell attributes to it, when he declares that Babylon has

> Rigd an Armd fleete, which euen now beates the waues,
> Boasting to make their wombes our Cities graues. (5.2.7–8).[20]

These monstrous wooden wombs deliver death rather than new life.

The Empresse anticipates such metaphors when she instructs her minions and compares a military invasion to painful parturition:

> Goe: cut the salt fome with your mooned keeles,
> And let our Galeons feele euen child-birth panges
> Till their great bellies be deliuered
> On the soft Faiery shoares: captiue their Queene,
> . . . .
> Blow vp, pull downe, ruine all, let not white haires
> Nor red cheekes blunt your wrath, snatch babes from breasts,
> And when they crie for milke, let them sucke bloud,
> Turne all their fieldes to lakes of gellyed goare. (4.4.114–17, 121–24)[21]

The Empresse commands a metaphorical birth that is inimical to maternal nurture, as she proposes to replace breast milk with blood. The final image of fields transformed into lakes conveys the disordered unnaturalness of her intention.

As was the case with allusions to maternity, Dekker's play once again implicates the Faerie Queene in the misogynistic imagery associated with her Babylonian antagonist. In one and the same scene, Titania's subjects compare both Babylonian and faerie warships to expectant mothers. Less than two hundred lines after he alludes to the hostile armada's entombing wombs, Florimell proudly reports to his queen:

> Your goodly ships beare the most royall freight
> That the world owes (true hearts:) their wombes are ful,
> Of noble spirits, each man in his face
> Shewes a Kings daunting looke, the souldiers stand
> So thickly on the decke, so brauely plum'd,

. . . .
                    . . . In such little roome
So many Faieries neuer dwelt at once,
Neuer so many men were borne so soone— (5.2.168–72, 178–80)

Not surprisingly, Florimell ascribes no malicious intent to Titania's navy. In fact, his phrase "royall freight" briefly implies a commercial rather than martial context, and his emphasis on "hearts" and "spirits" in the first few lines directs the audience's attention away from the material realities of combat. Nonetheless, he eventually reveals that stern soldiers congest the ships' decks, and his pun on "born/e" recalls the Empresse's earlier pun on "deliuered." If these faerie troops follow the "old grandams'" instructions (reported just twenty-four lines later) to "fight till th'art dead," the ships' wooden wombs will deliver at least some of their passengers to the grave. The grim equation between womb and tomb, then, which Florimell asserted openly when discussing the Babylonian fleet, rests here just below the surface. Thus, Dekker's representations of the Empresse and Titania and of the forces they command thwart his stated intention to differentiate sharply between the two fictive adversaries.

Menacing Wombs

The work of several critics writing about one of Dekker's principal sources, *The Faerie Queene,* illuminates the significance of the unflattering parallels that such images imply between the Whore of Babylon and the character who stands for Queen Elizabeth. Claire McEachern has suggested that depictions of the Whore and of Elizabeth sometimes resembled one another because, "far from defining itself in opposition to Roman rule, the Tudor state sought to appropriate its powers" (58). A particular instance of such appropriation bears upon Dekker's maternal imagery, as the monarch who decisively alienated England from the old mother Church in Rome sometimes portrayed herself as mother to the subjects she had thus orphaned. Louis Adrian Montrose argues more broadly that, since as queen regnant Elizabeth challenged "the homology between hierarchies of rule and of gender," the poet's stance toward the queen "becomes necessarily ambivalent— alternately or simultaneously adoring and contestatory—because, for the male subject, the authority and the other are now one and the same" ("Elizabethan" 309, 330). The images through which Dekker most often conveys such ambivalence point to aspects of Elizabethan rule, particularly those concerning royal succession, about which his play, written after the queen's death, voices retrospective uneasiness. Indeed, by attending to distinctive features of Dekker's play—its refashioning of the biblical Whore and depictions of diminished maternal power and privilege—as well as the historical moment that produced it, we can better understand how it participates in the broad patterns that McEachern and Montrose have observed and, more specifically, how it addresses the consequences of Elizabeth's embrace of metaphorical rather than literal motherhood.[22]

By portraying the Whore as emphatically maternal, Dekker diverges from his sources in scripture and apocalyptic literature. Although Revelation 17–18 does refer to the Whore once as "MOTHER OF HARLOTS," it focuses on her relationship with her paramours rather than with her offspring. In contrast to Dekker's three kings, who woo Titania and portray the Empresse as "our aged mother" (1.2.137), the "kings of the earth" in Revelation focus their erotic attention on the Whore, with whom they "have committed fornication and lived deliciously" (18:9). In fact, the far more maternal figure in Revelation is the Whore's opposite, the "woman clothed with the sun" of chapter 12 who first appears in the throes of childbirth and delivers a "man child who . . . was caught up unto God, and to his throne" (Rev. 12:2, 5–6). Similarly, in the "comoedia apocalyptica" *Christus Triumphans* (which Julia Gasper identifies as one of Dekker's sources), John Foxe portrays Ecclesia, the true church, as a mother of nations represented by the three allegorical characters Europus, Africus, and Asia (4.5.9, 4.8.52, 5.1.36, 5.4.1, 5.4.20–30, 5.5.18–19; Gasper 71–72). However, even when Foxe's Whore of Babylon, Pornapolis, supplants Ecclesia, deluded crowds greet the usurper as "bride of the lamb, supporter of truth," but not as mother, and Pornapolis continues to speak of herself as a "courtesan" (4.8.11, 26). In turn, Spenser's version of the Whore, the witch Duessa, portrays herself as more daughter than mother and as an oft-aggrieved maiden (1.2.22–23, 1.12.26, 2.1.21). By reshaping his source materials to stress the Whore's maternal identity, then, Dekker appears to be conveying his particular concerns.

Since Elizabeth and her admirers sometimes portrayed the queen as a mother to her subjects, troubled representations of the maternal body could convey dissatisfaction with aspects of her reign. The English occasionally turned Elizabeth's maternal rhetoric against her and worried aloud that she might prove to be an inattentive parent. John Puckering, for example, speaker of the Commons, employed familial metaphors to articulate the queen's duty to her subjects and to dissuade her from treating Mary, Queen of Scots, too indulgently: "She is only a cousin to you in a remote degree. But we be sons and children of this land, whereof you be not only the natural mother, but also the wedded spouse. And therefore much more is due from you to us all than to her alone" (qtd. in M. Axton 39). Here, in order to make the royal mother accountable to some other authority, Puckering seems willing to flirt with metaphorical incest, as he casts "this land" as both spouse and offspring to the queen. In 1566 Paul Wentworth, a member of the House of Commons, employed a shifting series of familial metaphors as he charged (far less delicately) that if the queen ignored certain of her subject's entreaties, "She may be reckoned of, not as a Nurse, not as a Mother of Countrye, but as a Step-mother, nay as a Parricide of her Countrey" (qtd. in C. Levin, *"Heart"* 87). In the recurrent rumors that Elizabeth had secretly given birth to children whom her attendants immediately murdered, we find a popular, literal counterpart of the figurative rhetoric that such elite speakers and writers were employing. If the queen acted as an uncaring mother in her political body, perhaps she did so in her natural body as well. In this context, Dekker's grim faerie grandams, as well as the elaborate parallels between Titania and the deeply flawed Babylonian matriarch, might express discontent concerning the aftermath of Elizabeth's reign.

The play's only (and surprisingly celebratory) account of childbirth sheds light on the particular aspects of Elizabethan rule that likely provoked such discontent. While Titania's forces are securing victory at sea and mustering in anticipation of battle on land, the allegorical character Plaine-Dealing excitedly announces a birth within the faerie camp at Beria (Tilbury). In turn, Titania greets the report enthusiastically and declares, "A child borne in our Camp! Give hem fame" (5.6.46). At first glance, this welcome news seems to contrast sharply with the grim representations of the maternal body that we have seen thus far. Upon closer inspection, however, this episode conveys, and perhaps clarifies, anxieties expressed in those other representations. The birth seems worthy of celebration in large part because it departs so thoroughly from the early modern conventions of childbirth, which, according to Adrian Wilson, "accomplished a reversal of the normal power-relations between wife and husband" ("Ceremony" 86).

In seventeenth-century England birth conventionally took place in a social and physical space inhabited exclusively by women and shut off from men. In addition to a midwife, invited female friends, "gossips," attended the expectant mother within the "lying-in chamber." That chamber was literally and symbolically closed, as keyholes were blocked up and heavy curtains obstructed daylight. For two or more weeks after the delivery, the mother remained in this chamber and continued to enjoy its privileges, excused from physical labor within the household and from sexual intercourse with her husband. Some early modern men were evidently wary of the liberties that wives enjoyed at the time of delivery and recuperation. A 1683 text entitled *The Woman's Advocate* answers objections that lying-in "'Tis a time of freedom, when women . . . have a privilege to talk petty treason" (qtd. in Wilson, "Ceremony" 82, 86). The hyperbolic reference to petty treason, which at the time included a wife's murder of her husband, suggests a keen awareness that the ceremony of childbirth temporarily disrupted the familial hierarchy (Dolan, *Dangerous* 21).[23]

The delivery that Plaine-Dealing announces in *The Whore of Babylon* bears little resemblance to the ceremony that Wilson has documented. The child does not emerge into the enclosed, womblike lying-in chamber surrounded by women; instead, he is born into the relatively open space of a military camp "amongst men at Armes" (5.6.35). The account of the child's birth mentions his mother, the only female who is definitely present, just once and quite laconically as simply "a woman" (5.6.35). Plaine-Dealing casts doubt on whether a midwife and gossips attended the birth, as he reports: "In steede of a Midwife, a Captaine shall beare him to the Fount; and if there be any women to followe it, they shal either traile pikes or shoote in Caliuers [muskets]" (5.6.48–50). Although arming these hypothetical women may seem to empower them, it also entails subjecting them to military discipline and denying them the "freedom" or "privilege" discussed in *The Woman's Advocate*. To the extent that women participate in this revised ceremony of childbirth, they are rendered peripheral or tightly controlled.

Forty lines later, Dekker once again depicts an erosion of maternal influence. During the play's concluding moments, the Empresse blames filial betrayal for her armada's defeat and denounces her adherents as "Scorpions to my brest, / Diseases to my bloud" and "disobedient, desperate, dampned sonnes" (5.6.89–90, 116). As she sees it, her followers have perverted the familial relationship, poisoning the breast that sought to nourish them. However, her words and actions almost immediately belie her interpretation of events and transform her fears of treacherous disobedience into self-fulfilling prophecies. Altering the tenor of her poisoning metaphor, she compares herself to a venomous creature, as she entreats supernatural forces to "turne me into / A speckled Adder"; moreover, she herself proposes to introduce poison into her body, as she boasts, "Earth, Ile sucke all thy venome to my brest" (5.6.110–11, 114). Embracing the role of venomous, unnatural mother, the rash Babylonian matriarch intends to prostrate her royal children: "This neck Ile yoke—this throate a staires Ile make / By which Ile climbe—" (5.6.124–25). In response, an irate and defiant Second King (representing the Holy Roman Emperor) threatens to subordinate the Empresse to his temporal authority and "thrust / A ring into thy nostrils" (5.6.130–31).

As the play concludes, the audience is left to wonder whether the Empresse's clumsy retraction—"I did but jest"—will placate the King, who remains silent. Moreover, when the Third King questions the sincerity of that retraction, observing, "You seeme still angry," the befuddled Empresse appears to surrender some of the authority that her son had threatened to wrench from her. "No; yes: leade the way," she sputters (5.6.132, 135). The compromising of maternal influence here parallels the restraint of maternal privilege in the radically revised ceremony of childbirth described earlier in this scene. This double linking of the climactic faerie victory with the limiting of maternal authority suggests that Dekker's menacing wombs convey ambivalence concerning the influence that mothers, particularly royal mothers, acquire through procreation.

Early Jacobean politics likely encouraged such ambivalence. By the time of this play's composition, the consequences of Elizabeth's determination to remain a mother in metaphor alone and to eschew procreation were evident. Her successor, who brought a Catholic consort to London, made peace with Spain, and seemed to favor leniency for English recusants, clearly had not fulfilled the play's prophesy that out of Titania's ashes a "second Phoenix" would rise "of larger wing, / Of stronger talent, of more dreadfull beake" to "shake all *Babilon*" (3.1.35–36, 144). Moreover, by attempting to negotiate a Spanish match for his eldest son in 1604 and 1605, James I imperiled the prospect that Prince Henry (1594–1612), whom Puritans reportedly "saluted . . . as one pre-figured in the *Apocalypse* for *Rome's* Destruction," might take up the role that his pacifist father shunned (Krantz 273–76).[24] English subjects likely worried that a Catholic bride might blunt Prince Henry's Protestant ardor and corrupt his heirs. The precedent offered by Henry's own mother, Anne of Denmark (1574–1619), probably fueled such concerns. In 1603 she led troops against Stirling Castle to wrest control of the prince's upbringing from the Protestant John Erskine (ca. 1558–1634), Earl of Mar. Ultimately, Anne achieved her objective not through the force of arms but rather by threatening not to join her husband in England at his coronation, where, even after James acquiesced to her wishes, she refused to receive the Protestant sacrament of Holy Communion. Dekker's ship-as-womb metaphor, formulated a few years after James's coronation, readily conveys the fears that a disorderly consort and rumored Spanish match might have aroused (Ardolino 3–4; Walsham 84–85; Williamson 115–16; Lewalski 20–21). As if echoing ancient gynecological lore that imagined the uterus to be an animate, independent entity hungry for seed, the allegorical character Time complicates the ship-as-womb metaphor and compares the Babylonian fleet to "roaring Whales [that] came with deuouring wombes / To swallow vp your kingdomes: foolish heirs" (5.6.59–60). These sea-borne "devouring wombs" might aptly represent the Infanta, who threatens to cross the ocean, consume the heir apparent's seed, and dissipate his Protestant zeal. Seen in light of a feared Catholic match, then, the ship-as-womb metaphor enables Dekker subtly to interrelate two different Spanish threats: the Armada of 1588, denoted in the metaphor's tenor; and the proposed marriage treaty of 1605, suggested by the metaphor's vehicle. Elizabeth had guided England past the earlier threat; however, her insistence on (at least the pretense of) virginity had severely limited her influence upon her successor and thus set the stage for the later threat. In Dekker's play, then, the paralleling of queen and Whore evident in other cultural artifacts produced during the Elizabethan and Jacobean periods conveys anxieties concerning the legacy even of a reputedly virtuous and magnanimous queen.

Perilous Analogies

"I am Richard II, know ye not that?" Queen Elizabeth famously declared six months after the Essex rebellion (Barroll 444–52).[25] The Pope Joan legend understandably might have troubled a woman so wary of historical analogies. Like the popess, Elizabeth governed a church; moreover, through the Royal Maundy and the ceremony of the royal touch, she presided over rituals that originated in or resembled liturgy. Like the popess, she reportedly fornicated with favorites—according to rumor, the queen simply succeeded in using royal progresses and other devices to conceal her pregnancies and deliveries. As we have seen in *A Concent of Scripture* and *The Whore of Babylon,* the words and images even in texts intended to compliment the queen all too readily suggested analogies between Elizabeth and the harlot of Revelation 17, the popess's apocalyptic counterpart. Further, like Joan, Elizabeth sometimes adopted masculine roles, if not attire, to achieve her objectives— in fact, John Knox characterized any queen regnant as "a woman clad in the habit of a man" (75). Of course, unlike the popess, Elizabeth never truly attempted to conceal her gender; however, such deceit was only one of the constellation of misdeeds articulated in Boccaccio's influential retelling of the legend. "God from on high was merciful to His people," the poet reports, "and did not allow a woman to hold so lofty a place, to govern so many people, and deceive them with such a wicked fraud, and He abandoned that unruly audacious woman to herself" (*Concerning* 232). Boccaccio's notion that female rule is an affliction from which a merciful God might relieve His people anticipates the views of some Elizabethan subjects like the Essex laborer who resolved in 1591 to "pray for a king," because "The Queene was but a woman," and "We shall never have a merry world while the Queene lyveth" (C. Levin, "'We'" 78). Like-minded Englishmen might infer from the precedent of Joan's career that after indulging the ambitions of an intellectually brilliant yet unruly woman (who had refused Parliament's pleas first to marry and then to name a successor), God might abandon Elizabeth to herself and thus to a predictable demise. Consequently, with very few exceptions, Elizabethan printers published only those accounts of Pope Joan that, like John Foxe's, portrayed her pontificate as only one, brief episode in the long course of events that culminated triumphantly in the restoration of the True Church under Elizabeth I.[26]

3 *Diagnosing Joan*

THE HERMAPHRODITE HYPOTHESIS

Aт тне 1992 аnnual meeting of the Endocrine Society, Maria I. New, a physician at the New York–Cornell Medical Center, delivered the President's Address, entitled "Pope Joan: A Recognizable Syndrome." In her lecture, New posed a question germane to this study: "If Pope Joan was a legend"—as New insists she "undoubtedly" was—"why as a civilization have we not lost interest in her after all these centuries?" In reply to this and a second, related question—"Why do so many people persist in thinking that her story could have been true?"—New observes: "The fact is, on a biological basis, it might have been. I have known a man who if he had lived in the Ninth [*sic*] century could have been Pope Joan." The "man" in question is a patient referred to New by his wife of ten years, who noticed that her husband seemed to experience menstrual bleeding. After explaining this patient's condition, New returns to the popess: "The endocrinological basis of the legend could be that Pope Joan had a recognizable syndrome: classical 21-hydroxylase deficiency," a prenatal condition in which the lack of a particular enzyme affects the adrenal gland and, in turn, disrupts hormone levels within the fetus. "From a medical perspective," New explains, "the story of Joan would be that Pope John VIII was a female pseudo-hermaphrodite who had a homosexual liaison, got pregnant, and delivered a child" (New and Kitzinger 5–6; New and Wilson). Here, New draws upon a classificatory system that Alice Domurat Dreger traces to the late nineteenth century, a period within the history of hermaphroditism that she dubs the "Age of Gonads." Within that system the term "female pseudo-hermaphrodite" designates someone with XX chromosomes whose external genitalia appear ambiguous and who possesses ovarian tissue but lacks testicular tissue. In other words, however much such a person's external organs might seem to defy easy classification as male or female, her or his internal organs "appear 'typically' feminine" (Dreger 11, 37, 140, 145–50). Physicians differentiate such individuals from the far rarer cases of "true hermaphrodites," who possess both ovarian and testicular tissue. By offering a medical perspective on the popess legend and suggesting that cases of genital ambiguity might explain its origins or staying power, New has, in a sense, attempted to diagnose Joan.

In doing so, she has manifested both a physician's professional bias and the difficulty of completely separating scientific and cultural discourses. Although her address ranges beyond endocrinology to discuss how hermaphrodites or androgynes have figured in myth, art, and popular culture, when New wishes to locate the "basis" of the Pope Joan legend, or perhaps of its longevity, she turns to biology. She thus appeals to the seemingly solid ground of anatomical sex underlying the slippery surface of culturally constructed gender. However, the peculiar way that she characterizes the circumstances surrounding Joan's reported pregnancy reminds us to heed Judith Butler's critique of the certainties that scientific discourse concerning sex appears to offer. According to Butler, like gender, sex is a cultural construct, an "effect" produced in part by compulsory or presumptive heterosexuality. Within our culture the "heterosexulization of desire," as she puts it, requires that each body fit into one of two discrete, asymmetrical categories, "male" or "female," and that a body express its sex by acting in accord with appropriate "masculine" or "feminine" gender norms. Those who do not conform to this pattern become unintelligible; "they appear only as developmental failures or logical impossibilities" (xxix, 10–11, 23–24). The bounds of gender intelligibility appear to constrain New's thinking, as she characterizes Joan's "liaison" as homosexual and thus forces the hermaphroditic body that she has posited for the popess, quite resistant to classification as "male" or "female," onto one side of the sexual dichotomy. Moreover, the physician's allusion to sexual orientation confuses rather than clarifies her hypothesis. By applying the adjective *homosexual* to Joan's encounter with an impregnating male, New chooses to define the popess's gender according to the masculine role that she assumed rather than according to the ovarian tissue that would have made such a pregnancy possible. To challenge the conviction that biology neutrally describes sex "as it is prior to the cultural meanings that it acquires," Butler has observed that cultural assumptions associating maleness with presence and activity "frame and focus" biomedical research into sex determination (139). In New's case the interaction between science and culture is simpler, as biological discourse, marked by terms such as *female pseudo-hermaphrodite,* simply gives way at midsentence, and the endocrinologist comes to accept the popess's masculine attire and historical designation as "John VIII" as adequate signs of his or her sexual identity. New's address thus demonstrates that, even for a physician well versed in hormones and chromosomes, the popess resists ready and straightforward classification and inscription in a binary gender system.

Centuries earlier, an English Catholic tract published at Antwerp in 1566 (and again in 1573) anticipated New by suggesting a physiological explanation for the cultural phenomenon of a female pope. That text presents a dialogue between Irenaeus, an Englishman defending Catholicism, and Critobulus, a German championing the Protestant cause. After Critobulus introduces the shameful case of Pope Joan, Irenaeus briefly and tentatively mentions hermaphrodites and then reviews documented, early modern cases of sexual transformation. Introducing a hypothesis that the prominent French jurist Etienne de Forcadel would explore in a 1580 legal treatise, Irenaeus suggests that such a change from one sex to another might explain the reports of a popess (Boureau, *Myth* 235).

Whereas New's address evidently received a positive reception, prompting its publication in the *Journal of Clinical Endocrinology and Metabolism,* Irenaeus's remarks provoked a far more hostile, derisive reaction. Within a year, undaunted Anglican controversialists had begun quoting and mocking Irenaeus's discussion of the popess, and decades later one such writer, John Mayo, still found the dialogue's physiological speculations so outlandish that he devoted two of the six chapters in his *Anatomie of Pope Joane* (1591) to ridiculing them. Moreover, even those hostile to the legend as an instrument for defaming the papacy came to see such speculations as part of the problem rather than a solution. The author of a 1687 text dedicated to exposing the "*Contrarieties, ridiculous Fables, and Untruths*" crammed into the popess legend refers to Joan simply as "this *Androgyne* or *Hermaphrodite*," eliding the distinction between transvestitism and anatomical ambiguity (*History,* Preface, 1, 4). Clearly, then, this sixteenth-century attempt at appealing to physiology in order to rehabilitate Joan and dissipate the legend's polemical force failed miserably. Here, I propose to investigate that failure. Why might Irenaeus's author think that, compared to a transvestite popess, a hermaphrodite pope or one who experienced an extraordinary sexual transformation would bring less disrepute to the papacy? In turn, at a time when respectable writers and physicians were documenting such cases, why did Irenaeus's antagonists find his suggestion ridiculous? As we shall see, the answers lie in the intense fear of effeminacy and in the multiple, often conflicting discourses concerning hermaphroditism and sexual transformation at play in early modern culture.

"Such a Pretty What If"

Irenaeus's remarks appear in Alan Cope's *Dialogi sex contra summi pontificatus, monasticae vitae, sanctorum, sacrarum imaginum oppugnatores, et pseudomartyres...*.[1] As the text's lengthy title announces, its six dialogues dispute Protestant martyrologies and mount a broad defense of the papacy, monasticism, sacred images, and the intercession of saints. Although Cope devotes particular attention to Matthias Flacius Illyricus (1520–75) and John Foxe, two polemical historians who reported Joan's pontificate, he spends only a few pages (out of over seven hundred) on the popess. Those pages might have occasioned little comment if their author had not proposed what John Jewel terms "such a pretty 'what if'" (*Defence* 656). Cope proceeds cautiously, resorting, it would seem, to apophasis to introduce the prospect of a hermaphroditic pope while denying that he means to discuss it: "Nor do I say here anything regarding hermaphrodites, about which there are complete books of the ancients" (Neque ego his quicquam dico de hermaphroditis & *herkinalson* de quibis veterum libri pleni sunt) (36). His polemical opponents, however, did not respect this subtlety. Jewel, who almost immediately incorporated Cope's conjectures into his own heated disputations with the Catholic Thomas Harding (1516–72), bluntly translates Cope's remark: "For thus he saith in effect: What if the pope were *Hermaphroditus?*" (*Defence* 656).

Cope's caution may signal some awareness of the ambivalence that greeted the hermaphrodite in early modern culture. Perhaps he hoped to associate the popess with the neo-Platonic interpretation of Genesis 1:27, which envisioned an originally androgynous Adam—"in the image of God created he him; male and female created he them"—whom God divided into two to fashion Eve (P. Cheney 177; Schwartz 269–74; Vavneh). Similarly, he may have hoped to suggest, as John Donne later does through his image of "a blessed Hermaphrodite," an integration of heavenly and earthly traits especially suited to the priestly vocation ("To Mr. Tilman after he had taken order"; Malpezzi). On the other hand, Cope may have recognized that, even for some of his coreligionists, a hermaphrodite pope was just as problematic as a female one. The prominent twelfth-century jurist Huguccio (died 1210) had argued that, in theory, hermaphrodites could receive spiritually valid ordination depending on which sex predominated in their physiologies. If the hermaphrodite were predominately male, the ordination would be valid; if predominately female or thoroughly mixed and sexually indeterminate, the ordination would be invalid. In practice, however, Huguccio notes, even a "male" hermaphrodite would be denied ordination due to physical deformity (Raming 62).[2] Writing in 1603, the exiled English Catholic Robert Persons articulates a less nuanced view. Before questioning the veracity of the Pope Joan legend, he challenges its significance, asking, what if "any Woman or *Hermaphroditus,* or any that had not byn baptized, or yf a layman and not Priest . . . had by error of men crept into the office of cheefe Bishopp?" (388). Each of these hypothetical candidates is incapable of fulfilling the papal office. Consequently, Persons explains, the Church would temporarily lack a true head, as it does after one pope has died and before a proper successor has been installed. In fact, drawing upon seventeenth-century French legal records, Ann Rosalind Jones and Peter Stallybrass report that hermaphrodites were "invariably" denied benefices (91).

Scholars (such as Marie Delcourt, Mircea Eliade, and Linda Woodbridge) who note the ambivalence surrounding hermaphrodites tend to focus on the tension between the androgyne as idealized philosophical or artistic symbol and the hermaphrodite as monstrous anatomical reality; in fact, however, early modern poetic and medical discourses concerning the hermaphrodite were each far less univocal than that neat opposition implies (Delcourt 45; Eliade 100; Woodbridge 140–41). According to Lorraine Daston and Katharine Park, in early modern medical writing two significantly different interpretations of the hermaphrodite competed and sometimes mingled. One approach, drawing upon Galen and Hippocratic writing, viewed hermaphrodites as neither male nor female but rather truly intermediate. In contrast, a second approach, rooted in Aristotle, saw them as individuals possessing "doubled or redundant genitalia," with only one set of genitals really functioning and the other resembling a tumor or growth. As Daston and Park point out, these two approaches carry very different implications. From the Aristotelian perspective, hermaphroditism was a superficial condition, concerning the genitals alone and not the whole organism. On the other hand, the "Hippocratic model was sexually charged: allowing for a spectrum of intermediate sexual possibilities, it posed a potential challenge to the male-female dichotomy and to the whole social and sexual order based on the dichotomy" (421–22). Although the Hippocratic view dominated the early Middle Ages, the Aristotelian perspective gained influence beginning in the thirteenth century but never completely displaced the alternative approach. Consequently, sixteenth-century thinkers inherited, as Daston and Park put it, "a subtle and eclectic body of theory that admitted both debate and difference of opinion on nearly all the central issues raised by the problem of generation" (422).[3] Through his hermaphrodite hypothesis, Cope wades into these muddy waters.

Ovidian Hermaphrodites

To discern how unstable the androgyne image was within sixteenth-century poetry, we might consider two Elizabethan reworkings of Ovid's watery hermaphrodite myth. Indeed, for Mayo, Cope's hypothesis evokes an Ovidian metamorphosis at the fountain of Salmacis rather than a prelapsarian Adam in the Garden of Eden. According to Ovid's narrator Alchithoe, the nymph Salmacis becomes infatuated with Hermaphroditus, as his name implies (the son of Mercury and Venus). After the youth initially rebuffs Salmacis's advances, she retreats, conceals herself, and observes Hermaphroditus bathing naked in a spring. Overcome by desire, she flings herself upon him, enwraps him in an embrace, and calls upon the gods to merge them forever. The gods comply, creating an androgynous "half-man" (semivir), who retains the name and consciousness of Hermaphroditus but not of Salmacis. Distressed, the youth entreats his parents to enchant the fountain so that whoever bathes in it will become a hermaphrodite like him (4.285–388). A few commentators, such as Giovanni Boccaccio and Marcus Vitruvius Pollio, interpreted the youth's transformation as a figure for the desirable softening or civilizing of barbarous customs. However, as Jones, Stallybrass, and Lauren Silberman have observed, most medieval and early modern mythographers saw Hermaphroditus's metamorphosis as a loss (of virtue, reason, potency) or a fall (into indolence, worldliness, incontinence). In turn, they viewed Salmacis, the woman who prompts that fall, as a vain, whorish temptress (Jones and Stallybrass 94–100; Silberman). The opening lines of Ovid's narrative encourage such censorious interpretations by proposing to explain the "ill-repute" of the fountain where the metamorphosis occurs ("Unde sit infamis"). Writing within this classical and medieval tradition, the influential Elizabethan translator Arthur Golding (1536–1606) contends that the story of "Hermaphroditus and Salmacis declare[s]" that idleness nurses voluptuousness, which, in turn, breeds sin, "which linking all toogither / Make men too bee effeminate, unweeldy, weake and lither" (Golding, Epistle, 113–16).[4]

The implications of *Salmacis and Hermaphroditus,* a 922-line epyllion published anonymously in 1602 but attributed to Francis Beaumont (1584–1616) in a 1640 reprint, could not be more different.[5] From the outset, Beaumont resists a harsh, moralizing interpretation of the myth. His first two lines portray the principal characters not as a fallen man and vicious temptress but rather as a "lucklesse payre, / Whose spotless soules now in one body be." Beaumont's opening summary of his subject matter contrasts sharply with Ovid's, which, in Golding's 1567 translation, invites readers to

Learne why the fountaine *Salmacis* diffamed is of yore,
Why with his waters overstrong it weakneth men so sore
That who so bathes him there, commes thence a perfect man no more.
 (347–49)

Whereas Ovid presents the metamorphosis as a decline from perfection, Beaumont purges the fountain of its ill repute and its waters of any explicit association with weakening, as he proposes to sing "of the strange inchauntment of a well / . . . Wherein who bathes, strait turnes *Hermaphrodite*" (The Author to the Reader). Beaumont tersely describes the metamorphosis without characterizing it as either degeneration or an improvement.

Through omissions from and additions to his classical source, Beaumont goes on to fashion a portrait of Salmacis that approaches the "spotless" character he promises, somewhat hyperbolically, in the poem's opening lines. Ovid employs several, nearly nightmarish similes to describe the aggressive embrace that precedes Hermaphroditus's transformation:

She held him still, and kissed him a hundred times and mo.
And willde he nillde he with hir handes she toucht his naked brest:
And now on this side now on that (for all he did resist
And strive to wrest him from hir gripes) she clung unto him fast:
And wound about him like a Snake which snatched up in hast
And being by the Prince of Birdes borne lightly up aloft,
Doth writhe hir selfe about his necke and griping talants oft:
And cast hir taile about his wings displayed in the winde:
Or like as Ivie runnes on trees about the utter rinde:
Or as the Crabfish having caught his enmy in the Seas,
Doth claspe him in on every side with all his crooked cleas [claws].
 (Golding 445–55).

As William Keach has noted, in his poem Beaumont retains only the least pejorative, vegetative simile and omits the other two (Keach 216). Of course, ivy might suggest parasitic exploitation, as in Prospero's well-known charge that his brother Antonio was "The ivy which had hid my princely trunk / And sucked my verdure out on 't" (*Tmp.* 1.1.86–87). Beaumont, however, portrays the vine's embrace as unthreatening and perhaps even admiring: "The flattering Ivy who did ever see / Inclaspe the huge trunk of an aged tree" (869–70). In contrast, the comparison to a "crabfish," or sea polyp, which the seventeenth-century translator George Sandys (1578–1644) glosses as "a ravenous fish: so called of his many feet wherewith he catcheth his prey"

(121), casts Salmacis as a mortal enemy who attempts to engulf and devour the youth. Further, that creature's tentacles invite phallic associations. Of course, the image of the phallic woman appears even more insistently in the initial simile in which the lowly snake attempts to strangle and ground the regal "prince of birdes" soaring aloft.[6]

In addition to omitting the two animal similes and thus diminishing Salmacis's association with the phallic woman, Beaumont adds material about another woman—or goddess—associated with castration and emasculation (Lacan 76; Mitchell 85). Psychoanalysis has long established blinding as a metaphor for castration, and according to Beaumont, Hermaphroditus's mother Venus blinds her elder son Cupid in order to repair a deficiency in her younger son (Mitchell 75). The goddess was disappointed to discover that Hermaphroditus's "eyes were somewhat dull"; consequently, "more the wanton boy to grace, / She puld the sparkling eyes from *Cupids* face" (69–70). In addition to mutilating her elder son, Venus complains of her husband Vulcan's impotence and, to dissuade Jove from pursuing Salmacis, threatens him with the loss of his phallic thunderbolts (202, 305–10, 329–34). By adding these episodes concerning Venus, Beaumont provides an alternative focus for the anxieties that the phallic woman might arouse. Such revisions have prompted Theresa M. Krier to observe that in Beaumont's poem Salmacis appears "not as an image of the horror of female lust but as a comically attractive tart" (8).

Beaumont's additions to Ovid also establish a context in which the actions Salmacis undertakes in response to her intense desire for Hermaphroditus appear to reflect or imitate the behavior of her superiors, the Olympian gods. According to Ovid, Salmacis distinguishes herself—"solaque naiadam" (unique among the naiads)—by failing to follow the divine virgin Diana in the hunt and preferring instead to adorn herself and admire her reflection in a pool. Beaumont uses the cautious clause "It is reported" (369) to distance himself from these assertions, which characterize the nymph as vain, idle, or even libidinous. Whereas Ovid characterizes hunting as bending the bow and racing on foot ("sed nec venatibus apta nec arcus flectere quae soleat nec quae contendere cursu"), Beaumont describes it bluntly and unattractively as "the savage and the bloody sport" (362), thus casting a more positive light on the nymph's refusal to join in the chase. Beaumont continues to part company with Ovid when he asserts Salmacis's resemblance to, rather than divergence from, the divine huntress. A few lines after detailing how Salmacis adorns herself, he reports that Bacchus at first mistakes the nymph for the "Virgin Diana that so liuely shone, / When she did court her sweet Endimion" (377–94, 417–18). Here, by alluding to a rare instance when the "Virgin Diana" takes the erotic initiative, "courts," and kisses the object of her affection, Beaumont reinforces the parallel between the conventionally chaste goddess and the sexually aggressive nymph (Berry 126–31).

Even before introducing Salmacis, Beaumont presents a digression suggesting that Hermaphroditus's charms could provoke lethargy and desire in any nymph and even in the "virgin-huntresse." As Beaumont tells it, "no Nymphes did now pursue the chase: / For all were strooke blind with the wantons face" (23–24). In order to eliminate this distraction, Diana resolves to take up her bow and slay the youth:

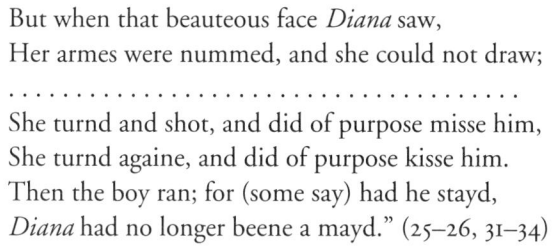

> But when that beauteous face *Diana* saw,
> Her armes were nummed, and she could not draw;
> . . . .
> She turnd and shot, and did of purpose misse him,
> She turnd againe, and did of purpose kisse him.
> Then the boy ran; for (some say) had he stayd,
> *Diana* had no longer beene a mayd." (25–26, 31–34)

Like Diana, Salmacis later discovers that infatuation with Hermaphroditus compromises her ability to command her own movements; after he rebuffs her advances, she attempts to withdraw, "But from his sight she had no power to pass" (823). In light of the goddess's experience, readers might find it difficult to reproach Salmacis for failing to behave more chastely than Diana. Moreover, Beaumont goes on to report that even Diana's brother Apollo dotes on Hermaphroditus, slipping away from "fayre *Leucothoes* side, / To dally with him in the vales of Ide" (37–38). Clearly, then, Hermaphroditus arouses a desire powerful enough to transgress the bounds of both avowed chastity and heterosexuality.

Several of the poem's other digressions focus on Jove's and Bacchus's attempts to seduce Salmacis and suggest that those experiences inform the nymph's aggressive approach to Hermaphroditus, thus qualifying her culpability. Building upon the physical resemblance that Keach has observed in Beaumont's descriptions of the nymph and of the rather effeminate boy (Keach 199), the poet establishes elaborate parallels between the gods' pursuit of Salmacis early in the narrative and the nymph's pursuit of Hermaphroditus later. Both the nymph and the youth have attracted the amorous attention of Apollo, who has "dallied" with Hermaphroditus (38) and "sport[ed] himselfe upon" Salmacis's "snowy hand" (466). Both incite an admirer's desire by bathing naked (245–47, 837–58), and both blush and attempt to retreat when confronted by an insistent suitor (439, 455–56, 660–63, 817–18). As she attempts to seduce Hermaphroditus, Salmacis even echoes Jove, alluding to the god's metamorphic encounter with Leda, six hundred lines after Jove does so while wooing Salmacis herself (123, 723–24). Like the student envisioned in humanist pedagogical theory and character- ized in Beaumont's early burlesque "Grammar Lecture" as a "soft imytating peece," Salmacis gains facility with (erotic) rhetoric by emulating magisterial models (Halpern 28–29; Eccles 406).[7] Such learning by imitation prepares her to show Hermaphroditus "With what a manly boldnesse I could woo the[e]" (716).

Whereas Salmacis's encounter with Jove instructs her in persuasion, the episode with Bacchus teaches her about coercion. As Salmacis forces herself on Hermaphroditus, "lock[ing] him fast" in her arms while he is "striving to get away" (873–74), she appears to imitate the "manly boldnesse" of Bacchus who earlier "forc[es] the lovely mayd to stay," "throwes her in the dewy grasse," kisses "the helpless Nymph upon the ground, / And would have stray'd beyond that lawful bound" (440, 458–60). At this point, Beaumont disturbingly implies that Bacchus's violence sustains, if not excites, the nymph's desire. Just before the god casts her to the ground, she is ambiva- lent: "faine she would have gone, but yet she staid" (456). The subsequent, enforced kisses, however, evidently effect a change, so that, as Beaumont tells it, by rescuing Salmacis from this assault, Apollo "'gainst her will . . . sav'd her maiden-head" (468). Apparently, for both Salmacis and Bacchus, "no" does not mean "no." Perhaps, then, Salmacis is projecting her own disguis- ing of desire, if not acceptance of sexual violence, onto Hermaphroditus. She appears to do so before forcing her embrace upon him, when she asserts, "onely thy tongue denyes, / And the true fancy of thy heart belyes" (805–6). Through his revisions, Beaumont does not eliminate Salmacis's sexual aggression from his narrative; however, he does suggest that it arises from the linking of desire and violence that her encounter with Bacchus fosters.

Beaumont also implies that Salmacis might have drawn Hermaphroditus into willing erotic union, eliminating any need to resort to force or appeal for divine assistance, were it not for the youth's self-absorption. After her ini- tial, flattering entreaty, "Her radiant beauty and her subtill arte / So deeply strooke *Hermaphroditus* heart" that she nearly wins his love (685–87). How- ever, the youth sees his own reflection in Salmacis's eye and becomes enthralled with what he mistakes for a "farre more beauteous Nymph" hid- den there. Whereas her extraordinarily "radiant" and "translucent" eye ear- lier captivates Jove and Bacchus, here it deflects Hermaphroditus into a narcissistic reverie (117, 424, 436). Salmacis attempts to eliminate the illusory competition by simply closing her eyes but finds the youth gone when she reopens them. As Keach and Ann Thompson have recognized, the poet sets the stage for these narrative details by repeatedly alluding to Narcissus, whom Golding interprets as a representation of "scornfulnesse and pryde" (Keach 213–14; Thompson 102–3; Golding, Epistle, 105). Beaumont asserts, for example, that Salmacis's fountain is part of the river where the ill-fated youth fell in love with his own reflection (399–402) and notes (in Salmacis's voice) that through his exceptionally smooth face Hermaphroditus resembles Narcissus (757). As if to ensure that even the most obtuse reader will recognize the point, immediately after Salmacis perceives the youth's self-infatuation, she admonishes him to

> Remember how the gods punisht that boy
> That scorn'd to let a beauteous Nymph enjoy
> Her long wisht pleasure; for the peevish elfe,
> Lov'd of all others, needs would love himself. (703–6)

For the nymph at least, Hermaphroditus's evident narcissism renders his resistance to her advances "peevish" rather than virtuous. Neither of the principal characters appears quite as "spotless" as the epistle to the reader promised. Nonetheless, the material that Beaumont adds to Ovid's narrative affects the portraits of the youth and nymph differently, darkening the character of the victim, Hermaphroditus, and introducing extenuating circumstances regarding the aggressor, Salmacis.

Beaumont's reinterpretation of the myth continues in his concluding description of the fountain's metamorphic properties, as he departs from his source to characterize the transformations that occur there as a blessing. As Hermaphroditus calls upon his divine parents to enchant the fountain, Ovid again stresses debility and diminution:

> That whoso commes within this Well may so bee *weakened* there,
> That of a man *but halfe a man* he may fro thence retire. (478–79, my emphasis)

Whereas Golding's translation, following Ovid, focuses on subtraction— "but halfe a man" (semivir)—Beaumont offers a more balanced description attending not only to what is lost, "a manly shape," but also to what is gained, "halfe a virgine":

"Grant that who e're heated by *Phoebus* beames,
Shall come to coole him in these silver streames,
May nevermore a manly shape retaine,
But halfe a virgine may returne againe."
His parents hark'ned to his last request,
And with that great power they the fountaine *blest.*
And since that time who in that fountaine swimmes,
A mayden smoothnesse seyzeth halfe his limmes. (915–22)[8]

Beaumont expands upon Ovid's simple "comes into this pool" (in hos fontis
. . . venerint) to elaborate the fountain's visual and tactile pleasures and to
imagine the motivations of subsequent bathers. In fact, since Galenic medicine contended that a hot, dry bodily temperament produced masculine
traits, but a cold, moist condition produced feminine ones, Beaumont's
additions hint that the bather intent on cooling himself in the "silver
streames" may, to some degree, embrace the gender transformation that the
fountain effects (Maclean 30–31, 41–42). To represent the fountain's effect
upon bathers, Beaumont turns away from Ovid's "weakening" (enervet)
(286) and "softening" (mollescat) (386) and chooses instead the more desirable "mayden smoothnesse," recalling the extraordinarily smooth face that
Hermaphroditus possesses even before his transformation. Most notably,
whereas in Ovid's original the gods have "stained the fountain with an
impure drug" (incesto fontem medicamine tinxit) and in Golding's translation have "infected" it "with an unknowne strength" (480), in Beaumont's
they have "blest" it.[9] Beaumont thus departs from his source by casting both
Salmacis and the transformative properties of her fountain in a more positive
light.
    Of course, inspired by his "sportive Muse," Beaumont may have wished
to violate convention and provoke his audience with self-consciously "wanton lines"; the playful conclusion of his epistle to the reader suggests as
much:

I hope my Poem is so lively writ,
    That thou wilt turne halfe-mayd with reading it. (The Author to the
    Reader)

Indeed, in light of the conventional analogy between Elizabeth I and the
classical goddess of justice, the epyllion's satirical description of the corrupt
court of Astræa, "Full of dark angles, and of hidden wayes, / Crooked Mæan-

ders, infinite delays," seems to manifest the poet's disregard for Elizabethan orthodoxies (177–78; Yates 29–87).[10] Such disregard may also inform the poem's representation of another of the queen's divine analogues, Diana, whose frailties and frustrations seem to parallel Elizabeth's. Like the queen, who sometimes found it difficult to exercise as much control as she wished over the erotic lives of her courtiers and maids of honor, Diana finds that, thanks to Hermaphroditus, she has lost command of her nymphs who, "strooke blind with the wantons face," no longer "pursue the chase" (23–24).[11] In another possible parallel, a year after Elizabeth had consented to the execution of the handsome but troublesome royal favorite Robert Devereux (1567–1601), Earl of Essex, Beaumont writes of Diana's intention to slay the handsome wanton who threatens the proper order of her court. Further, like the queen, who, according to persistent rumors, bedded lovers and gave birth to illegitimate children, Diana wavers in her chastity and, if Hermaphroditus had consented, would have "no longer bene a mayd" (33; C. Levin, *"Heart"* 66–90). Indeed, in this poem Hermaphroditus commits himself to virginity more wholeheartedly than Diana does. Perhaps, then, Beaumont's portrait of the youth offers implicit commentary on Elizabeth's avowed virginity and refusal to marry. By 1602, that policy, combined with the queen's resistance to naming an heir, had set the stage for a perilous succession crisis.[12] Consequently, the proud self-absorption that motivates the virginity of Beaumont's narcissistic Hermaphroditus may have seemed to underlie the queen's as well. We should not be surprised, then, to find that a writer so ready to interrogate the conventions of Elizabethan propaganda would also rethink Ovidian mythography.

Whereas Beaumont, perhaps emboldened by anonymous publication, declares his lines "wanton" and appears to embrace the opportunity to flout poetic and political orthodoxies, Edmund Spenser, through his use of problematic hermaphroditic imagery, seems to have unintentionally aroused the disapproval of powerful Elizabethan readers and to have promptly repented his transgression. In 1596, when Spenser, a writer more ready to craft than to critique royal propaganda, published the second, expanded edition of *The Faerie Queene,* he added Books IV–VI and altered the conclusion of Book III. The 1590 edition closes with a joyous embrace between the knight Scudamour and his wife, Amoret, after her rescue from the dungeon of the sorcerer Busyrane. In contrast, the 1596 edition adds new obstacles to the lovers' happiness and postpones their reunion until the tenth canto of Book IV. To accommodate this change, Spenser substituted three new stanzas for the five that had concluded the first edition (3.12.43–47). The lines dropped from the

1596 text include a metaphorical description of the two lovers' passionate greeting:

> No word they spake, nor earthly thing they felt,
> But like two senceles stocks in long embracement dwelt.
>
> Had ye them seene, ye would haue surely thought,
> That they had beene that faire Hermaphrodite,
> Which that rich Romane of white marble wrought,
> And in his costly Bath causd to bee site:
> So seemd those two, as growne together quite. (3.12.45a–46a)

Through its references to bathing and Roman origins, as well as its apparent vegetative metaphor ("two senceles stocks . . . growne together quite"), Spenser's passage recalls Ovid's narrative, which compares the merging of Hermaphroditus and Salmacis to the grafting of a twig onto a tree.[13] More important, as both Donald Cheney and Richard Axton have noted (D. Cheney 193–94; R. Axton 37), Spenser's image draws upon an iconographic tradition exemplified by an emblem in the Calvinist Barthélemy Aneau's *Picta Poesis* (1552). In Aneau's woodcut, entitled "Matrimonii Typus," man and woman intertwine to form a tree, while Moses on one side and a satyr on the other look on. Spenser, then, appears to be operating within established conventions.

In the 1596 edition, however, he deletes this image and portrays the lovers' reunion quite differently. At the conclusion of Book III Scudamour despairs of ever recovering Amoret and abandons his vigil at the House of Busyrane. When he finds his wife ten cantos later in the Temple of Venus, she prefers to remain with the goddess and resists his attempts to retrieve her. In this later edition, the couple has grown apart rather than together, so that, as Scudamour tells it, they resemble the hunter and hind or the ill-fated Orpheus and Eurydice. The hermaphrodite appears this time not as a metaphor for their union but rather as a modestly clothed, coolly autonomous goddess. Scudamour finds Venus standing upon an extraordinary altar within her temple and explains:

> The cause why she was couered with a vele,
> Was hard to know, for that her Priests the same
> From peoples knowledge labour'd to concele.
> But sooth it was not sure for womanish shame,

Nor any blemish, which the worke mote blame;
But for, they say, she hath both kinds in one,
Both male and female, both vnder one name:
She syre and mother is her selfe alone,
Begets and eke conceiues, ne needeth other none. (4.10.41)

Here, the hermaphrodite is doubly secreted behind both a veil and the
priests' efforts to obscure her androgyny. Whereas the lovers' embrace in the
1590 edition of Book III "empassiond" the chaste Britomart as she looked
on, this figure transcends sexual interdependence and, shrouded as it is,
thwarts voyeuristic excitement.

As if to explain his text's revision, Spenser opens Book IV by reporting a
censorious critic's charges against the 1590 edition:

The rugged forhead that with graue foresight
Welds kingdomes causes, & affaires of state,
My looser rimes (I wote [know]) doth sharply wite [censure],
For praising loue, as I haue done of late,
And magnifying louers deare debate;
By which fraile youth is oft to follie led,
Through false allurement of that pleasing baite,
That better were in vertues discipled,
Then with vaine poemes weeds to haue their fancies fed. (4.Proem.1)

Spenser disputes this accusation, attributing it to the poor judgment of those
"that cannot loue, / Ne in their frosen hearts feele kindly flame" (presumably
the Lord Treasurer, William Cecil) and asserting that "To such therefore I
do not sing at all." Nonetheless, he admits to some occasional second
thoughts concerning the final cantos of Book III (4.Proem.2, 4.Proem.4).
"Amorets hart-binding chaine" provokes his own tears of pity so intensely
that he "oftentimes doe[s] wish it [his account of her suffering] neuer had
bene writ" (4.1.1). Although disapproving "Stoicke censours" did not induce
Spenser to abandon such erotically charged episodes as the "Castle Ioyeous"
(3.1) and "Bower of Bliss" (2.12), some combination of the hostile reception
and authorial misgivings that Spenser discusses at the opening of Book IV
may have prompted the removal of the lovers' embrace and the hermaphrodite image from the conclusion of Book III. Since a skillful and politically
aware writer such as Spenser could evidently miscalculate concerning the
hermaphrodite's reception, Cope's misstep seems more understandable.

Turning Woman

In fact, as Cope speculates concerning the popess's sexual anatomy, he passes over the hermaphrodite quickly and focuses his attention instead on his second conjecture concerning sexual transformation. He proceeds cautiously, as if recognizing which aspects of his supposition are most controversial: "This, perhaps, you may concede to me that sometimes through the generosity of nature males are made from females, while conversely men sometimes change into women" (Hic tu fortasse, vt ex feminis mares aliquando fieri naturae benignitate mihi concedas; at contra tamen viros in mulieres vnquam transire) (36). Here, Cope leads with women transformed into men, which several early modern writers acknowledged as an extraordinary but real phenomenon. The French physician Ambroise Paré, for example, devotes a chapter of his tract *Des monstres et prodiges* (*On Monsters and Marvels*) (1573) to such occurrences and cites some of the same sources as Cope: Pliny and the sixteenth-century Portuguese physician Amatus Lusitanus (1511–68). In turn, while commenting on Ovid's mythological *Metamorphoses,* the early seventeenth-century translator George Sandys asserts, "Women, if we give credit to histories either ancient or moderne . . . have often beene changed into men"; Sandys goes on to discuss several of the same fifteenth-century Italian cases (recorded by Giovanni Pantano) that Cope mentions (Sandys 103, 336). The difficulty arises with Sandys's closing phrase: "but never men into woman."

Writing several decades before Sandys, Paré shares the Englishman's conviction and attempts to explain the reasons behind it. He maintains that whereas "women can degenerate into men" ("les femmes se peuvent dégénerer en hommes") we "never find in any true story that any man ever became a woman, because Nature tends always toward what is most perfect and not, on the contrary, to perform in such a way that what is perfect should become imperfect" (*On Monsters* 32–33; *Des monstres* 30).[14] Paré's odd suggestion that by "degenerating" women illustrate a natural striving for perfection may signal tension or confusion in the text and surely encourages closer scrutiny.[15] Here, as in the twentieth-century genetic research that Judith Butler has critiqued, cultural assumptions about gender appear to inform biomedical claims about sex (J. Butler 137–39). The adjective *true* in Paré's closing assertion about accounts of men transformed into women raises questions about the structure of his reasoning. Is the physician working inductively from the absence of empirical evidence of men changed into women to formulate a conclusion about the principles informing nature? Or is he working deductively from assumptions about nature and perfection to discount reports of such transformations? For Paré and Sandys (who seems to echo the Frenchman), are such transformations simply impossible to believe?

The two men certainly stop short of acknowledging or disputing a prominent report of the sort of sexual transformations that they consider impossible. To support his claim, Cope cites Decimus Magnus Ausonius's Epigram LXXVI, a fourth-century C.E. Latin text that recounts the transformation of a peacock into a peahen and of a Campanian youth into a girl (2: 199–201). Of course, poetry might not merit the same evidentiary status as natural history. Nonetheless, we should be wary of overly facile explanations for the omission of Ausonius from Paré's and Sandys's texts, since, in their own discussions of sexual transformations, Paré's contemporaries, Guillaume Bouchet and Johann Weyer, chose to note (and discount) Ausonius's anecdote (Parker 360; Weyer 345–46).

Significantly, Paré and Sandys do not address Ausonius or any of the (presumably untrue) stories of men changed into women implied in Paré's remarks. Their silence may express unquestioning certainty that renders further discussion unnecessary. On the other hand, it may mask the uncertainty evident when the seventeenth-century English physician Sir Thomas Browne (1605–82) considers the topic in a passage that contradicts and revises itself as it goes along. After asserting that "the mutation of sexes" is "observable in Man," Browne continues: "For hereof beside Empedocles or Tiresias, there are not a few examples: and though very few, or rather none which have emasculated or turned women, yet very many who from an esteem or reality of being Women have infallibly proved men" (2: 213). Here, Browne's pairing of "esteem or reality" suggests that at least some cases of women transformed into men could be attributed to temporary misperception of the individual's true sex. More important, the references to Tiresias and Empedocles—who reports in Fragment 117, "I was once already boy and girl" (36)—as well as Browne's initial formulation, "very few," momentarily hold out the possibility of "emasculated" men.

The significant silences in Paré's and Sandys's discussions of such transformations parallel silences that inform Jewel's and Mayo's responses to the *Dialogi*. In fact, these responses seem as notable for what they omit—arguments that engage Cope's speculations—as for what they assert—the outlandishness of Cope's approach. Both writers quote and translate the passage in which Cope recounts two fifteenth-century Italian cases of women transformed into men, as he advances his physiological explanations for the popess narrative. Although both writers acknowledge that Cope has appealed to the "possibility of nature," they both characterize the proposed sexual transformation as miraculous. Choosing terms that evoke the Eucharistic controversy, Mayo describes Cope's "surmise" as "verie Catholicke and substanitall" (36). The derisive tone evident here dominates Mayo's and Jewel's discussions of the *Dialogi*. Jewel, for example, sarcastically characterizes the Catholic's reasoning as "discreet" and "handsome" (*Defence* 656), and Mayo bluntly exclaims, "What a vaine illusion and Maygame" (36). They do not question the veracity of Cope's Italian anecdotes, which include substantiating details such as the names of an affected woman, her husband, and the region where they lived. Nor do they challenge the disputable analogy between women changed into men and men changed into women. They even fail to note that, according to canon law, a hermaphrodite could not legitimately occupy the papacy any more than a woman could. In short, they don't dispute or engage with Cope's propositions in any substantial way. Instead, resorting to a strategy that Cope anticipates when he alludes to those who will ward off his speculations through ridicule ("risu excepturos"), they only mock (36).

Taking Cope's ideas seriously in order to refute them would have entailed confronting the profound instability of gender and fear of effeminacy in early modern culture. No doubt, the one-sex model of the body—which originated with Galen in the second century C.E., survived through the sixteenth century, and underlies accounts of sexual transformation—encouraged such fears (Laqueur 8, 19–20). This model implies that the sexual organs of men and women are, as Stephen Greenblatt has succinctly put it, "mirror images of each other" (*Shakespearean* 79). According to Paré, "women have as much hidden within the body as men have exposed outside" (32). The uterus and ovaries are an internal scrotum and testicles; the penis is a cervix and vagina inverted and pushed outside the body by vital heat (Fletcher 34). In fact, heat alone determines whether a fetus will become male or female, and, as Paré explains, in rare cases when such heat "is rendered more robust, vehement, and active," the organs once "hidden" within an adult woman's body could emerge in inverted male form, changing her into a man (Paré, *On Monsters* 33; Maclean 32–33). In the one-sex model, as in Judith Butler's conception of gender, biological sex does not function as a stable substrate underlying gender (Laqueur 8). Assessing the implications of these ancient physiological theories, Peter Brown has observed that "lack of heat from childhood on could cause the male body to collapse back into a state of primary indifferentiation. No normal man might actually become a woman; but each man trembled forever on the brink of becoming 'womanish.' His flickering heat was an uncertain force" (P. Brown 10–11; Jones and Stallybrass 86).[16]

In fact, for much of their childhood, early modern boys experienced such a state of "primary indifferentiation." They wore ankle-length skirts, like their sisters', until the age of six or seven when they were "breeched," that is, dressed in distinctly masculine attire and transferred from the care of a nurse or mother into the hands of male authorities, such as the schoolmasters directing their educations, master craftsmen guiding their apprenticeships, or fathers instructing them in the family trade (Buck 81; Orgel 15–16, 25). Anne Buck has suggested that this breeching constituted a minor ceremony often eagerly anticipated by the child and his family. In 1674 Elizabeth Legh wrote to her husband that their son was "count[ing] the hours . . . for the coming of his breeches." Anne, Lady North reported that her grandson's 1679 breeching generated nearly as much excitement as a wedding: "You cannot believe the great concern that was in the whole family. . . . Never had any bride that was to be dressed upon her wedding night more hands about her." This event was so momentous because it revealed for the first time, as one father put it, "how proper a man" the boy would be (qtd. in Buck 149–51). Memories of being without breeches and the masculine status they signified, then, could fuel sixteenth- and seventeenth-century Englishmen's fears of effeminacy.[17]

Additionally, the unusual structure of the Elizabethan body politic may have made Jewel and Mayo especially uneasy with the sort of metamorphosis that Cope imagined. As the subjects of a queen regnant, in the eyes of some of their contemporaries, these Englishmen had already been rendered womanish. Writing in 1558 with Mary Tudor in mind, John Knox speculates that if classical authorities such as Aristotle were alive to see

> a woman sitting in judgment, or riding from parliament in the midst of men, having the royal crown upon her head, the sword and the scepter borne before her, in sign that the administration of justice was in her power: I am assuredly persuaded, I say, that such a sight should so astonish them, that they should judge the whole world to be transformed into the Amazons, and that such a metamorphosis and change was made of all the men of that country, as poets do feign was made of the companions of Ulysses; or at least, that albeit the outward form of men remained, yet should they judge their hearts were changed from the wisdom, understanding, and courage of men, to the foolish fondness and cowardice of women. (43)[18]

Here, through the eyes of venerable ancients, Knox envisions two gender transformations. In the first, most hyperbolic scenario, the "whole" social world, both men and women, is changed into viragos. Thomas Laqueur has argued that under the one-sex model, "To be a man or a woman was to hold a social rank, a place in society, to assume a cultural role, not to *be* organically one or the other of two incommensurable sexes" (8). Knox evidently imagines that feminine rule erases the distinctions between the social ranks and cultural roles assigned to men and women, so that gender distinctions disappear altogether. The second scenario rests upon an imperfect analogy between the Ithacans on Circe's island and the Englishmen on Mary Tudor's; those Englishmen are changed not outwardly but inwardly and not into beasts but into women. Knox's allusion to the seductress Circe implies another significant analogy, this time between erotic and political subjection. Scholars have accumulated abundant evidence—including Romeo's well-known complaint that Juliet's "beauty hath made me effeminate" (3.1.113–14)—demonstrating that early modern thinkers believed erotic devotion to women rendered men womanish (Orgel 25–26; Laqueur 122–28). Here, Knox suggests that political devotion produces the same effect. In the Elizabethan context, Knox's analogy seems especially apt, since the subjects of the unmarried queen often intermingled erotic and political discourses, casting her in 1581 royal entertainment, for example, as the "The Fortress of Perfect Beauty" besieged by the "Foster Children of Desire" (Montrose, "Shaping" 55). According to Francis Bacon (1561–1626), the son of Elizabeth's Lord Keeper, the queen invited and enjoyed such discourse: "she allowed herself to be wooed and courted, and even to have love made to her; and liked it; and continued it even beyond the natural age for such vanities" (Bacon 11: 460). As subjects to such a queen, then, Jewel and Mayo experienced a particular, political threat to their masculinity.

Jewel's own notorious brush with apostasy, moreover, may have made him especially uneasy with narratives of unstable personal identity, like those implied in Cope's hypothesis. After the accession of the Catholic Mary Tudor in 1553, the Protestant Jewel was stripped of his fellowship at Oxford. Although, like many other Reformers, Jewel's mentor Peter Martyr (1500–62) fled to the Continent, Jewel remained at Oxford, taking refuge in Broadgate Hall and teaching a small number of devoted students. In 1554 Jewel gave in to pressure and publicly signed articles assenting to Catholic doctrines concerning transubstantiation. Nonetheless, within a year, he too was forced to flee England to escape prosecution for heresy. Because he had assented to papist articles, some Continental Protestants approached Jewel with hostility and suspicion, viewing him as "a stranger craftily brought in to preach, who had both been at Mass and also subscribed Blasphemous articles" (qtd. in Booty xxii). Consequently, before the congregation at Frankfurt, Jewel declared contrition for his cowardice and inconstancy, traits that humoral medicine associated with the cold, moist physiologies of women (Maclean 41–42). Even after the accession of Elizabeth and Jewel's return to England, polemical opponents such as Henry Cole (ca. 1500–80) and Thomas Harding sought to discredit Jewel by citing his subscription to Catholic articles (Booty xix–xxiii; *Dictionary* 10: 815–16). Since a moment of apparent doctrinal vacillation haunted Jewel for much of his career, and since humoral theory assumed that physiology determined psychology, he may have found Cope's hypothesis regarding physiological instability particularly disconcerting.[19]

Perhaps, then, the gibes that Jewel directs at Cope express an unintended truth. Twice within his one-paragraph discussion of the *Dialogi,* Jewel sarcastically notes the extraordinary rhetorical potential of Cope's conjectures. First, he advises his polemical opponent Thomas Harding that if he had adopted Cope's proposition he "might soon have put us out of countenance." Since, as we have seen, Cope's ideas rest upon disputable assumptions regarding physiology and canon law, as a defense of the popess, they could not truly discountenance his Protestant adversaries. However, by casting doubt on the stable gender of any man, rather than the sexual identity of a single ninth-century pope, Cope's conjectures may have provoked something approaching the profoundly disorienting effect that Jewel mockingly envisions, as he concludes his discussion of Pope Joan: "If you had taken this same way, then all this story had been a fable, and a woman had been a man; and we had been utterly confounded" (*Defence* 656). Cope's effort to rehabilitate Joan failed, then, because his tactic was at once too feeble—too dependent on dubious ideas about biology and canon law, as well as on the unpredictable reception of the androgyne in early modern culture—and too potent—too capable of arousing profound anxieties that his opponents chose not to confront. Cope's attempt to diagnose Joan, like the twentieth-century New's, exposes confusion in competing discourses concerning gender and biological sex.

4 Canonizing Joan

NECROMANCY, PAPACY, AND THE
REFORMATION OF THE BOOK

In 1548 POPE JOAN became an English author and a magician. That year, at least, the English Protestant polemicist and antiquarian John Bale credited Joan with writing a book on necromancy and therefore included her story among the brief literary biographies presented in his *Illustrivm maioris Britanniae scriptorum . . . summarium,* arguably one of the earliest attempts to fashion an English literary history (Simpson 216–17; Ross 57; King, *English* 66).[1] The French poet Martin le Franc had earlier credited Joan with composing prefaces to the Mass; however, amid the religious tumult of the sixteenth century, Bale's report was more provocative and resonant (S. Taylor 268, 275; Boureau, *Myth* 156). In subsequent decades Joan's necromantic literary enterprise became part of the popess legend, disputed by the Catholic controversialist Robert Bellarmine and recounted, often with direct citations to Bale, in Protestant texts such as Matthias Illyricus Flacius's 1565 *Historia ecclesiastica* (*Magdeburg Centuries*); Johann Wolf's 1600 *Lectionum memorabilium et reconditarum centenarii XVI;* and the 1599 *Historia de Donne Famose, or The Romaine Iubile* (Walpole 419; Morris 162; Wolf 1: 239; *Historia* C2v). As we shall see in this chapter's first section, Bale's report fits easily within misogynistic witchcraft lore and legends regarding necromancer popes such as Sylvester II and Alexander VI but seems at odds with some elements within the popess legend and with Bale's celebration of learned and literary women in texts such as the 1548 *Summarium* and Bale's subsequent revision and expansion of that work, the *Scriptorvm illustrium Maioris Brytannie . . . Catalogus* (1557, 1559).[2] A full understanding of Bale's report, then, requires examining it, as this chapter's second section does, in the context of his polemical career and his other additions to the popess legend and in light of what Jennifer Summit terms the Protestant "reformation of the book." Such an examination reveals how Bale's representation of Joan addresses his ambivalence regarding the origins of his antiquarian enterprise, which was prompted by the dissolution of English monasteries—a policy that he promoted—and by the destruction of the monastic libraries—a consequence that he regretted.

Engagement with monastic culture, as either a participant or a critic, marked much of Bale's career. Educated initially by Carmelite friars and later at Cambridge, where he earned a doctorate of divinity, Bale served as prior of Carmelite houses at Maldon and Ipswich. In a radical break with his Roman past, in 1536, two years after the Act of Supremacy declared Henry VIII head of the Church of England, Bale left the Carmelites, married, and took up a post in Suffolk as a secular priest, free from the confines and rules of a monastic community or religious order. Imprisoned for heretical preaching in 1537, Bale won release through the intervention of the antiquarian and royal chaplain John Leland (ca. 1506–52) and the privy councilor Thomas Cromwell. Evidently under Cromwell's patronage, Bale composed and produced polemical dramas portraying Catholic corruption and error and, in the case of the allegorical history play *King Johan,* promoting royal supremacy. Upon Cromwell's fall and execution in 1540, Bale fled to the Continent, where, for the next eight years, he wrote polemical tracts and edited texts by other Protestant writers.

A decade after he left the Carmelites and Henry VIII dissolved English monasteries, concern with religious orders and monastic culture continued to inform much of Bale's writing. Having staged monks' sexual immorality in his polemical drama, Bale set about chronicling it in the revealingly entitled *Actes of Englysh Votaryes Comprehendynge their Vnchast Practyses and Examples . . .* (1546)—"votaryes" here referring to those whose vows bind them to life in a religious order. At the same time, he worked to prevent or undo some consequences of the dissolution, a reformist program that Bale's portrayal of monastic corruption in the *Votaryes* and in his earlier plays implicitly promoted or defended. Influenced by his friend Leland, Bale recognized that the closure of the monasteries scattered and imperiled the contents of their libraries. Consequently, like Leland (whose own efforts were cut short by an incapacitating mental illness), Bale composed lists of English books and authors, making it possible to preserve what remained extant and to document, at least, what had already been lost. As Thomas Fuller's memorable characterization of Bale as "*Biliosus Balaeus*" might lead one to expect, he retained a polemical component even in these antiquarian projects (King, *English* 59). Bale organized the *Scriptorvm illustrium* around a view of Christian history as a struggle between true and false churches and incorporated within the *Scriptorum illustrium* a history of the papacy (published separately as *Acta romanorum pontificum* in 1558 and later translated by John Studley as

The Pageant of Popes in 1574) informed by that same view. In fact, due to the inclusion of that papal history, Bale devotes two entries in the *Scriptorum illustrivm* to Joan, foregrounding her career as pope in one and as a writer in the other (King, "John Bale"). As we shall see, in the latter entry, as in his earlier tracts and polemical drama, Bale draws attention to the moral deficiencies of monastic culture, which despite its failings had preserved Britain's literary antiquities during the Middle Ages.

Smooth-Tongued Women and Necromancer Popes

In some respects, Bale's introduction of necromantic writing into the Pope Joan legend seems quite predictable. One of the earliest written accounts of Joan's career, a passage from Etienne de Bourbon's *Tractatus de diversis materiis praedicabilibus* (Treatise concerning Diverse Materials for Preaching) (ca. 1260), set the stage for her association with necromancy by asserting that, after securing a place in the Roman Curia through diligence and learning, Joan became a cardinal and ultimately pope "with the devil's help" (Boureau, *Myth* 118; Pardoe and Pardoe 16–17). Centuries later and just a few years after Bale published his account of Joan the scriptor, in a tract bluntly entitled *Historia di papa Giovanni VIII che fu meretrice e strega* (History of Pope John VIII, Who Was a Whore and a Witch) (1557), the Italian Protestant Pier Paolo Vergerio (1498–1565) made a charge much like Etienne's, asserting that Joan seized the papacy through magical arts ("malis artibus") (D'Onofrio 119; Boureau, *Myth* 242). Other writers such as Martinus Polonus and Giovanni Boccaccio had attributed Joan's rise to the extraordinary intellectual accomplishments she achieved in part by eluding conventional strictures that denied women access to monastic education. As sixteenth-century depictions of Friar Bacon and Doctor Faustus demonstrate, necromancy could exemplify learning that, like Joan's, transgressed established boundaries. As James I notes in his dialogue *Daemonologie* (1597, 1603), in its narrowest, root meaning *necromancy* refers to consulting the dead (*nekros*) to divine future events (*manteia*); the term itself thus foregrounds knowledge as the principal object of "this black & unlawfull science" (Weyer 133; *OED* 10: 284; James VI and I 6). Bale's report of Joan's authorship, then, elaborates elements—demonic assistance and transgressive learning—already present in the popess legend.

Quite likely, Bale's report also drew credibility from medieval witchcraft lore, which contended that those most attracted to magic and superstition were libidinous, verbally adept women—a category to which Joan certainly belongs. According to the widely circulated *Malleus maleficarum* (The Witch Hammer) (1486), far more women than men were "infected with the heresy of witchcraft" and evil superstitions (Kramer and Sprenger 47).[3] Philomathes, an interlocutor in James I's dialogue *Daemonologie,* sets the ratio at twenty women for every man "giuen to that craft" (James VI and I 30). Even a skeptic such as the physician Johann Weyer (1515–88), who denied that witches or magicians accomplished the feats attributed to them, claimed that the female sex was especially vulnerable to the demonic illusions that are mistaken for magic (181).[4] As Stuart Clark has noted, the association between women and witchcraft rested upon "entirely unoriginal foundations," namely, the Aristotelian view of women as "deformed" men and Christian denigration of them as the source of sin (Clark 114).

As they attempt to explain "why superstition is chiefly found in women," the Dominican inquisitors Heinrich Kramer (1430–1505) and James Sprenger (died 1505), writing in the *Malleus maleficarum,* repeatedly cite women's speech, their Siren-like voices, "slippery tongues," and mouths "smoother than oil" (44, 46). They borrow this last phrase from Proverbs 5:3–5, where it refers only to the adulterous "strange woman" whose "feet go down to death" and "steps take hold on hell"; here, however, they apply it to all women. These Dominicans seem to have reasoned that since women are generally loquacious and "unable to conceal from the fellow-women those things which by evil arts they know," witchcraft would spread easily among them. Speech so concerns Kramer and Sprenger that, as they set out to explain "why a greater number of witches is found in the fragile feminine sex than among men," they cite a dangerous trinity: "the Tongue, an Ecclesiastic, and a Woman," three things "which know no moderation in goodness or vice" (42). As an eloquent woman who usurps ecclesiastical office, the popess brings together all three. In fact, even when focusing on Joan's ecclesiastical rather than literary career, Bale stresses eloquence as her principal talent. Writing in the papal history that he includes within the *Scriptorvm illustrium,* Bale at first notes Joan's accomplishment "in all sciences" (in omnibus artibus); however, he soon departs from the precedent provided by Boccaccio, a source who elaborates a broad foundation for Joan's learning in the trivium and in "liberal and sacred letters" (in liberalibus & sacris literis), and in contrast focuses narrowly on her verbal facility, her "ready tongue" (lingua promptissima) and the richly ornamented speech she employs in debates and lectures ("in disceptationibus ac lecturis publicis ornatissime loqueretur") (Boccaccio, *Ioannis Boccatii* LXXIIIv; Bale, *Scriptorvm illustrium* 1: 116; Bale, *Pageant* 56r). Bale's Joan thus excels at the smooth speech that, according to Kramer and Sprenger, inclines women toward witchcraft.[5]

Bale's Joan also manifests the vice that, according to these Dominican inquisitors, above all others attracts women to magic and superstition. "All witchcraft comes," they insist, "from carnal lust, which is in women insatiable. . . . Wherefore for the sake of fulfilling their lusts they consort even with devils" (Kramer and Sprenger 46). Women, they contend, are "more carnal" than men, and the women who are most prone to superstition are those most moved by sexual desire: "adulterous drabs and whores" (44, 47, 54). Clearly, Bale's "whore pope" (Papa meretrice) fits easily into such company. Once again the contrast with Boccaccio is instructive. The popess's Italian chronicler reports a period of celibacy between the death of Joan's first lover and her election to the papacy and insists that virtue and saintliness ("honestate ac sanctitate") informed her private life at that time. Only after she dares to assume the papal office and falls under the devil's influence ("suadente diabulo") does she give herself over to lust ("in ardorem devenit libidinis") (*Ioannis Boccatii* LXXIIIIr). Bale, on the other hand, reports no period of abstinence, identifies Joan with the Whore of Babylon, and notes that her son was conceived through fornication ("puerum ex fornicatione conceptum") (*Scriptorvm illustrium* 1: 116). Bale's popess thus resembles the insatiable women of the *Malleus maleficarum,* ready to "consort even with devils." In several ways, then, she seems predisposed to delve into magic and conjuring.

Bale's report about Joan's authorship not only draws upon these broad notions regarding witchcraft and magic but also extends particular parallels between Joan and Pope Sylvester II (reigning 999–1003), a reputed sorcerer who, as Bale explains immediately after citing Joan's necromantic writing, conjured Satan to aid his rise to the papacy. According to Bale, the pontificates of Joan and Sylvester mark the beginning and end of a particular Antichristian phase of papal history (*Scriptorvm illustrium* 1: 116, 142; *Pageant* 55v, 72r). Moreover, as if drawing attention to parallels between their pontificates, Bale transforms Sylvester's given name from "Gerbertus" (as it appears in earlier authoritative texts by the papal historian Platina and the English chronicler William of Malmesbury, ca. 1090–1143) into "Gilbertus," the masculine form of "Gilberta," the given name that Bale (following Boccaccio) assigns to Pope Joan (Platina 1: 264; William of Malmesbury 172). Like Joan, who traveled with her lover to Athens where, according to Bale's account, she "profited in all the sciences," Sylvester pursued transgressive learning with an erotic accomplice. Forsaking the Benedictine abbey where he had begun his career, Sylvester journeyed to Moorish Spain to investigate "devilishe artes" and "prophane sciences" (*Scriptorvm illustrium* 1:

142; Pageant 56r, 72v). Determined to possess the prized text owned by the Saracen magician who had taught him "both sorcerye and ambitio[n]," Sylvester "inveigled" (allured or seduced) the magus's daughter, "wyth whom beinge in th[e] house he had good acquaintance," to steal her father's conjuring book; then, text in hand, he escaped to France. Although Bale stops short of asserting that Sylvester's intimacy ("domestica familiaritas") with his mentor's daughter was sexual, she does seem to play Medea to Sylvester's Jason (*Scriptorvm illustrium* 1: 142). In fact, as if determined to eroticize this episode one way or another, William of Malmesbury quotes Ovid's *Amores* (3.4.17), a meditation on sexual jealousy and desire, to explain Sylvester's yearning for the magus's closely guarded text (William of Malmesbury 174). As if to confirm that the intellectual pursuits of these two pontiffs were transgressive, Bale's narratives link erotic and intellectual desires and satisfactions.

In a further parallel between Bale's accounts of Joan and Sylvester, each pontiff's false confidence, fostered by an intellectual failure, occasions a catastrophe set in motion during a disrupted ceremony. Joan disregarded her advanced pregnancy and undertook a public procession during which she went into labor, revealing her true sex. This brilliant woman who had "profited in all the sciences" failed to comprehend the workings of her own body. Similarly, Sylvester, who reportedly was clever enough to command (and in some accounts even create) a brazen head that spoke and foretold the future, failed to interpret correctly this instrument's oracular utterances. When the head declared that Sylvester would not die until he had said Mass in Jerusalem, the pope felt certain that he would enjoy a long life and began "to waxe carelesse." Not recognizing that the Palace of the Holy Cross in Rome was also called "Jerusalem," he rashly celebrated Mass there and immediately fell ill with a lethal fever. Before dying he confessed and ordered his own dismemberment, commanding that his hands and tongue, with which he had blasphemously offered sacrifices to Satan, should be cut from his body. This violence inflicted upon the body of a disgraced pope recalls details present in Jean de Mailly's and Etienne de Bourbon's thirteen-century accounts of the popess (but absent from Bale's) in which, after her deception has been exposed, Joan is dragged behind a horse (her feet bound to its tail or hooves) and stoned to death. In Bale's accounts of the downfall of both pope and popess, the body's frailty draws attention to the empty pretensions of papal ceremonies (*Scriptorvm illustrum* 1: 143; *Pageant* 73r; Pardoe and Pardoe 16–17).

Bale also links both pontificates to apocalyptic prophecy. In *The Image of*

Both Churches, which John N. King has characterized as the "first full-length Protestant commentary on Revelation," Bale articulates an influential interpretation of Christian history as a contest between the followers of the true, apostolic church and of the Antichristian, Roman church (King, *English* 61). As I have noted, that interpretation informs the history of the papacy that Bale includes in the *Scriptorvm illustrium;* moreover, it prompts him to associate Joan with apocalyptic imagery. Within that papal history, the heading Bale assigns to the section that includes Joan's pontificate makes her place in apocalyptic prophecy quite clear: "in regno meretricis magnae; quae sedet super bestiam, Apoc. 17. usque ad Syluestrum secundum" (from the reign of the great whore who sits upon the beast in Apocalypse 17 up to Sylvester II) (1: 116). As we saw in chapter 2, the sexually immoral woman who, as Bale tells it, took two clerical lovers (the monk with whom she traveled to Athens and the cardinal who impregnated her) invites comparisons to the biblical "MOTHER OF HARLOTS," the Whore of Babylon. Further, for Bale, the obeisance that monarchs such as the Holy Roman Emperor Louis II and King Aethelwolf of England performed before Joan (as Pope John VIII) seems to fulfill the prophecy that the Whore would "reigneth over the kings of the earth" (Rev. 17:5, 18). Not surprisingly, Bale endorses the notion that Joan's pontificate "was suffered by Gods especiall prouidence . . . to bewraye the whore of Babilon in a Pope . . . that the elect might beware of her" and "Antichrist might be knowen" (*Pageant* 56v–57r). Similarly, Sylvester II, who rose to the papacy in the millennial year 1000 C.E., "by the helpe of the devil, whom he w[ith] coniuration raysed out of hell" (*Pageant* 73r), fulfilled another Revelation prophecy, that after Christ's thousand-year reign is "expired, Satan shall be loosed out of his prison" (Rev. 20:7). Bale's accounts of these two pontiffs thus parallel each other not only in their narrative details but also in their apocalyptic significance.

Such parallels, as well as witchcraft lore suggesting that lustful, smooth-spoken women were "giuen to that craft" and reports asserting that Joan rose to the papacy through transgressive learning if not demonic assistance, certainly provide a foundation for Bale's statement concerning Joan's necromantic writing. However, in some respects that statement fits awkwardly into other traditions surrounding Joan, into Bale's larger polemical and editorial projects, and even into the *Scriptorvm illustrium* itself. First, notwithstanding Etienne's reference to demonic aid, an equally if not more persistent thread within the Pope Joan legend involves accounts of *antagonism* between devils and the popess. For example, according to the anonymous *Chronica minor* (ca. 1261), Joan's disguise and pregnancy came to light not, as in other accounts, when she fell into labor but when during a papal assembly a demon publicly exclaimed, "O Pope, Father of Fathers, disclose the childbearing of the woman pope" (Papa, Pater Patrum, Papisse Pandito Partum) (Boureau, *Myth* 140; Pardoe and Pardoe 18). The Franciscan chronicle *Flores temporum* (ca. 1290) elaborates this narrative as well as the exclamation, reporting that the demon was afflicting an unfortunate demoniac, and after interrogators asked when the demon would depart, he announced, "Pope, father of fathers, publish the childbearing of the woman pope. And then I will tell you when I will withdraw from the body" (Papa, pater patrum papise pondito partum. Et tibi tunc edam, de corpore quando recedam) (Pardoe and Pardoe 19, my translation). As we have seen, Dietrich Schernberg's play *Ein schön Spiel von Frau Jutta* (1480) dramatizes this episode, as Jutta (Joan) expels a demon who was possessing a youth and defying the commands of all other exorcists. In retaliation, the enraged spirit reveals Jutta's sex and pregnancy, concluding, "That's what she gets for expelling me; / otherwise I would have left her in peace" (ll. 767–68). These texts, unlike Etienne's, foreground conflict rather than collaboration between devils and the popess.

Further, Bale is an unlikely spokesman for distrust of learned and literary women. His predecessors, Johann von Tritheim and John Leland, chose titles for their inventories of authors and texts that convey little concern for writing by women: *Catalogus illustrium virorum Germaniae* (1496) and *De viris illustribus* respectively. In contrast, in the title Bale assigned to his catalog he signals the inclusion of women by using, rather than *vir,* the term *scriptor,* which although grammatically masculine could refer to a male or female writer. Moreover, he admiringly edited Princess Elizabeth Tudor's *Glass of the Sinful Soul* (1548), a translation of a devotional tract by Marguerite de Navarre (1492–1549). In his conclusion to that edition, Bale proudly declares, "No realme under the skye hath had more noble women, nor of more excellent graces, than have thyse realme of Englande," and goes on to reveal that these "excellent graces" include "beauty, wit, wisdom, science, languages, liberality, policies, [and] heroical force," virtues exemplified by several women to whom he devotes entries in the *Scriptorvm illustrium:* the lawgivers Marcia Proba and Cambra of Sicamber, the Briton poet Claudia Rufina, and the sainted abbess Hilda of Whitby who "not only disputed in the open Synod of Streneshalce . . . but also wrote a treatise against Bishop Agilbert" ("Conclusion" 97–100; *Scriptorvm illustrium* 1: 12–13, 20–21, 81). Further, as he discusses the case of Eleanor Cobham (died ca. 1454), a "famous and honourable" woman whom "in hate of her name and belief" papist bishops "accused of sorcerous enchantments," Bale demonstrates an awareness that charges of necromancy could be trumped up to attack women of conviction ("Conclusion" 101). Similarly, as Jennifer Summit has noted, in his editorial commentary on the *First Examination of Anne Askew,* another of his catalog's illustrious writers, Bale condemns the "blynde Romysh beggeryes" of popish texts who denounce learned "schole women" (*Examinations* 30–31; Summit 149). According to Summit, far from fearing feminine learning, Bale envisions a lost, repressed history of learned women dissenting from Roman orthodoxy, a history that "prefigures and grounds the history of English Protestantism" (149). Presenting Joan as a negative exemplum of feminine intellectual accomplishment therefore would not advance Bale's broader polemical project.

Finally, Bale's statement regarding Joan's book is brief and tentative. Whereas he boldly asserts that Pope John VIII was a woman—"mulier erat"—and cites authorities such as Platina, Boccaccio, and Sabellico (Marco Antonio Coccio, 1436–1506) to justify his certainty, Bale relates the report of her authorship more cautiously, attributing it to hearsay ("dicitur") and failing to ground it in any textual authorities: "Scriptis dedisse dicitur haec ingeniosa & docta mulier *Necromantica quaedam. Lib. 1*" (This ingenious and learned woman is said to have put into writing certain necromantic matters, being one book) (2: 122). The vague phrase "certain necromantic matters" contrasts sharply with the precise titles included, for example, in the *Scriptorvm illustrium* entries that immediately precede and follow Joan's: *De officiis ecclesiae* for Walafrid Strabo, a German monk whom Bale credits with Anglo-Saxon ancestry ("ex Anglosaxorum genere"); and *Vitam Eamundi martyris* for St. Abbon, a French monk who earned his way into Bale's catalog by directing the monastery school at Ramsey (2: 121, 123). Further, although, as we have noted, the *Scriptorvm illustrium* includes two separate entries devoted to Joan (one each for her ecclesiastical and literary careers), Bale associates her with necromancy only in the one brief sentence quoted earlier. In fact, although he asserts that many men have obtained the papacy through demonic means, unlike Etienne de Bourbon, Bale does not assert that Joan did so. As if recognizing that his report of the popess's sorcerous writing conflicts with the emphasis he places on learned women's resistance to Roman apostasy in his conclusion to *Glass of the Sinful Soul* (a text published the same year as his account of Joan the scriptor), Bale articulates that report cautiously (Summit 149). How then did that report, so at odds with the role Bale assigned to learned and literary women, contribute to the Protestant polemical enterprise to which Bale devoted so much of his writing?

Idolatrous Prayer and Pious Conjuring

In answer to the question that I have just posed, examining the intersection of necromancy and cross-dressing in Bale's polemical drama and probing the meaning of "*Necromantica quaedam. Lib. 1*," the phrase he uses to describe Joan's book, reveals that Bale's cautious and somewhat surprising reference to the popess's literary activities amounts less to an attack on learned woman and more to a critique of what many Protestants considered medieval Catholicism's idolatrous approach to devotional books. For Bale, that critique grew urgent as the dissolution of the monasteries, a policy that he had promoted, threatened to eradicate texts that constituted, as he put it, "lyuelye memoryalles of our nacyon" (*Laboryouse* A7v). As an extreme illustration of the failings of medieval Catholic literary culture, the popess's writing could demonstrate the need to disrupt that culture, as the dissolution of the monasteries and monastic libraries surely did.

The traits attributed to a cross-dressing sorceress in Bale's allegorical drama *A Comedy Concernynge Three Laws of Nature* (ca. 1538) demonstrate that by later adding necromantic studies to Joan's biography, Bale made her a particularly apt representation of idolatry, a vice that purportedly infected medieval Catholicism's treatment of prized books. In the play's second act, Infidelitas summons the seemingly inseparable pair "Sodom[ismus] Monach[us]" and "Idol[olatria] Necro[mantic]," the latter of whom resembles the popess in several respects (stage directions 2.388, 398). The text's colophon confirms the implications of these characters' names by recommending, "Let Idolatry be decked like an old witch, Sodomy like a monk of all sects" (121). As if inviting comparisons to Pope Joan, Bale characterizes Idololatria as a woman "wele seane [distinguished] in phylosophye" (2.411; Happé 162) and a cross-dresser. Alluding, it would seem, to the conventions of transvestite theater and conflating actor and character, Infidelitas asserts, "Sumtyme thu wert an he!" and Idololatria replies, "Yea, but now Ich am a she" (2.425–26). As both Alan Stewart and Garret P. J. Epp have noted, a traveling troupe such as Bale's would have needed to double the role of Idololatria with parts in the play that require an adult male actor—Hypocrisy, for example, who appears "as a grey friar" (Stewart 13; Epp 68). Far from obscuring this theatrical transvestitism, Bale foregrounds it, as Infidelitas compares Idololatria to several effeminate or transvestite men from ancient history and mythology, including Hercules, who dressed in women's clothes while enslaved to Queen Omphale; Cleisthenes, a beardless Athenian mocked in Aristophanes's *The Clouds* (354); and the Roman demagogue Publius Clodius Pulcher (died 52 B.C.E.), who, in order to pursue a liaison with Julius Caesar's wife, allegedly disguised himself as a woman to slip into Caesar's house during the exclusively feminine rites of Bona Dea (*Comedy* 2.433–35; Hornblower and Spawforth 350, 1067). These men, as Infidelitas explains:

> . . . themselves oft transfourmed
> Into a womanys lyckenes,
> With agylyte and quyckenes;
> But they had Venus' syckenes,
> As writers have declared. (2.437–41)[6]

Here, as in Bale's account of Joanna Anglica, who put on men's apparel "the more to enioye her louers company," sexual desire ("Venus' sickness") prompts the lustful to cross-dress and thus blur gender boundaries (*Pageant* 56r).

In fact, the failure to observe conventional boundaries functions as a recurrent motif within the portraits of Idololatria and her companion. In addition to the various illicit sexual acts suggested by the name Sodomismus, the play hints at incest. A few lines after characterizing Idololatria as "My muskyne [pretty face] and my mullye [darling]" (*OED* 10: 75, 133), who "though she be somewhat old" is "myne own sweetheart of gold," Sodomismus, whom Idololatria initially addresses as son, in turn refers to her as "good mother" (2.398, 477, 479, 481, 495).[7] Looking on and evidently recognizing the impropriety of this coupling, Infidelitas observes:

> What wylt thu fall to mutton?
> And playe the hungry glutton
> Afore thys company?
> Ranke love is full of heate;
> Where hungry dogges lacke meate
> They wyll durty puddynges eate,
> For want of befe and conye. (2.484–90)

Even the description of Idololatria's sorcery blurs sixteenth-century distinctions between necromancy and witchcraft. Bale associates this character, on the one hand, with the necromancer's practices of telling men's fortunes and "fetch[ing] the devyll from hell" (2.412, 416), and, on the other hand, with more mundane vengeful mischief characteristic of witches (and later of Shakespeare's Robin Goodfellow), who might threaten to make ale go flat, if, as Idololatria puts it, "the bruar please me natt" (2.451). Bale points to the logic underlying this preoccupation with blurring, as he alludes to Romans 1:23–27. Idolatry, which Bale characterizes as a perversion of the heart and soul (2.684–90), involves mistaking the proper object of spiritual devotion and consequently worshipping "the creature more than the Creator" (Rom. 1:25). According to Paul, God abandons idolaters "through the lusts of their own hearts" to sodomy, a parallel corruption of the flesh that involves mistaking the proper object of erotic attraction (Rom. 1:24). Drawing upon scriptural authority, Sodomismus asserts this link between physical and spiritual corruption:

As Paul to the Romans testify,
The Gentiles, after Idolatry,
Fell to such bestial sodomy
That God did them forsake. (2.603–6)

By portraying Idololatria as the mother of Sodomismus, Bale allegorically expresses this Pauline view that the spiritual sin of idolatry leads to (gives birth to) the fleshly sin of sodomy. Further, as mother and lover, necromancer and witch, woman and sometime cross-dressed man, Idololatria aptly represents the "categorical confusion," to borrow Epp's phrase, embodied in idolatry (Epp 64). Joanna Anglica, a licentious woman disguised as the Vicar of Christ, also aptly figures categorical confusion. Joanna's misdirected study of necromancy rather than divinity, an element that Bale later introduces into the popess legend, intensifies such associations.

Unlike Idololatria, however, Bale's Joanna Anglica writes about but does not necessarily practice necromancy—he never explicitly charges the popess with conjuring. To understand the import of stressing the popess's literary rather than sorcerous activities, and to recognize the particular form of idolatry that Joan the scriptor represents, we must consider what sort of book the phrase "*Necromantica quaedam*" might denote: an erudite demonology like the one James I would later write, a witch hunter's handbook like the *Malleus maleficarum,* or a conjuring book or grimoire like those that Edmund Spenser's Archimago consults (*Faerie Queene* 1.1.36–37)? Although Bale provides no explicit answer to this question, we might infer one from the sentence that immediately follows his terse reference to Joan's writings. As we have seen, evidently implying an analogy, Bale turns from Joan to Sylvester II, who through sorcery loosed Satan and obtained the papacy and who, according to the separate biographical sketch that Bale devotes to him, stole his Saracen mentor's prized conjuring book. Additionally, by the early seventeenth century, two such conjuring books had been attributed to papal authors. The *Enchiridion of Pope Leo,* a book of charms that, according to dubious legend, Pope Leo III (reigning 795–816) gave to Charlemagne, was published at least as early as 1584 in Lyons, in 1633 in Mainz, and in 1660 in Rome.[8] In 1629 and again in 1670 another conjuring book appeared in print, this time attributed to Pope Honorius III (reigning 1216–27) and prefaced by what purports to be a papal bull extending to all Catholic clergy the power to command demons (E. M. Butler 89; Davis xxvi–xxviii).[9] In light of these early modern reports that popes possessed or composed conjuring books, as well as the close association between Pope Joan and Sylvester II, Bale's report concerning the popess's necromantic writing quite likely refers to such a text.

In that case, Joan's writing offers a hyperbolic illustration of medieval Catholic textual practices that, according to Jennifer Summit, English Protestants found sorely in need of reform. Summit has interrogated the notion, prominently advanced by John Foxe and echoed by modern scholars, that the invention of the printing press, with the resulting increase in literacy and book ownership, gave rise to Protestantism. Such a causal narrative oversimplifies the historical situation, she contends, by disregarding the Catholic print culture that preceded the Reformation in England and was marked by books of hours and other devotional texts. Protestantism therefore entailed a "renegotiation of textual conventions"; as Summitt puts it, "the reformation of England's religious identity was a reformation of the book" (112, 122).

English Protestants perceived at least two profound failings in Catholic textual practices. First, Catholic devotional books often functioned as vehicles for indulgenced prayer, promising readers remission (for themselves or others) of anticipated punishments in purgatory. In fact, an explanation of the indulgence to be earned by reciting a prayer conventionally preceded its text in such books. As one might expect, Protestants committed to justification by faith attacked such salvific prayer and the books that facilitated it. In 1538, for example, William Marshall exhorted readers to reject "pestilent infections of bookes" that "greate promises and perdons have falsly a[d]uanced" (qtd. in Summit 119). Similarly, the 1547 *Certayne Sermons or Homilies, Appointed by the Kynges Majestie* condemned "lady psalters" and the well-known indulgenced prayer book *The Fifteen Oes* as "papisticall supersticions . . . which were so esteemed & abused to [th]e great prejudice of Gods glorye and commanundements, that they were made most high & most holy things, whereby to attaine to the eternal life, or remission of synne" (K1; Summit 119). Second, Protestants charged that Catholic practices cultivated an idolatrous veneration of the devotional book as material object. For example, while attacking "the idolatrous superstitio[n] of the elder world" in a 1578 treatise, the Protestant Edward Dering focused on books "which Satan had made, Hell had printed, and were warranted unto sale under the Popes priuiledge, to kindle in mens hartes the sparkes of superstition" (qtd. in Summit 116). Further, *The Seconde Tome of Homelyes* (1563) hints at idolatrous veneration as it condemns medieval books of hours as "graven bookes, and paynted scripture of the glorious gylt ymages and ydolles, all shynynge and glytterynge with metal and stone, and covered with precious vestures" (qtd. in Summit 123). If this description calls to mind ornate medieval reliquaries, the association is apt, since some devotional books, namely saints' lives, were thought to possess the miraculous properties of saints' relics (Summit 115; Wogan-Browne and Burgess xi; Boureau, "Franciscan" 16–18).[10] According to Summit, the "reformation of the book," the Protestant response to such medieval Catholic conventions, entailed locating a book's value in a symbolic rather than material realm and understanding the reading of prayers as an expression of faith rather than an efficacious ritual practice.

As one might infer from the Protestant Dering's reference to Satanic books made by hell, the textual practices surrounding pre-Reformation devotional books overlapped with those surrounding grimoires (manuals for summoning demons). Both indulgenced prayer books and grimoires assigned ritual efficacy to reading and reciting prepared texts. Moreover, the blessings proffered in prayer books extended beyond the reduction of time that a soul would spend in purgatory to include safe and swift childbirth, protection from sudden death or pestilence, revelation of the exact date of one's death, or simply a wish (Summit 115, 121; Thomas 43). Bishop John Hilsey may have had such blessings in mind in 1539 when he warned the readers of prayer books against "goodly printed prefaces, promisinge to the sayers therof many things both folyshe and false" (qtd. in Summit 121). Such promises intensify the resemblance between prayer books and grimoires, which proposed to invest readers, through the services of conjured demons, with the power to cure disease, uncover hidden treasure, and reveal the future (Scot 218, 228, 240; *Liber juratus* 62, 64, 65). Not surprisingly, the Anglican bishop Jeremy Taylor (1613–67) perceived parallels between ritually efficacious prayer and magical spells, contending that Catholics suppose "prayers themselves *ex opere operato* . . . do prevail," and "like the words of a charmer they prevail even when they are not understood" (qtd. in Thomas 42).

The authors of grimoires too fostered their resemblance to prayer books through what Barbara Mowat has identified as an intensely religious tone informing those texts (8). Such books recommend confession and pious prayer in preparation for summoning spirits (*Liber juratus* 71; Scot 238). A thirteenth-century grimoire, for example, contends that only "clean," shriven Christians can succeed in "Magical Art" and goes on to present roughly one hundred prayers, including some standard Catholic ones, under the headings "Psalter" and "Litany" (Mathiesen 146, 148, 151).[11] Rather than following the "shortest cut to conjuring" and "abjur[ing] the Trinity," as Marlowe's Mephistophilis recommends (*Doctor Faustus* 1.4.54–55), the author of another such text invokes the triune God, asking "protection of my bodie and soule" as well as "grace and divine power over all the wicked spirits." For this writer, conjuring and prayer are complementary rather than antagonistic practices. He directs those attempting to conjure a particular spirit, Bealphares, to recite the Twenty-second and Fifty-first Psalms as well as "a *Pater noster* an *Ave Maria,* and a *Credo*" (qtd. in Scot 241). He also addresses Jesus Christ in a prayer of his own composition, asserting "by blessed Marie thy mother, . . . and by all thy saints, and by all the sacraments which are made in thine honour, I doo worship and beseech thee, I blesse and desire thee, to accept these praiers, conjurations, and words of my mouth" (qtd. in Scot 226–27). At such moments, as prayers and conjurations intermingle, grimoires seem to echo medieval prayer books.

Additionally, like the "idolatrous" devotional texts that Reformers condemned, grimoires derived much of their value from their material rather than symbolic properties. These books circulated in manuscript and rarely appeared in printed editions until after the sixteenth century. As Mowat has noted, both E. M. Butler and Grillot de Givry explain the paucity of early, published grimoires by contending that, as conjuring books, printed texts had "no practical value" (Mowat 6; E. M. Butler 48). The grimoire must be copied by hand, preferably by the magician's own hand using a consecrated pen and consecrated paper. However accurately a printer might reproduce the grimoire's words and symbols, the circumstances of its production would render it "useless." Like the "graven bookes" condemned in the 1563 *Homelyes,* grimoires derived inordinate value from their properties as material objects rather than signifying instruments. As the author of such a book ("*Necromantica quaedam. Lib. 1*"), then, Joan illustrates the worst aspects of medieval Catholic book culture.

Moreover, Bale crafts a biographical sketch of Joan the writer that emphasizes her association with a key institution within medieval textual culture: the monastery. Whereas Bale's sources such as Boccaccio and Platina describe Joan's lover vaguely as a young student or learned man, as Alain Boureau has noted, Bale introduces a new detail by specifying that her first paramour and accomplice in her transvestite deception was a monk from the abbey at Fulda (Boureau, *Myth* 239). Bale alludes to this detail again as he tauntingly concludes his entry on the popess, observing that Joan's career "could have been placed among the grander miracles of Boniface the Great, apostle of the Germans, insofar as he founded the monastery at Fulda: if the monastic writers of Chronicles had not been silent, because her first lover was a monk and the next a cardinal" (Poterat & hoc inter Bonificii magni Germanorum Apostoli maiora miracula poni, quod ille condidisset Fuldense coenobium: si non tacuissent Chronicorum scriptores monachi, utrumque eius amasium fuisse monachum, posteriorem vero Cardinalem) (*Scriptorvm illustrium* 2: 122). Here, Bale attacks monastic culture on two counts, citing the immorality of Joan's lover and the intellectual dishonesty of the monastic chroniclers who expurgated ecclesiastical histories. In the 1557 edition of the *Scriptorvm illustrium,* Bale inserts a paraphrase of Jakob Curio's account of the popess that further intensifies her connection to monasticism. Curio (1497–1572) characterizes Joan's travels to Athens and Rome (recounted originally by Martinus Polonus) as "wandering through many Greek and Latin monasteries" (per Latina & Graeca multa uagantem coenobia) (*Scriptorvm illustrium* 2: 122). Joan thus appears as a product of monastic culture in at least two respects. Her erotic attachment to a monk incites her transvestite disguise, and her sojourn through various monasteries hones the intellect and learning that would enable her rise to ecclesiastical heights.

Bale's particular conception of authorship, which seems rooted in what David Hult has characterized as the "profoundly intertextual nature of medieval literary creation," further implicates monastic culture in Joan's necromantic writing (Hult 92). Notably, Bale does not characterize his book as a catalog of authors (*auctores*), a term that implies original writing from one's own materials; instead, he reports on the lives and works of writers (*scriptores*), suggesting those whose writing may draw upon or derive from others' texts (Minnis 95). Moreover, his catalog includes editors and translators, such as William Caxton and the young princess Elizabeth Tudor. Even on the title page of his play *A Comedy Concernynge Three Lawes,* Bale casts himself as that text's "compiler," a term that at that time could denote the author of an original work but had for centuries meant more narrowly one who assembles and arranges the writings of others (*Comedy* 66; Minnis 94–95; *OED* 3: 605–6). According to John N. King, by employing that term, "Bale associates himself with medieval commentary traditions that presuppose incremental accumulation and assimilation of the work of predecessors." On the title page of the *Scriptorvm illustrium,* as Bale simultaneously announces his debt to precursors (including Bede, John Boston, and John

Leland) and somewhat surprisingly presents himself as an author—
"au[c]tore Joanne Baleo"—he may be appealing to that medieval tradition
by evoking the Latin root *augere,* meaning, as King has noted, "to increase or
augment" (King, *English* 69). If Joan's necromantic book is viewed as the
product of such "incremental accumulation and assimilation," then its iniquity reflects the iniquity of the institutions that shaped her intellectual and
moral development, in particular Catholic monasticism.

Ambivalence concerning the policies and events that set his antiquarian
enterprise in motion gave Bale reason in 1548, when he invented Joan the
scriptor, to use the popess legend to illustrate the iniquity of the Catholic
book culture centered and preserved in monasteries. Scholars have recently
argued that as a playwright under the patronage of the privy councilor
Thomas Cromwell, Bale played a substantial role in the Henrician propaganda campaign against monasteries. Alan Stewart contends that Bale's plays
"appear to have been custom-written, or at least custom-performed," and
that the itinerary that his traveling troupe followed in the late 1530s suggests
that performances were scheduled to generate support or understanding for
the closure of local monasteries and priories (4–5). A character such as
Sodomismus, decked "like a monk of all sects," would certainly fit into such
a campaign.

In time, Bale found that the dissolution of the monasteries, thus promoted through his drama, produced grievous consequences that, in turn,
prompted his cataloging endeavors. New owners of monastic properties
often showed little interest or concern for the religious houses' libraries: "A
great nombre of the[m] which purchased those superstycyouse mansions,
reserved of those lybrarye bokes, some to serve theyr iakes [latrines], some to
scoure theyr candelstyckes, & some to rubbe their bootes" (*Laboryouse* B1r).
Writing, he claims, on the verge of tears, Bale wishes that the "profitable
corne," that is, the "worthy workes of men godly mynded, and lyuelye memoryalles of our nacyon," had not "perished wyth the unprofitable chaffe,"
that is, "those laysy lubbers and popyshe bellygoddes" (*Laboryouse* A7v–A8r).
He warns, "Oure posteryte maye wele curse thys wicked facte of our age,
thys unreasonable spole of Englandes moste noble Antiquytees, unless they
be stayed in tyme, and by the act of pryntynge be brought into a no[m]bre
of coppyes" (*Laboryouse* B2r). Cataloging these antiquities sets the stage for
the preservation effort thus envisioned.

Joan's necromantic writing, rooted in her education and experience in
medieval monasteries, could readily represent the "chaffe" that, according to
Bale, found its way into monastic libraries. Although admittedly based on an
ill-defined rumor—"dicitur"—Bale's reference to Joan's book of necro-

mancy suggests to readers of the *Scriptorvm illustrium* that, whatever reckless excess accompanied the dissolution, some contents of the monastic libraries, "dregges of the deuyll," as Bale puts it in his 1549 additions to Leland's *The Laboryouse Serche for Englandes Antiquities,* were better off discarded or destroyed (G3). Although, as Bale makes clear, their contents should have been handled with greater caution and discrimination, the monastic libraries could not have been completely protected from the trauma of the dissolution. Perhaps, then, for Bale the sorcerous writings of the popess demonstrated that those libraries and the literary culture they fostered and exemplified too needed reform.

"Doubting Harts"

As if demonstrating the difficulty that writers often encountered when attempting to manipulate the popess legend for polemical purposes, Bale's critique of Joan the scriptor assumes the validity of early modern witchcraft lore, a system of thought challenged in the sixteenth and seventeenth centuries by growing skepticism. As Stephen Greenblatt has observed, evidence of serious skepticism regarding witchcraft appeared at least as early as the eleventh century, when Bishop Burchard of Worms (died 1025) asserted in a penitential canon (known as the *Canon episcopi*) that belief in witchcraft constituted a sinful and heretical relapse into paganism ("Shakespeare Bewitched" 18). That view proved so influential that Kramer and Sprenger began their 1486 *Malleus maleficarum* by responding to Burchard's assertion (in "the work of Episcopus") and attempting to confute writers who "have tried to maintain that there is not such a thing as magic, that it only exists in the imagination of those men who ascribe natural effects, the causes whereof are not known, to witchcraft and spirits" (2). A century later, in the preface to his 1597 *Daemonologie,* King James asserts that he undertook that treatise "to resolve the doubting harts of many" (James VI and I xix). Indeed, James so vigorously censured the "damnable opinions" of the skeptic Reginald Scot, who was "not ashamed in publike print to deny, that there can be such a thing as Witch-craft," that after the king's death stories spread alleging he had ordered that every available copy of Scot's *Discoverie of Witchcraft* (1584) should be burned (James VI and I 110–12). According to Henry Paul, Diane Purkiss, and Joanna Levin, however, even the royal demonologist James I, after acceding to the English throne, shifted his focus from promoting Continental witchcraft theory to discrediting false claims of witchcraft and demonic possession (Purkiss 203, 207; J. Levin 25; Paul 75–127).[12] Looking back on James's reign in his 1655 *Church History,* Thomas Fuller (1608–61) boldly claims that the "frequency of . . . forged possessions wrought such an alteration upon the judgment of King JAMES, that he receding from what he had written in his *Demonologie* grew first dissident, and then flatly to deny the workings of Witches and Devils, as but Falsehood and Delusions" (qtd. in Paul 85). For readers who, like James, acquired a "doubting hart," Joan's alleged necromantic writing would no longer signify, as it seemed to for Bale, the popess's collaboration with demonic forces.[13] What, then, would it signify?

As the title of Samuel Harsnett's *Declaration of Egregious Popish Impostures* (1603) demonstrates, anti-Catholic polemics could readily accommodate the skeptical view of witchcraft, exorcism, and demonic possession. At the opening of his tract Harsnett (1561–1631) reduces witchcraft to metaphor and identifies it with Catholicism, asserting that the "two grand witches in the world," namely *"Lying wonders,* and *Counterfeit zeale,"* have "many yeeres since combined and united themselves in the Pope of Rome, and his disciples" who, in order to "bewitch" the "affections" of lay Catholics, falsely claim for themselves "the soveraigne power of our saviour Christ, with authority to commaund uncleane spirits" (A2r–A2v). Similarly, Reginald Scot contends that Catholics, who fail to recognize that miracles have ceased, are "of all others" the "most credulous, and doo most mainteine the force of witches charmes, and of conjurors cousenages" (89–90, 261). After all, they have "the word and authoritie of the pope himselfe, and others of that holie crue," as well as the precedent of their numerous "charmes, conjurations, blessings, curssings" (130–31). Scot makes no apologies for using the expression "conjurations"—"for so their owne doctors terme them"—and goes on to indict devotional objects such as the agnus dei medallion, "holie water, salt, candles, &c: conjured by their holie bishop and preests" (261), as well as prayers like the following: "The signe of the crosse defend me from evils present, past, and to come, inward and outward" (133). Scot perceives insistent parallels between the practices of "massmongers" and "witchmongers," as each affirms the power of similarly ineffectual charms (135). For skeptics such as Harsnett and Scot, Joan's alleged devotion to necromantic studies would illustrate (perhaps somewhat hyperbolically) Catholics' embrace of *"Lying wonders."*

Although Bale's brief formulation "Scriptis dedisse dicitur . . . *Necromantica quaedam. Lib. I"* (*Scriptorum illustrium* 2: 122) might appeal to Protestants on either side of the early modern witchcraft controversy, the discussion that follows it decidedly aligns Bale with those who, as Scot puts it, "mainteine the force" of charms. For skeptics, the necromantic writing he attributes to Joan might demonstrate the emptiness and falsehood of Catholic learning, and for those who believed in the power of conjuring, it might hint at the papacy's dependency on demonic forces. Bale, however, immediately sets aside the caution that characterizes the potentially equivocal statement "she is said to have put into writing" and presents far less guarded assertions concerning Sylvester II, who obtained the papacy through conjuring, and "many more" (alii multi) necromancer popes who, he contends, continue to practice sorcery "even to this day" (in hunc usque diem) (2: 122). As skepticism regarding witchcraft and sorcery grew, such assertions would undermine Bale's credibility and cast doubt on his other claims. The controversialist and cardinal Robert Bellarmine dismissed Protestant additions to Martinus Polonus's foundational popess narrative— including details that Bale added regarding Joan's ties to the monastery at Fulda and the "bookes of witchcraft" she allegedly wrote—discounting them as "all mere fancies inuented without witness or reason" (qtd. in Walpole 418–19).[14] Those who doubted the force of charms would have been inclined to agree that the claims of a writer, such as Bale, who contended that sorcerers had loosed Satan from hell and conjured their way to the papacy were indeed "mere fancies." For such readers, Bale's attempt to use the popess's grimoire to demonstrate the need for, as Summit puts it, "a reformation of the book" would prove profoundly ineffective.

5 *Playing Joan*

POPISH PLOTS IN THE THEATRE ROYAL

On the evening of November 17, 1679, as many as two hundred thousand Londoners witnessed a spectacle that reportedly cost its Whig sponsors twenty-five hundred pounds. The torches carried by 150 hired porters illuminated a float bearing a pope in effigy, embraced and counseled by the devil and attended by cardinals, Jesuits, and friars. The procession stopped at Temple Bar before the statue of Queen Elizabeth, decked for this occasion with a golden shield inscribed "The Protestant Religion and Magna Charta [*sic*]." While singers performed a dialogue between "Cardinal Norfolk" (Philip Cardinal Howard) and Protestant "Plebeians," the papal effigy was prostrated before the queen's statue and then tossed into a bonfire (*Solemn Mock Procession of the POPE . . . 1679; Solemn Mock Procession of the Pope . . . 1679*). A year later, the procession grew to nine floats, as Tory "Abhorrers," "poor deluded Nuns," and others joined the papal entourage (*Solemn . . . 1680;* F. C. Brown 61–63). The English taste for such pageants had revived in 1673 when rumors of a secret alliance between Charles II (1630–85, reigning 1660–85) and Catholic France mixed with news of an impending marriage between the English heir presumptive, the future James II (1633–1701, reigning 1685–88), and a Catholic princess. For the next fifteen years pope burnings, often orchestrated by Whig political organizations, celebrated and encouraged militant Protestantism on significant dates and occasions, particularly November 5 and 17, the anniversaries of Guy Fawkes's Gunpowder Plot and of Queen Elizabeth's accession. These incendiary ceremonies disappeared only after the openly Catholic James II abandoned his throne and fled to France at the end of 1688 (Miller 183–87; Cressy 179–82).[1]

The heated political and cultural climate that prompted Whig clubs to stage such pageants also inspired writers and printers to disseminate scandalous accounts of Pope Joan. As I note in the introduction, between 1675 and 1689, a period that roughly corresponds to the height of pope burnings, English printers brought out four texts devoted to the popess, at least one in multiple editions.[2] Although several of these publications rehash arguments and citations from earlier English polemics, one attempts something relatively novel. *The Female Prelate: Being the History of the Life & Death of Pope Joan, A Tragedy,* the first extant English play devoted to the popess, was performed at the Theatre Royal in 1680 and published in separate editions in 1680 and 1689. As the play's oddly compounded title—*the History . . . A Tragedy*—indicates, within extant English discourse concerning the popess, this text marks a transition from the putatively historical to the openly fictional.[3] It omits not only the sometimes laborious citations found in the other Restoration treatments of the popess but also most chronological signposts. It specifies, for example, neither the date nor the duration of Joan's pontificate, nor her predecessor nor successor. In fact, the play's description of all true Saxons praying their rosary beads and saying morning litanies implies either extraordinarily rapid and thorough success for the eighth-century evangelization of Saxony or a relocation of the play's action to sometime after the ninth century, when, in the most influential accounts, Joan's pontificate allegedly occurred (*Female* 28).[4] As it adds to and alters Pope Joan materials from the medieval chronicles, *The Female Prelate* expands the legend's traditional focus on clerical corruption to dramatize ecclesiastical threats to temporal rulers. In doing so, it appropriates the legend's concern with sexuality, gender confusion, and feminine autonomy to manifest, if not fuel, the political anxieties that the pope burnings staged.

To that end, the play introduces a revenge plot concerning two generations of Saxon dukes and presents motivations or explanations for Joan's transvestitism, papal election, and ultimate exposure unlike any that appear in the oft-cited medieval chronicles. In *The Female Prelate,* Joan, or more precisely "Joanna Anglica," travels through Europe and pursues her education in Athens and Rome as an unaccompanied and undisguised woman. She cross-dresses as a monk only later to carry out her deadly revenge against the Duke of Saxony, an unfaithful lover whose passion for her wanes two years after he seduces Joanna into becoming his adulterous mistress. She, in turn, wins election to the papacy by falsely incriminating the duke as a plotting heretic and then accepting the cardinals' gratitude for murdering such a traitor to Rome. When the duke's legitimate son and heir discovers the pope's crimes and disguise, he denounces her to cardinals and commoners alike. Unnerved, Joanna falls into labor and confirms at least some of the younger Saxony's charges by delivering an "abortive Bastard" (60). To conclude, the play returns to familiar ground, as two cardinals discuss an alleged statue of Joan in Rome and the pierced porphyry chair, where subsequent papal candidates reportedly sat while a manual examination established their masculinity.

More than chronology and anti-Catholicism link this play to the pope burnings described here. The play's author, Elkanah Settle (1648–1724), reportedly composed a description of the 1679 pageant, entitled *London[']s Defiance to Rome,* and more certainly devised the November 17, 1680, ceremony. Briefly John Dryden's rival for patronage and play-going audiences, Settle now lives mostly in footnotes as a combatant in literary quarrels with Dryden and a butt of jokes in Alexander Pope's *The Dunciad.* Settle dedicated the 1680 edition of *The Female Prelate* to the Whig leader Shaftesbury (Anthony Ashley Cooper, 1671–1713), who allegedly hired the playwright to design the 1680 pope-burning pageant. Early in 1681, through a tract entitled *The Character of a Popish Successour,* Settle contributed further to Shaftesbury's campaign to exclude the Duke of York from inheriting his childless brother's throne (*Dictionary* 17: 1210–12; F. C. Brown 11–15, 21–26, 36–37). The playwright repeatedly shifted allegiances during his career, but such political inconsistency seems to befit a period that found Whig leaders at the same time inciting popular anti-Catholicism and quietly accepting payments from France's Catholic king (Harris 101–2; A. Gardiner, *Ancient* 194; J. R. Jones 147–51).[5] By interrelating the pamphlet, pageant, and play that Settle composed early in the 1680s while still allied to Shaftesbury, we can discern how *The Female Prelate* performs a wide-ranging critique of Catholic spirituality, theology, church polity, and sexual mores. Further, by attending to the multiple instances of transvestitism in the text, we can uncover moments when the play ranges beyond the author's apparent intention and interrogates religious belief itself.

The Restoration Context

As more topical and openly propagandistic spectacles, the pope-burning ceremonies address Restoration politics more directly than does Settle's play; consequently, examining them provides insight into what made the popess legend an apt vehicle for dramatizing Catholic threats to England and its monarch. As we shall see, for reasons rooted in both polemical traditions and seventeenth-century social and political developments, Restoration controversialists contended that disguise and feminine usurpation characterized Catholicism. The November pageants foregrounded these two themes, and the Pope Joan legend powerfully merged them. For example, *The Burning of the Whore of Babylon,* the title assigned to a 1673 account of the first Restoration pope burning, invokes the Tudor equation between Church of Rome and Whore of Babylon (*Burning* 3; Miller 183). In turn, through her deceptive appearance and notorious sexual indiscretion, the popess seemed to embody that equation, as Humphrey Shuttleworth implies at the opening of his 1675 tract *A Present for a Papist:*

A Woman Pope (as History doth tell)
In High Procession Shee in Labour fell,
And was Deliver'd of a Bastard Son;
Thence *Rome* some call *The Whore of Babylon.*

In fact, Settle's Joanna invites the play's audience to identify her with the scarlet seductress of Revelation 17, as she compares her own reign in Rome to the legendary exploits of the Assyrian Queen Semiramis, the so-called strumpet who reportedly founded Babylon (*Female* 5).[6]

Further, Settle's November 17, 1680, pageant demonstrates that English controversialists drew upon recent history and current events, in addition to legend and allegory, to identify women who might persuasively exemplify Catholicism. In 1667, by publishing his translation of Gregorio Leti's *Life* of Olimpia Maldalchini Pamfili (1594–1646), the manipulative sister-in-law of Pope Innocent X (reigning 1644–55), Bishop Henry Compton alerted English readers to the career of a woman who, according to the text's English title, "governed" the Roman Church from 1644 to 1655. As if inviting comparisons to the popess, Compton characterizes Donna Olympia as a metaphorical transvestite "who in the City of *Rome* acted a Man in Womans apparel and in the Church a woman wearing the breeches" (1). Not surprisingly, then, in his 1675 *Present* Shuttleworth cites Donna Olympia as further evidence of papal fallibility (A3v). By 1680, she had apparently become such a recognizable figure that Settle devoted the penultimate float in his November 17 pageant to this matron seated in a chair of state (according to at least one illustration) and attended by "poor deluded Nuns" (*Solemn . . . 1680;* F. C. Brown 63; Kenyon 172).[7]

Elizabeth Cellier, the recusant at the center of the notorious "Meal-Tub Plot," also figured prominently in Settle's pageant. He depicted her twice, once on a painted banner and again in effigy on the first float (F. C. Brown 62). A year earlier, when she was accused of scheming to discredit the Whigs by concocting evidence of an impending Presbyterian coup d'état, Cellier, the so-called Prelate-Bess, had inspired comparisons to Pope Joan.[8] Another of her nicknames, "Joan of Arque," followed the pattern established in

Compton's portrait of Donna Olympia and associated Cellier too with both transvestitism and attempts to appropriate putatively male authority. Indeed, Cellier may have invited comparisons to amazons and viragoes by boldly defending herself with voice and pen, if not with sword (A. Gardiner, Introduction iii, xi). After discrediting her accuser and securing acquittal in a one-day treason trial in June 1680, she further vindicated herself in a tract entitled *Malice Defeated*. This counterattack so angered government authorities that they tried her again a few months later for libel and sentenced her to the pillory as well as a fine (*Dictionary* 3: 1326; Kenyon 189–90, 199). By thus keeping her name before the London public, Cellier only enhanced her value to Whig propagandists like Settle.

Several of the best-known details concerning Cellier's case associated it with femininity and anticipated images or plot devices in *The Female Prelate*. The "Meal-Tub Plot" derived its name from the vessel in which Cellier concealed documents that the scoundrel and convict Thomas Dangerfield had forged and would later use to incriminate her. That tub appeared with her effigy in Settle's pageant and linked the plot to the domestic domain where women might cook up dangerous plans or potions (F. C. Brown 62). Moreover, the tub's contents, fabricated evidence of a Whig conspiracy, offer a precedent for the forged correspondence that Settle's Joanna uses vindictively to implicate her unfaithful lover in an alleged heretical plot (Kenyon 189–90, 199). Further, as one of few occupations that enabled women to earn wages and to work outside the home, midwifery provided Cellier with an unusual degree of female autonomy—an attribute that, as we shall see, Settle's Joanna prizes. Of course, like her meal tub, Cellier's profession also associated her conspiracy with a distinctly feminine domain, in this case, childbirth. In fact, Cellier would later argue in 1688 that midwifery "*ought to be kept as a secret amongst Women as much as is Possible*" (qtd. in A. Gardiner, "Elizabeth Cellier" 25).[9] Cellier's contemporaries exploited the metaphorical opportunities that her profession afforded, as they charged, for example, that she had "midwived into the world" tracts "begot" by convict priests (A. Gardiner, Introduction x). In fact, as Frances E. Dolan has pointed out, earlier polemicists had employed the midwife metaphor to describe the male plotter Guy Fawkes (*Whores* 39). No doubt, the rhetorically potent figure of a secretive midwife delivering fresh plots intrigued Settle, who used images of grotesque fecundity in *The Female Prelate* when he described Joanna as an endlessly fertile, brooding, "hatching Basilisk" (59–60).

In fact, the veiled image of a popish midwife's hand seems to appear in a variation on the Pope Joan legend that Settle introduces into the play's closing moments. As I note in chapter 1, medieval chroniclers described a cere-

mony in which a pope elect sat in a pierced, porphyry chair so that "one of
the younger cardinals may make proof of his sex" and thus prevent a repeti-
tion of the Pope Joan fiasco (Adam of Usk 215; Pardoe and Pardoe 32). As
Cesare D'Onofrio has noted, the pierced chairs resemble the birthing stools
whose use spread from ancient Italy to early modern Germany (D'Onofrio
172–83; Shorter 55–56). After announcing Joanna's miscarriage and exposure,
Settle dramatizes the establishing of this ceremony with one significant sub-
stitution:

> SECOND CARDINAL. But my good Brothers,
>   How shall we guard our Mother Churches Brightness
>   From new pollutions; fence her holy Throne
>   From new impostors; from all future Sorceries?
> FIRST CARDINAL. Oh Brothers, by immediate revelation,
>   Touch'd with a Spark from yon Celestial Orb,
>   I've have [*sic*] found that happy glorious great design,
>   For which our yet even unborn Heirs shall thank me.
> THIRD CARDINAL. Oh speak!
> FIRST CARDINAL. Thus then the Coronation Porphyry,
>   On which *Romes* installed Bishop, Heavens
>   Lieutenant takes his great Commission,
>   Shall thro' it have that subtle concave form'd
>   Thro' which a reverend Matrons hand—
> SECOND CARDINAL. Now by yon Stars inspired by some good
>   Angel,
>   I guess thy glorious purpose. (*Female Prelate* 60)

As her hand, in Settle's version, replaces the young cardinal's and reaches up
through the pierced seat of what looks like a birthing stool to examine the
candidate's genitalia, this matron resembles a midwife. Settle's First Cardinal intensifies that resemblance by alluding to maternity and posterity as he
characterizes this procedure as a service to "our Mother Church" and a boon
to "yet . . . unborn Heirs." As this image points ahead to the later popish
midwife "Prelate-Bess," it discloses the futility of the cardinal's "glorious
great design" to preclude a future Pope Joan. In fact, the imagery and diction
of the prelates' dialogue emphasize that futility. In order to "fence" and seal
off the "holy Throne," they decide to perforate the coronation chair. The
ingenious prelate's word choice hints at a pun, since in order to lock women
outside the cardinals' subtle conclave, he would invite a matron to explore
inside the porphyry's "subtle concave." Like the polemically embellished

career of Cellier, who according to one tract had "from Hee-Popes . . . the Miter won," this matron's crucial role in the ceremony of papal succession implies the impossibility of curbing women's influence within Catholicism (*Scarlet Beast* 8 [misnumbered], 4).

The pope-burning ceremonies also reveal that the royal consorts, arguably the most influential Catholic women in England, aroused Protestant suspicions and fears. Recall that the first such pageant to be staged during Charles II's reign followed fast upon James's marriage to the Catholic princess Mary Beatrice of Modena (Miller 183; Kenyon 16). King Charles's reputed "effeminate" and lustful subjection to women likely intensified fears concerning Catholic consorts (Owen 9–10). Further, Restoration revisionists who portrayed Charles I as an Anglican martyr blamed his misfortunes on the papist Queen Henrietta Maria (Miller 85; Dolan, *Whores* 129–36).[10] Moreover, during Charles II's reign, the royal chapels maintained in London briefly by the queen mother and permanently by the Catholic Queen Catherine of Braganza provided a haven for Roman rites.[11] Thus, papist queens consort appeared to impede England's complete conversion to Protestantism.

Further, thanks to Titus Oates's questionable testimony concerning the Popish Plot, servants of both Queen Catherine and the Duchess of York were depicted in the pope-burning pageants. If Charles II's would-be Benedictine and Jesuit assassins failed to shoot or stab him dead, then allegedly the queen's Catholic physician Sir George Wakeman would poison him (Kenyon 52, 111). Although Wakeman was ultimately acquitted, his effigy (complete "with Jesuits' powder in one hand, and an urinal in the other") found a place in the 1679 pope-burning pageant, just ahead of the pontiff's cross bearers. Moreover, a 1679 broadside account of the procession designates Wakeman as "the Pope's doctor," thus equating queen and pope (*Solemn Mock Procession of the Pope . . . 1679* 238). The Duchess of York's sometime secretary, Sir Edward Coleman, a reckless busybody who had conducted treasonous correspondence with Louis XIV's confessor, allegedly paid part of Wakeman's blood money—and that earned his effigy its own burning shortly before his execution late in 1679 (Kenyon 35; Miller 184). In fact, at his most reckless and with great harm to his credibility with the king and the Privy Council, Oates (1649–1705) even charged that the queen had consented to her husband's assassination. For Oates, the king's notorious adulteries provided a motive for murder, as, for Settle's Joanna Anglica, a lover's infidelities did. The Popish Plot thus added the queen and the Duchess of York to the Restoration gallery of dangerous popish women (Kenyon 110–15).[12]

The fears aroused by such well-known Catholic women may have drawn evocative force from broader sociological trends. Patricia Crawford reports that from 1660 to 1720 more English women than men were presented for recusancy (192). This statistic may reflect the evolution of anti-Catholic legislation. By imposing fines, the 1559 Act of Uniformity focused its coercive pressure on Catholic men, who might seek to preserve family property by conforming, and only subsequent legislation, enacted in 1610 and 1657, addressed the problem of recusant wives directly. Further, both Crawford and Dolan argue that religious persecutions effectively enhanced the significance of recusant wives by driving Catholic practices from the male-dominated public sphere and into the private household where women exercised their greatest influence (Crawford 60; Dolan, *Whores* 52–53, 65–67). Before their own arrests, Cellier and her patroness and alleged coconspirator Lady Powis (Elizabeth Herbert) seemed to illustrate the enhanced significance Crawford posits, as they provided moral and material relief to Catholics imprisoned in response to Oates's accusations—Cellier even housed thirty students from the Jesuit College at St. Omers who wished to testify in defense of accused plotters (*Dictionary* 3: 1326; Kenyon 189; A. Gardiner, "Elizabeth Cellier" 25).[13] In light of both popular iconography and social reality, then, in Restoration England a female pope served as an apt sign of Catholic threats.

So too did a pope cloaked in an improbably successful disguise. After all, Andrew Marvell's influential *Account of the Growth of Popery and Arbitrary Government* (1678) had denounced Catholicism itself as an "imposture" (Marvell 4: 251; Owen 141–43). Further, Restoration anti-Catholicism relied in several ways on theories of improbable disguise. To magnify the threat posed by a small Catholic minority (roughly 4.7 percent of the total population), Settle, for example, depicted "Popish Ingeneers under the Mask of Protestants" in his November 17 pageant (*Solemn . . . 1680;* F. C. Brown 62–63). Similarly, in testimony concerning the Popish Plot, Titus Oates had implied that thousands of such "Ingeneers" lurked in England. Although a 1676 census ordered by Bishop Henry Compton counted only 2,069 adult recusants in the diocese of London, Oates claimed that 20,000 London Catholics planned to murder 100,000 Protestants (Miller 9, 23, 156; Kenyon 24–25). Jonathon Scott has argued that sensational reports concerning the defeat and martyring of Continental Protestants in Hungary, Bohemia, and the Netherlands fueled such fears, as did revelations that Charles II had received secret subsidies from Catholic France and consequently could not be trusted to protect English Protestantism (113–22). In fact, Restoration reinterpretations of the Civil War had established a precedent for displacing such distrust of the monarch onto crypto-Catholics. Writers like Settle, who characterized Charles I as a "Royal Martyr . . . that seal'd the *Protestant Faith* with his blood," could not comfortably regard the king's executioners as radical Protestants (*Character* 11). William Prynne's theory that covert papists had contrived the Civil War and regicide offered an attractive alternative. Those who believed, for example, that John Milton had successfully concealed his true Catholic sympathies might have been prepared to believe that a popess could successfully conceal her gender (Miller 85–86, 155–56).[14]

Predictably, then, in both *The Character of a Popish Successour* and *The Female Prelate,* Settle implies that masquerade is a typical Catholic practice. In the pamphlet, to demonstrate that no "Shape or Hypocrisie" is too "scandalous" for a Catholic monarch acting upon papal commands, Settle cites Mary Tudor's broken promises of religious tolerance for Norfolk and Suffolk. He employs the imagery of masquerade, as he asserts that once Queen Mary's "Soveraign Power was securely established . . . his pious Holiness had bid her safely pull the Vizor off" (*Character* 5).[15] In the play, although Settle's cardinal of Milan does not address disguise specifically, he does endorse covert attacks on the Church's enemies, as he answers his own question concerning popish tactics:

Does the Weak Traveller face the roaring Lion,
Or spotted Leopard, and grapple Arm to Arm?
No, foolish Prince.

Consequently, when battling Rome's enemies, Catholics need not restrict themselves to "open hostile Arms" (*Female* 16). To demonstrate his popess's command of the stealth that this cardinal recommends, Settle multiplies the instances of disguise present in the chronicle accounts of Joan's career. She first masquerades as the Benedictine monk Theodore in order to carry out her deadly revenge against the Duke of Saxony, her unfaithful lover. To that end, she impersonates Saxony in incriminating letters addressed to a heretic named Damasus. Once she has murdered the duke and fled the Saxon court, she assumes yet another identity as John, later the cardinal of Reims. Caught in one scene without her masculine costume, Joanna saves herself from arrest by playing the part of what a priest ambiguously terms "my Mistriss" (*Female* 44). Moreover, spurred by lust for the dead duke's adult son, she even masquerades as the younger Saxony's new bride to steal the pleasures of his marriage bed. In the society in which Joanna prospers, even the most intimate contact does not necessarily uncover disguise.

The one disguise that Settle borrows from his sources (probably John Bale or John Foxe) links Joanna to one of the most powerful papist institutions in Restoration England: the Benedictines. According to Claudius Agretti, minister apostolic in Flanders, in 1669 theirs was the second-largest order in the kingdom, concentrated in London and surpassed only by the Jesuits (Miller 40; Kenyon 24). Charles II had forged a special relationship with the order during his exile, a point that his lord chancellor, Clarendon (Edward Hyde, 1609–74), noted during 1663 debates over recusant legislation (Miller 101–2). One monk, John Huddlestone (Huddleston), had protected Charles by hiding him from Oliver Cromwell's pursuing troops after they routed his army at Worcester in 1651. Consequently, when the king banished English and Irish priests from the court in 1675, Huddlestone was the lone exception— he also later participated in the king's deathbed conversion to Catholicism (C. Hill 97; Miller 22). The order's prominence may have spurred Oates to feature it prominently in the plot he recounted. His earliest statements named a Benedictine, Thomas Pickering, and a Jesuit lay brother, John Grove, along with Wakeman, as the king's would-be assassins. He later added that the Benedictine prior, a Father Howard, donated six thousand pounds to support the conspiracy and that, if the plot succeeded, under the new regime another Benedictine, James Corker, would preside as bishop of London (Kenyon 64–65). With Oates's help, the order thus earned a float in Settle's 1680 pageant, just before the Jesuits (F. C. Brown 73). Since, by dramatizing the career of a medieval pope, the playwright could not easily discredit the hated Jesuits (who were not founded until 1534), he instead took aim at their more ancient colleagues who had carried popery to England with Augustine in 596 (MacDougall 34).[16]

Further, the source of Joanna's skills as an impostor proves at least as significant as their particular manifestations, since they appear to result from her training in medieval Catholic philosophy. Whereas in the earlier chronicle accounts, Joan's cross-dressing precedes and evidently enables her academic career, Settle's Joanna travels through Europe and pursues her education in Athens and Rome as an unaccompanied and undisguised woman. By thus departing from the order of events in his sources, Settle frees himself to invert that causal sequence. As Joanna describes her training, she echoes humanist and Protestant charges that Scholastic dialectic encouraged sophistic debate rather than the pursuit of truth (Perreiah 10; Rummel 22, 30, 141):

So far I fadom'd [fathom'd] into Books, Men, Manners,
Reason, Religions; I could take all Forms:
The perfect Christian, or complete Philosopher;

Could give the Earth and the Heavens first Foundation
To Nature, or to Natures God at pleasure:
Dispute on both sides, and on both sides vanquish. (*Female* 22)

If arguing *in utramque partem* amounts to protean shape-shifting, then
Joanna's Catholic theological training functions as an apprenticeship for her
subsequent impersonations. Thus, the Roman churchmen in Settle's play,
who rage at Joanna's deception, have merely reaped what their pedagogy has
sown. The devil has not, as they suggest, simply "put" this whore "upon"
them; rather, their institutions have participated in her formation (*Female*
60). Consequently, for Settle, she aptly represents what is dangerous and dis-
tasteful about those institutions.

Popery and Monarchy

In 1680 and 1681, as he voiced his distaste for Catholicism in *The Female
Prelate* and other texts addressing the Exclusion Crisis, Settle confronted a
rhetorical challenge. Although he sought to warn his various audiences
about, as the subtitle of *The Popish Successour* puts it, "What England might
expect from" a Catholic monarch, he seemed reluctant to defame an heir
presumptive directly—even the spectacular November 17 pope burnings of
1679 and 1680 apparently stopped short of that (Miller 185; F. C. Brown
62–63). Consequently, he set out to portray popery as a threat to monarchs
(whether Catholic or not), as well as to subjects. In *The Female Prelate,* then,
Settle modifies the traditional Pope Joan legend to dramatize how trust in
Catholic institutions ruins two generations of Saxon dukes. As he reveals
how the elder duke's adulterous affair with Joanna led to his lethal poisoning, Settle illustrates the peril one invites by sharing intimacies with popish
clerics. In turn, as he depicts the younger duke's fatally belated conversion
from faithful son of Rome to impassioned dissenter, Settle dramatizes the
high cost of an incomplete or delayed recognition of Catholic ideology's
infectious corruption. Moreover, as the younger duke bequeaths his antipapal ardor to his subjects and descendants, he seems to invite Settle's Restoration audience to embrace its Saxon heritage and take up his unfinished struggle against the ideas and institutions that fashioned the popess.

In Settle's view, no Catholic monarch was truly sovereign. The young
Duke of Saxony learns this when he naively invokes the "divinest Justice" of
the conclave of cardinals to convict his father's murderer, the cross-dressing
Joanna, who by then has become the cardinal of Reims (*Female* 10). Rather

than condemning Reims (Joanna), the Roman prelates credit her fabricated evidence of the elder Saxony's heresy; embrace their admittedly murderous colleague; and assert Rome's rightful "power / To Judge a King, and doom a Sovereign Head" (15). Further, they decree that the bowl used to poison the elder duke should "be consecrated, / As an Eternal Relick to the Chappel at *Loretto*" (16), thus sensationally demonstrating that, as Settle charges in *The Popish Successour,* Catholic principles "consecrate Daggers, and kill Kings" (12). When young Saxony objects, Joanna deposes and excommunicates him; then, as a "private Malefactor" surrounded by tortured heretics in a Roman prison, he learns how, as Settle puts it in his pamphlet, "popery" teaches all nations by "scourging, and wracking, and broiling 'em into the fear of God" (*Female* 19; *Character* 12).

For Settle, a deposition like the one young Saxony suffers was only the Roman Church's most blatant breach of a prince's sovereignty. In *The Popish Successour,* he contends that Catholic theology, which "makes humane Merit the path to Salvation," effectively invests clerics with temporal sway: the pope, "the undisputed Keeper of the Keys of *Paradise,*" can manipulate a prince by specifying the "Work" that can save his soul. Particularly after the Counter-Reformation, which encouraged sacramental piety and prescribed more elaborate and searching penitential procedures, the most immediate instrument of such papal manipulation was the prince's confessor (Haliczer 21–24). Catholics and Protestants alike seemed to recognize this significant relationship between priest and prince. As we have seen, Coleman corresponded with Louis XIV's confessor to promote the Catholic reconversion of England; in turn, Oates forged letters to incriminate the Duke of York's spiritual advisor (Kenyon 59, 85–89). Similarly, concerning Louis XIV's broken assurances that he would leave Flanders unmolested, Settle wondered whether the French king's "*Confessour* found some *Jesuitical* Loop-hole" to free His Most Christian Majesty from his oath (*Character* 6). Such a mingling of spiritual and temporal roles enables Joanna, disguised as the monk Theodore, to fabricate the correspondence that posthumously convicts the elder Saxony as a heretic. In *The Female Prelate,* Settle thus suggests that confessors menace even those to whom they seem to minister.

The extraordinary relationship between Saxony and Joanna hyperbolically illustrates the dangerous intimacy between confessor and penitent. Shortly after Joanna (disguised as Theodore) returns to the Saxon court, the duke's confessor conveniently dies—a death that Settle uncharacteristically does not blame on his villainess. Once the masquerading Joanna begins serving as the duke's new spiritual advisor, her juxtaposed roles as mistress and "Ghostly Father" appear to resemble one another. In passages that echo each

other, both Joanna and young Saxony agree that the duke's "Soul was all
. . . [the monk's] own"; moreover, each adds a bodily reference—"His
Bosom," "His Ear, his Hand"—to these assertions of complete possession
(23). Employing a potentially erotic term like "Favourite," Joanna describes
a relationship that extends beyond spiritual counsel:

> I was this Prince's Father's Confessor,
> His Favourite, Friend, Confident.
> Nay the whole Circle of his Deeds, Thoughts, Counsels,
> All center'd in my Heart. (10)

In light of such assertions of intimacy, an audience might be excused for feel-
ing momentarily puzzled concerning a later passage in which Joanna shifts
from celebrating her successful disguise—"absolute Proteus"—to describing
the unfaithful duke's newest fiery passion. Does the beloved "new Face" in
the following lines refer to Saxony's new mistress, Leonora, or to Joanna's
new identity as Theodore?

> Oh, an absolute *Proteus!*
> Bore my Disguise so well.—In short, his Love
> To this new Face, unlike my harder Fate,
> Took every day new Fire, out-ran all bounds,
> And flow'd as fast as e'er it ebb'd to me. (25)

A reference to self-defeating bawdry in the next two lines ultimately clarifies
the passage:

> Whilst I by being his Priest, his Conscience Confident,
> Was Bawd to that Intrigue that had undone Me. (25)

Nonetheless, the temporary uncertainty concerning the identity of the "new
Face" illustrates how Settle blurs the distinction between confessor and
lover—a distinction that the papacy struggled to enforce by issuing bulls in
1561 and 1622 that expressly condemned confessors' soliciting of sexual acts
from their penitents (Haliczer 56).

The elder duke's murder illustrates (again hyperbolically) dangers inherent in maintaining such close relations with Catholic clerics. The assassin's
weapon, a noxious bowl filled and lifted to Saxony's lips, literalizes a
metaphor that Settle employs in *The Popish Successour.* According to that
pamphlet, the Roman clergy's rhetoric intoxicates if not poisons Catholic

monarchs: "When *Rome* by her insinuating Witchcrafts has lifted the full
Bowl of her Inchantments to his [a monarch's] Lips what will his holy
enthusiastick Rage do less than the hot-brain'd drunken *Alexander*?" (6–7).
In turn, as the duke's son recounts his father's murder, he juxtaposes speech
and potion, the tenor and vehicle of Settle's metaphor in *The Popish Successour*:

> . . . his savage Confessor.
> That cursed Slave that fed upon his Smiles,
> Fill'd the dire Bowl, and whilst the canting Villain
> Was whispering Heaven into his Ear, could lift
> Damnation to his Lips. (*Female* 2)

Further, the inflammatory physiological effects of Joanna's poison nicely
parallel the psychological effect suggested by the pamphlet's allusion to the
enraged and "hot-brain'd" Alexander:

> We found him raving, all his veins on Fire,
> His restless bed more like a Funeral Pile. (10)

Lest the audience should overlook the poison's metaphorical significance,
one of Settle's cardinals makes it clear by comparing speech and venom, as
he admonishes Joanna (as Reims) against answering the young duke's testimony with slanderous accusations:

> Mark what you say, bold Lord; Take heed you lay not
> An Imputation on a Princely Family;
> Add Crimes to Crimes, and with invenomed Breath
> Attempt to play the Poysoner o'er again. (12)

The Catholic clergy poisons the minds of princes, as Joanna, its most
debased representative, poisons the body of her princely former lover.

Of course, these hard lessons in the relationship between popery and sovereignty alter young Saxony's view of Rome, but his conversion lacks the
theological and psychological insight needed to persuade others to challenge
popery. Here, the heretic Damasus serves as a foil against which to measure
the young duke's development. Saxony recoils at the first charge of his
father's apostasy, proclaiming the dead duke's "unshaken constancy to
Rome"; however, he eventually comes to echo the words of his father's
alleged coconspirator Damasus (14). Although that "Rebel to Rome" has

died at the stake three years before the play opens, Damasus's words enter the text through an intercepted letter from him to the elder Saxony, which Joanna (as Reims) produces to justify the duke's murder. In the letter, Damasus rejoices that the duke is evidently ready "*to strike your dagger in the Gates of Rome,* and lay the Scarlet prostitute in Ashes." He also exhorts the elder Saxony to "*continue still to believe, that* Romes *usurpt Supremacy . . . is maintained by an Impostor.*" Finally, Damasus hails his aristocratic ally as a Hercules destined to destroy the hydra that the Pope and "*all his Limbs the Cardinals*" constitute (12–13). Like the heretical letter writer, young Saxony eventually characterizes the pope as a "Scarlet Whore," usurper, and impostor (12, 19, 58). Also like Damasus, he sees the pope as a "monstrous Hydra" with papal servants as its stinging appendages (13, 35). Saxony's critique, however, is both less broad and less profound than Damasus's. The duke refers to a literal whore—or at least a woman who revels in her sexual excess. Once she is exposed, even the cardinals, the "Limbs" of that "monstrous Hydra," recognize Joanna as a usurper and impostor. Unlike Settle in *The Popish Successour,* Saxony focuses on individuals rather than ideology. He does not analyze the Church's venal formula for salvation, which, according to Damasus, renders Rome a "publick Mart of Souls" (13). Consequently he is unprepared to mobilize the Roman populace in his final assault against Joanna.

Young Saxony enters the final scene carrying the body of his wife (murdered at Joanna's command) and intending to emulate Mark Antony's oration over Caesar's corpse. However, he finds that Romans have degenerated from their ancient virtue. Catholicism's mercenary spirituality has infected their consciousness and eroded their self-reliance. Before Saxony appears, one Roman explains to another that he never attends church, because he trusts that the "Shoals of Church-men," maintained in part by his donations, will worship for him. A clever man, he implies, either pays or prays, but he does not do both (55). Accustomed to depending on clerics to solve his problems, this man drolly urges Saxony to do the same:

Well sir, I understand you are a Prince, and that your good Lady is dead, and you'd have us make her alive again. We can do you no good in it; 'tis not every man that lives in *Rome* can do that Job, but if you'll speak to the Pope, or one of his Cardinals they'll do it for a word speaking. (57)

When Saxony asserts that the Pope is the problem rather than the solution, another citizen reveals that changing the rabble's allegiance will be costly:

Take heed Sir, what you say; the Pope!
But that you have greas'd us in the fist [bribed us], or else— (58)

Saxony's rhetoric cannot answer this demand. His failure to appreciate fully the "German Heretick['s]" critique of popery dooms Saxony to share Damasus's fate: as the Roman commoners exclaim, "Burn him, burn him," the duke, condemned to the stake, makes his final exit (25, 60).[17]

The pervasive corruption thus manifested in the play's denouement casts doubt on C. A. Patrides's observation that "by the end of the 'tragedy' order is fully restored" (178). Admittedly, this comment seems accurate if we assume that Joanna's iniquity and female prelacy represent the sole disorder in the play. After all, once the Roman cardinals observe Joanna in labor and thus discern her true gender, they resolve to rid themselves of the popess by casting her body—dead or alive—into the Tiber. Further, their descriptions of her unfortunate newborn—"abortive . . . half-got, weak, untimely"—do not suggest that it could survive to pose any subsequent threat. As Raymond D. Tumbleson has noted, however, *The Female Prelate* has dramatized disorder that seems more formidable than a "puny" fetus and too widespread to eliminate by drowning one impostor. Like the commoners who rely on them, those same cardinals—"willful blind deluded Prelates"—have proven deaf to Saxony's pleas for justice and his reports of Joanna's masquerade (59). In the aftermath of her miscarriage and exposure, these prelates contemplate even more dissembling, as they debate whether Joanna should be memorialized or torn "From *Romes* great Annals . . . for ever" (60). Like young Saxony, they focus on individuals rather than ideology. Consequently, once they devise a method for assuring the masculinity of future popes, they feel protected from the threat Joanna represents. An unfounded bravado then intoxicates them and informs the text's final lines:

Now Devils we defie your utmost power,
Romes awful Throne shall be profan'd no more,
Put Whores and Bawds upon us, if you can,
Romes Mitred Head hence forth shall be a Man. (60)

Settle's play has illustrated what the cardinals ignore: far more than Joanna's gender and promiscuity pollutes the Roman Church.

In light of his Saxon stock, the duke's admittedly incomplete religious enlightenment presages a later, more profound resolution of Christianity's disorders. As he passes from naive loyalty to "*Romes* Majesty" and "the blessed Prelacy" to disillusioned cursing of the Roman Church, young Saxony's nationality gathers significance (58). It casts him as both an ancestor of Protestantism and a representative of the English national character. Late in the seventeenth century, especially in light of Catholic military advances in the Low Countries and southern Germany, Protestantism seemed to be a northern European phenomenon (Kenyon 3, 15; Miller 67, 90). As Settle reports it, the "late Secretary St. Coleman" assumed as much when he wrote "*That the pestilent Northern Heresie was to be rooted out*" (*Character* 7). Once deposed (but before discovering Joanna's gender), the duke, whom the cardinals address as "Bold German" and whose rhetoric echoes the "German Traytor *Damasus*" (12, 14), vows that he will not be Rome's last German enemy, as he confers his hatred for Joanna onto his own heirs and former subjects. He promises his foe that in "Morning-Letan[ies]" each man who is no "Bastard to the Blood of *Saxony*"

> . . . shall place thee before Wars, Plagues and Famines;
> Whilst his each Bead that drops a Prayer to Heaven,
> Shall blend a Curse to thee. . . .
> . . . .
> By Heavens, the very Girls through all my *Saxony*,
> That have no weapons above their Needles,
> Shall in revenge of thy detested Name,
> Limb that curst Head in their embroydered Toys,
> And execute that Monster in Effigie.
> Nay, by my Soul, I will bequeath my Dukedom
> To Painters and Engravers to revenge me.
> There's not that humblest Roof in all the Principality
> Of *Saxony,* that shall not have thy face
> Drawn to the life in Hell. Nay, every Portal
> To a Stable, or a Jakes
> Shall have thy Picture drawn upon a Gibbet. (28)

Settle, the designer of political pageants, must have expected that a propaganda campaign sown into embroidery, etched into buildings, and recited in daily prayers would erode Rome's prestige long after Joanna's pontificate had ended. Presumably such expectations prompted Pope Pius V, according to Elias Hasenmuller's sixteenth-century account, to order that a statue, allegedly depicting Joan and her child, should be removed from Rome and cast into the Tiber (Pardoe and Pardoe 48–49). By enlisting fellow Germans in his revenge, then, the duke prepares the ground in which the later, more enduring "Northern Heresie" will take root.

Since for more than a century historians and controversialists such as John Bale and Sir Edward Coke (1552–1634) had been valorizing England's Saxon past, Settle may have expected his audience to recognize that such proto-Protestant ground might have been found in Britain as well as Germany (MacDougall 45, 47, 55). According to Bale and John Foxe, a Saxon church, untainted by popery, flowered in England before Augustine's seventh-century evangelization (MacDougall 34, 38). In *The Popish Successour,* Settle appears to draw upon such histories to imply that his compatriots are innately resistant to popery, as he concedes that even within a Catholic monarch, "perhaps the stubborn *English Genius* will not easily bend to the superstition of *Rome*" (12).[18] Thus, the duke's Saxon ethnicity, with its historical ties to the "English Genius," points back to primitive Christian purity as well as forward to a cleansing northern Reformation.

Thus informed, we can take up F. C. Brown's invitation to read this play as political allegory (21). Disaster awaits, if the English people, like young Saxony, fail to comprehend fully and learn from their ancestors' deadly and polluting infatuation with popery, the scarlet whore who masquerades in clerical robes. If, like the duke who travels to the Tiber's banks to wed the beauteous Angeline, they seek the sacred in Rome, they will find there a whorish pope with an insatiable desire to defile virtue.[19] She will divide them from their souls' "dearest Oracle," as Joanna forcibly separates young Saxony from his bride. Like Settle's hero, they will find themselves stripped of their sovereignty and bedded with a "false Angelick Vision" that

> To his deluded Sense appear'd so fair,
> As left no track to shew the Fiend was there. (39)

If they recognize the truth too late or naively rely on their ability to persuade benighted papists, they will end their days, like the duke, as martyrs.

"Better to Marry"

The path that ultimately leads Joanna to her identity as a scarlet whore, like that identity itself, illustrates Anglican charges against Catholicism. As her self-interested attempt at celibacy degenerates into vile sexual license, Joanna's behavior vindicates Protestants' suspicions concerning the Catholic glorification of lifelong virginity. Here again Settle departs from medieval accounts, like Giovanni Boccaccio's and Ranulph Higden's, in which Joan seems to embrace sexuality as a force that facilitates her exploits, as she begins her career by traveling (cross-dressed) with a male lover. In contrast, Settle's popess at first forswears sexuality (Boccaccio, *Concerning* 231; Higden 6: 332). As Joanna tells it, she initially resolved to live celibate, due not to piety but to her fear of erotic love as a pernicious threat, especially to feminine autonomy. She asserts that her "Sexes Fate" is to dote "on its destruction," and consequently, she characterizes a "Breach" in a virgin's "Adamantine Walls of Honour" as the place "where love and Ruine enter" (22–23). According to Tudor Reformers, Catholics acted upon a mistaken disdain for even marital sexuality as "unclean," which parallels Joanna's broad distrust of the erotic (Crawford 45; Yost 157). That distrust draws added force from her conviction that for women love entails subordination. As she tells it, fortified with that insight, Joanna's Radigundian "Pride" preserved her "guarded innocence" at least temporarily:

> Who yields to Love, makes but vain Man her Lord:
> And I who had studied all the greater Globe,
> Scorn'd to be Vassal to the lesser World. (22)

The charge that pride motivated Catholic insistence on clerical celibacy suggests another parallel with Settle's popess. Focusing on hierarchies of class rather than gender, the Protestant George Joye (died 1553) contended that papist prelates resisted clerical marriage because the married state would diminish their apparent superiority over the laity and because matrimonial duties would erode their wealth and power—as the 1603 Anglican *Homily of the State of Matrimony* observed, despite wives' subjection, husbands must "yield something to the woman" (qtd. in Dolan, *Taming* 174, 176; Yost 160). Neither Joye's proud prelates nor Joanna, the woman who will eventually masquerade as one, choose to "yield" any of their autonomy to a spouse.

Not surprisingly, concerning celibacy Joanna's gender makes a difference. As Patricia Crawford has suggested, early modern Protestants saw a woman's choice of lifelong celibacy as especially suspect. According to *The Law's Resolutions of Women's Rights* (1631), all women "are understood either married or to be married" (Book 1, B3v, excerpted in Dolan, *Taming* 198). In the 1630s Bishop John Williams acted upon such ideas when he admonished two women residing at the Ferrar's Protestant community at Little Gidding against their wish to make vows of chastity (Crawford 46; B. Hill 111). With perhaps comic hyperbole, a gentleman in a 1662 play by Margaret Cavendish (ca. 1623–73) goes so far as to say that "those women which restrain themselves from the company and use of men, are damned" (qtd. in B. Hill 128). Moreover, physiology seemed to confirm what ideology asserted. Although the "superstitious and rash" monastic vows condemned in *The Anatomy of Melancholy* (1638) bind both men and women to virginity "against the laws of nature," Robert Burton's persona, Democritus Junior, contends that a unique malady afflicts (celibate) maids, nuns, and widows. He has in mind hysteria, which early modern physicians imputed to sexual abstinence, and he therefore recommends marriage as "the best and surest remedy." As Burton's remarks demonstrate, seventeenth-century medicine provided an additional rationale for Protestant distrust of celibacy, and that rationale differentiated between men's and women's abstinence. Indeed, although Democritus Junior admits to being a "bachelor" and "lead[ing] a monastic life in a college," he apparently does not suffer from this particular malady (Burton pt. 1, 414, 417–18; Veith 37–38, 114–18, 123). Evidently, as Protestants saw it, men could be trusted to recognize whether or not they had received God's gift of chastity and to act accordingly, but women (whether Protestant or Catholic) could not. By choosing an option that Protestant ideology would not offer her, even at the start of her career Joanna seems to arrogate unwarranted authority.

Joanna's career after she loses her virginity illustrates the consequences that Reformers anticipated from such mistaken attempts at celibacy. George Joye and John Ponet (ca. 1516–56) contended that imposing celibacy on those who had not received God's gift of chastity led to whoredom: the concupiscence that was not remedied through lawful marriage would erupt into fornication (Yost 161–63). Joanna's career appears to substantiate this claim, since after the elder Saxony storms her virginal "Fort," she descends into progressively less restrained and more grotesque sexual adventures. Five (apparently chaste) years intervene between her murder of the elder duke and the beginning of a discreet, two-year affair with her henchman Lorenzo. However, when the resemblance between father and son kindles her desires for the younger Saxony, she begins to portray her own lust as "th'unnatural Monster" (28). When Lorenzo proposes a lurid double bed-trick to delight that monster, her appetites become not only boundless and uncontrolled but also sadistic (34). After she has bedded the duke and Lorenzo the duchess (while the unsuspecting newlyweds imagine that they embrace each other), she exultantly characterizes herself and her henchman as "Ravishers" and their victims as "the kind Sacrifice" flying "to the fire" (38). At this point, sacrilege and prostitution compound with fornication as she resolves, "I'll melt the Crown from the gilt Martyr's Head" for gold to procure lovers and "t'adorn my bed" (40).

Eventually, Joanna's fortunes decline and turn her fiery imagery against her. When a near-fatal prison blaze interrupts another tryst with the unwitting duke, Joanna seems destined to take the Duchess Angeline's place this time as a burnt offering rather than a conjugal partner. Her holocaust metaphor returns as Saxony, awakened by smoke, reports:

> A strange prophetick horrour tells my Soul
> That we are mew'd up for sacrifice. (42)

Caught without her papal robes, Joanna must bribe her way to safety. Even so, the jailers who rescue her from one fire initially threaten her with another, as they propose to burn Joanna as a witch. As the fires in this scene proliferate, we sense a metaphor at work. Indeed, when Joanna cowers before the approaching flames and exclaims, "By Hell, I scorch already," Settle's plot appears to literalize the Pauline admonition, so favored by Reformers, "better to marry than to burn" (1 Cor. 7:9; *Female* 43). In an attempt to evade the choice that Paul poses, Joanna has presumed to possess the gift of chastity, which Protestant ideology and early modern medicine resisted ascribing to women. The flames that relentlessly pursue her through this scene portray most specifically the failure of that attempt and more generally the disasters that can result from popery's misguided exalting of virginity.

The Transvestite Effect

Thus far, we have observed how Joanna's career illustrates a Whig critique of popery as a pernicious ideology and a threat to English sovereignty. Shifting our focus to the play's second, more easily overlooked transvestite, the popess's page Amiran, reveals traces of a second, less restrained critique that threatens to erode the play's prized distinction between Protestantism and Catholicism. As befits a character whose presence signals the collapse of distinctions, early in *The Female Prelate,* Amiran herself resists definite categorization. The play's second scene (1.2) opens with the promise of revelations, since, while addressing his two attendants (Lorenzo and Amiran), John/Joanna, the cardinal of Reims, stresses intimacy, privacy, and authentic identity:

Now my best love, we are in our private state
I thy kind *Juno,* thou my faithful *Jove,*
And our sworn Loyal *Ganimede* alone,
And now we are our selves. (4)

A suspicious audience, or at least one that has read its Ovid, might wonder
about the adjectives "kind" and "faithful" or about the evident harmony
among Juno, Jove, and Ganymede—indeed, Lorenzo will eventually prove
to be inconstant and John cruel. Yet the classical allusions gain credibility
seven lines later, when John/Joanna confirms at least one thing that the comparison to a goddess implied: she has "lived an undiscovered Woman" (4).
But what truths does the allusion to Ganymede reveal about Amiran? Very
few, since it introduces the red herring of homosexuality without disclosing
her true gender.[20] To the small extent that Amiran manifests sexual desires,
they are aroused, like Joanna's, by young Saxony's courage, and unlike her
two companions, she does not pursue a physical relationship with any character in the play. An audience that is not privy to Settle's list of dramatis personae must wait until Joanna addresses Amiran as "Girl" in act 3 to learn that
she is a "Woman in the Habit of a Page" (28).

The audience's complete and unrelieved ignorance of Amiran's personal
history surpasses this temporary ignorance of her gender. Consequently, to
posit the experiences that have shaped her behavior, the audience can only
emulate young Saxony's unfounded speculations:

Perhaps some honest humble Cottage bred thee,
And thy ambitious Parents poorly proud,
For a gay Coat made thee a Page at Court,
And for a Plume of Feathers sold thy Soul. (49)

His failure to perceive accurately even this "Page['s]" gender illustrates the
futility of imagining a past for Amiran. Thus hobbled, the audience can construct only the barest motive for her transvestitism: presumably, she cross-
dresses to serve Joanna in ecclesiastical precincts otherwise closed to women.
This rationalization of her cross-dressing as a means to an end or a response
to social constraints exemplifies what Marjorie Garber terms "progress narratives" (8, 67–71). Such a narrative might explain, for example, that Shakespeare's Portia of Belmont cross-dresses in order to participate in court proceedings before returning to her role as Bassanio's bride. In Garber's view,
such an interpretation promptly reaffirms the binary opposition between

male and female, since it views the cross-dresser not as a "third" but "as male or female manqué"; the progress narrative thus avoids the transvestite figure's challenge to binary thinking. Amiran, however, never appears without her male disguise and, consequently, never progresses beyond female manqué. *The Female Prelate* thus provides neither a vision of Amiran as anything other than transvestite nor the details needed to craft an elaborate progress narrative that could comfortably explain away her cross-dressing. Consequently, the play compels its audience to confront rather directly this transvestite's "power to disrupt, expose and challenge" (Garber 10–11, 16).[21]

Amiran exercises such power in act 5, scene 1, when she begins to depart from Joanna's instructions and to act upon her own initiative. In that scene, for example, she (perhaps unconsciously) discredits notions of easily generalized and essential gender differences. Of course, the medieval accounts of Pope Joan had already cast some doubt on such notions, since reports that none of Joan's contemporaries equaled her intellectual accomplishments conflicted with Aristotelian and Galenic theories concerning the female intellect's physiologically determined deficiencies (Maclean 42–43; Jordan 32; Morris 84–85). For her part, Amiran focuses on emotion and volition rather than intellect. As act 5 opens, she prepares to carry out Joanna's orders and to poison the young duke in prison, but overcome by indeterminate emotions—"Pity, Conscience, Love, / I know not which"—she wavers in her resolve. Drawing perhaps upon assumptions about feminine compassion articulated in Aristotle's *Historia animalium* (9.1), she attributes these misgivings to her gender:

> . . . there's something
> In Murder so beyond a Female Villain.
> As my Soul startles at the thought. (48)[22]

However, within a few moments Amiran contradicts her generalization concerning female villains, as she reports that seven years earlier Joanna Anglica, an explicitly feminine "Sorceress" and "Hag," poisoned the duke's father. Moreover, Amiran's own metaphors draw attention to this contradiction. After she shifts allegiances and decides to reveal his enemy's secrets to young Saxony, Amiran imagines that the truth she tells is a "Killing Story" that the duke cannot physically endure:

> Break, break, great heart, thou'rt too much lost to live,
> And for the last, the greatest fatal stab;
> For I must tell you all. (50)

Since Amiran can stab metaphorically and Joanna can poison literally, the capacity to murder does not, as Amiran implied, distinguish men from women.

Similarly, Amiran's account of the elder duke's murder destabilizes the categories of sexual victim and victimizer. Even though she must rely on the popess alone for information about Joanna's career in the Saxon court, the tone of the page's account differs markedly from that of her mistress's earlier narration. As we have seen, Joanna has insisted upon her former determination to restrain the "high Spring Tide" of lust within her veins and to preserve her maidenhead. In keeping with this self-representation, she draws upon familiar poetic conceits and portrays her defdowering by the elder Duke of Saxony as a violent invasion:

> The Fort was storm'd, and my proud Heart surrender'd.
> My Virgin Spoils were the great Duke of *Saxony*'s. (22)

In contrast, Amiran describes this besieged virgin as "That *Syren* [who] first defil'd your Father's Bed," a "Sulphurous Mine that blew his soul up." She further charges that Joanna "doubly, doubly poyson'd" the elder Saxony's blood—first, it would seem, figuratively through lust or sexual contact and then literally through the fatal bowl (50). She thus seems to encourage the audience to metonymically transfer the defiling from the duke's bed to his person. This characterization of the adulterous duke as victim of Joanna's poisonous defiling seems strained, since after conducting a two-year affair with Joanna and concealing it from his wife and son, Saxony turned his attention to yet another mistress, named Leonora. Without access to any new information about the popess's past, Amiran has reversed the roles of victim and victimizer, thus casting doubt on the distinction between them.

Amiran's obviously revised exposition gains no credibility from its conspicuous and self-interested incompleteness. The duke mistakenly imagines that Joanna's page has overcome shame and "now wouldst . . . tell me all"— Amiran herself says she "must" do just that (49–50). Yet she never reveals her own transvestite disguise. As if to remind the audience of this continued deception, Settle's Saxony addresses Amiran as "Boy" three times within two pages of dialogue and once as he asserts the young page's newfound candor: "thou't a Convert, / A gentle honest boy" (50–51). Since Amiran is not a "boy," Saxony's description reminds us that she has not been as "honest" as she pretends.

Amiran's role in Settle's play appears to exemplify a particular dynamic that Garber has posited. "The apparently spontaneous or unexpected or supplementary presence of a transvestite figure in a text," she argues, "indicates a *category crisis elsewhere*," that is, "a failure of definitional distinction, a borderline that becomes permeable" (11, 16–17, 36–37). A transvestite can absorb and reflect the discomfort resulting even from crises that do not principally concern gender. In a related process of displacement, Jacobean moralists' concerns over cross-dressing, for example, manifest anxieties about gender but also, Garber contends, about the porous boundaries between social ranks—in this instance, class is the site of Garber's "crisis elsewhere."[23] In several respects, Amiran is an "unexpected or supplementary presence" in *The Female Prelate.* Whereas Lorenzo may derive from the unnamed, impregnating lover in earlier versions of the Pope Joan legend, Amiran appears to be Settle's invention, unprecedented in the medieval chronicles. The play's second transvestite also seems secondary in that she contributes only modestly to the plot. By the time that Amiran changes sides and turns informant, Saxony has already learned through the prison fire that he has bedded his father's poisoner and thus that both pope and poisoner are a woman who had once disguised herself as the monk Theodore. In fact, as if the duke could not be trusted to recognize the face illuminated next to him during the prison blaze, in that same scene his father's ghostly apparition inscribes "M U R D E R" in fiery letters on the chamber wall (43). Admittedly, Amiran does reveal that the popess began her career as the elder Saxony's secret mistress Joanna Anglica and that she has now ordered the murder of young Saxony and his bride (50, 52). The turncoat page also releases the duke from his imprisonment in time for him to see the dying Angeline and to deliver his ineffectual appeal to the Roman masses. Nonetheless, Amiran's absence from the play's final scene, in which the principal characters (Joanna, Lorenzo, and Saxony) appear, seems to confirm her secondary status.

Amiran, the play's "supplementary" transvestite, signals one of Garber's "category crises elsewhere," this time along the troubled boundary between popery and all religion, between anti-Catholicism and irreligion. Fears of apostasy trouble young Saxony in *The Female Prelate,* as fears of atheism trouble Settle in *The Popish Successour.* As the duke addresses his fatally poisoned wife, he worries:

Ah no, my *Angeline;* when thou art dead,
I am afraid my wrongs so high will rise,
Make such complaints against my angry stars,
Till in despair

I curse the Author of my wretched Being;
Then in my wild Apostate fury die,
And never meet thee more. (54)

Although a few lines later Saxony does "abhor" the night of his creation, he stops short of cursing his Creator. Nonetheless, his apprehensions seem justified, since with his final words (addressing Joanna and whoever else will listen) he craves not the Christian Church's reformation but its absolute corruption:

Farewel thou Royal rank Church Whore, farewel,
. . . .
Brood on *Romes* cursed Chair, Brood like a hatching Basilisk:
Entail thy Lust t'a thousand Generations
And warm the Nest for all thy bloody Successors:
May not that Beast of Prey, a Pope Succeed thee,
But be thy Bastard, Not a Cell nor Cloyster
But be thy Brothel.
And not a fawning Cardinal but thy Bawd:
. . . .
May all thy race be Cardinals, Popes, Abbots,
Monks, Friars, Priests and all be damn'd together. (59–60)

With all the play's principled dissenters incinerated in the prison fire or at the stake and all the Church's clerics thus blasted by Saxony's curse, only the antipapist sentiment that the duke has bequeathed to his homeland holds out the promise of a revived and purified Christianity.[24]

Settle concludes *The Popish Successour,* like *The Female Prelate,* with the specter of irreligion. In the pamphlet's final paragraph, he predicts that in England an antipapist backlash will follow the reign of a Catholic monarch. The consequences of such a reign would thus effectively "undo" the parties on either side of the religious divide. Only the faithless could prosper in such times: "Why nothing but an Atheist, he that believes there is no God, and so makes the name of the most fashionable Religion, the Bawd to his Pleasures and preferments; or at best that Latitudinarian Believer, that can kneel to a Crucifix to day, and burn it to morrow. This and this onely Principle, can be safe under a Papist" (*Character* 22).[25] Settle's time servers thus mimic Joanna's Protean flexibility—recall "I could take all Forms: / The perfect Christian, or complete Philosopher" (*Female* 22). For his own part, at a startling, earlier moment in his pamphlet, Settle grimly mirrors his "Latitudinarian Believer" and ignores sectarian distinctions, as he suggests not that all religions are equally good but rather that they are all equally and unrepentantly destructive: "Religion . . . from the beginning of the World, thro' all Ages, has set all Nations in a Flame, yet never confesses it self in the wrong. . . . But Religious Frenzy leaves that eternal Intoxication behind it, that where it commits all the Cruelties in the World, 'tis never sober after to be sorry for 't" (*Character* 6–7). As he paints with this broad brush, Settle seems to second an imprisoned heretic in *The Female Prelate* who, casting his eyes about a chamber of horrors, exclaims:

> . . . No wonder nothing,
> But Cruelty and Torments fill this place;
> For here Religion reigns, that pious Cormorant;
> Religion, that devouring Savage reigns;
> Yes, we are Hereticks.
> Those bugbear monstrous things, design'd for slaughter. (41)

It seems unlikely that Settle fully intended such indiscriminate condemnations, since elsewhere in *The Popish Successour* he denounces atheistic unbelief as "wretched" and "despicable" and celebrates Charles I as a "Royal Martyr" untainted "with the least blemish of Irreligion" (*Character* 5, 11; F. C. Brown 65; *Solemn . . . 1680*).

As Settle's polemical attack strays beyond Catholic theology and church polity to question religion more generally, Amiran's full role in the play becomes clearer. The transvestite pope's transvestite page encourages the audience to doubt her by falling short of promised candor and radically reshaping Joanna's personal history. Moreover, by contradicting her own assertions concerning female villainy, Amiran discredits a neat, binary view of gender. Since she thus undermines certainty on several counts, Amiran readily serves as Garber's "third," absorbing and disclosing displaced anxieties aroused when, at certain isolated moments within his play and pamphlet, Settle casts doubt on even the Protestant religion. Like his "blind deluded Prelates," who expect to restore order by simply initiating manual examination of papal candidates, Settle appears to have overestimated his ability to contain the disruption of religious belief or sentiment that a tyrannous popess (whether fictive or real) might unleash.

Afterword

In 1972, seven hundred years after Jean de Mailly first committed it to writing, the popess legend entered a new medium with the release of a film entitled *Pope Joan* (or alternatively *The Devil's Imposter*). As originally conceived and shot, this film portrayed a troubled, twentieth-century woman's attempt to appropriate the popess legend in order to structure her experience. Like the texts by Cooke, Cope, Bale, and Settle analyzed in the preceding chapters, it thus attempts a narrative appropriation but, as if in response to those earlier failures, also foregrounds and engages with the difficulties involved in just such an attempt. That engagement, however, was thwarted when the film suffered the sort of textual castration that, according to the Protestant polemicists cited in chapter 1, Catholics readily inflicted upon ancient and medieval manuscripts. In this case, such gelding produced a film that disappointed viewers and critics, as well as its screenwriter and star. More important, the gelded film demonstrates that in the twentieth century, as it had in the sixteenth and seventeenth, the popess legend resisted attempts to appropriate it, doing so in this instance even when that attempt explored the difficulties of such appropriation.

Many of the creative artists who worked on the film brought strong records of accomplishment to the project. The director, Michael Anderson, had established himself with films such as *1984* (1956) and the Academy Award–winning *Around the World in Eighty Days* (1956). After playing leading roles in Ingmar Bergman's *Persona* (1966), *Hour of the Wolf* (1968), *Shame* (1968), and *The Passion of Anna* (1969), Liv Ullmann, appearing in her first English-language film, starred as Joan. The supporting cast included talented, experienced actors such as Olivia de Havilland, Trevor Howard, and Maximilian Schell. Maurice Jarre, who composed the score, had received Academy Awards for the historical epics *Doctor Zhivago* (1965) and *Lawrence of Arabia* (1962). Although a relative newcomer, the screenwriter

John Briley would go on to write *Cry Freedom* (1987) and the Oscar-winning screenplay for *Gandhi* (1982). When *Pope Joan* was commercially released, however, critics panned it as "a complete nonstarter" (Strick 9). Students of the popess legend have concurred: Rosemary Pardoe and Darroll Pardoe contend that the film could hardly be worse, and C. A. Patrides goes further, suggesting hyperbolically that this film's "prodigious vulgarity" may have finally "interred" the popess legend (Pardoe and Pardoe 86; Patrides 181).

Ullmann and Briley have offered an explanation for such damning appraisals: the film that Patrides and Pardoe and Pardoe have decried is not the one the director and cast made. The movie was written and filmed with a modern frame narrative. "It was the story of a girl who starts following Christian leaders and then begins preaching herself, [and] has a mental breakdown," Ullmann explains. "In the director's version there is intercutting between the modern girl and her vision. It is the story of a woman in an asylum who *thought* she was Pope Joan." After the completion of the director's cut, however, the film was reedited. "When it was cut by the director it was a beautiful picture," Ullmann insists. "But someone else took it for six months and recut it, redid the music, and it came out a completely different picture," one with all the modern shots removed. Whereas medieval scribes or early modern printers allegedly expunged Pope Joan from the chronicles, those who reedited the film deleted everything *but* the medieval popess. Without the modern shots, mostly depicting incidents that parallel those of the medieval plot, "you are left," as Ullman puts it, "with the story within the story, which makes for a strange story" (99).[1]

In a letter graciously answering my request for a copy of his screenplay, Briley, who was also credited as the film's associate producer, has confirmed and elaborated Ullmann's account, fixing blame on an editor "whose previous experience had been the Hammer-horror films."[2] Whether or not that editor bears full responsibility for the film's flaws, this episode appears to constitute a paradigmatic tale of the homogenizing pressures at work in the commercial film industry. Several of those who worked on the film, De Havilland and Jarre in particular, had admired the original cut and expected great things. On the only two occasions when that version was screened (both in New Haven, Connecticut), Briley asserts, preview audiences reacted enthusiastically. However, the reediting that Ullmann describes was, in the screenwriter's estimation, disastrous, as was the American opening of the recut film. Briley reports that he, in turn, recut the recut film for its English premiere but, because he was working from a married print (a print that carries image and sound on the same piece of film), Briley could only eliminate, as he puts it, "the grossest absurdities." He could not restore the modern frame narrative, which, as far as I can determine, has been lost, rendering the "disastrous" reediting irreversible.[3] Such irreversibility heightens the parallel between that reediting and the textual gelding that early modern Protestants feared and suspected.

Although the much disparaged reediting may, of course, serve as a convenient scapegoat for a failed project, the account offered by Ullmann and Briley does raise the question: how did the removal of the modern frame alter the film's meaning?[4] Most significantly, that removal eliminated the film's most forceful and persistent suggestions that the popess narrative and its ninth-century context relate meaningfully to late twentieth-century American culture. Briley's screenplay suggests that the modern Joan's identification with the popess is not merely delusional but also insightful and thus encourages the audience to contemplate the logic underlying that identification and the meanings it suggests.

To that end, Briley creates clear parallels between details in the popess legend and the life of the modern Joan. Her childhood as the daughter of an itinerant preacher, for example, resembles that of the popess, whose father, according to sixteenth-century accounts, was an English priest traveling in Germany presumably as a missionary (Bale, *Scriptorvm illustrium* 2: 122–23). Several such parallels are underscored in dialogue between physicians treating the modern Joan. The script presents the medieval scenes as the dramatization of the story told to a psychiatrist by the modern Joan, who, we learn, has read an old printed volume on Pope Joan and now believes she is the medieval popess. After listening to his patient recount her ninth-century experiences, the psychiatrist (who has also glanced quickly at an *Encyclopedia Britannica* entry on the popess) anticipates information that his colleague uncovers about their patient's twentieth-century past concerning, for example, her male traveling companion, a counterpart to the monk who accompanies Joanna Anglica at the start of her transvestite career. Impressed by such prescience, the colleague asks the psychiatrist, "You learned something from her then?" After his reply, "A little," the screenplay calls for a silent pause that, it seems, would encourage the audience to contemplate just how much he has learned from his patient (Briley 139). Further, the modern Joan dies of complications from a concealed pregnancy, and when the psychiatrist (who apparently has overlooked some details in the encyclopedia entry) learns that the medieval popess reportedly suffered a similar fate, he exclaims, "My God—no wonder she identified with her" (Briley 140). What insights does the modern Joan's identification with the popess, thus endorsed by the authoritative voice of her psychiatrist, convey?

As one might expect in a film released while soldiers waged the Vietnam

War and demonstrators protested against it, some of these insights concern troubled and often violent international relations. Allusions to the peace and nuclear-disarmament movements frame the screenplay. Briley wrote and the director shot two possible openings for the film, and both begin with the modern Joan standing on a speaker's platform before a crowd of "mostly young people" bearing "banners with Crosses and peace symbols." In one opening Briley specifies "CND [Campaign for Nuclear Disarmament] signs," and in the other Joan's first words, the first words spoken in this version, allude to nuclear weapons and assert an analogy between ancient Rome and twentieth-century America: 'The Romans had the ultimate weapon too! And where are the Romans now?" (Briley 1, A). Twice more near the end of the film, the script calls for shots of such a crowd, in one case extending "as far as the eye can see" (Briley 119, 138).

In Briley's screenplay, Carolingian dynastic conflicts—the ninth-century counterpart of the Cold War hostilities these crowds seem to be protesting—shape the popess's career. They unleash the recently and superficially Christianized Saxon warriors who attack the nunnery where Joan has made a life, forcing her into the countryside and prompting her to adopt a masculine disguise. Later, these conflicts propel Joan toward the papacy, as Leo IV recommends "Cardinal John" as his successor in order to avoid endorsing a candidate too closely identified with one of the two great-grandsons of Charlemagne, whose competition for territory and influence threatens, as Leo puts it, to "produce a kingdom of destitutes" (Briley 107).[5] The parallel Briley draws between medieval and modern political and military rivalries suggests that the Cold War struggle is no more idealistic than dynastic conflicts in which, to secure a useful alliance, an emperor crowned by the pope in Rome authorizes his Saxon subjects to revert to paganism.

Briley's screenplay also foregrounds conflict between the forces (medieval and modern) represented by the Carolingian emperors and the popess. Late in the film, the popess confronts the emperor-elect Louis II, who, leading a column of troops, approaches the steps of the Lateran Church on horseback and threatens to have the newly elected "Pope John" cast into the Tiber. Joan, however, threatens excommunication and the resulting loss of popular or even military support, forcing Louis to back down (Briley 119–24). Briley alludes to this scene in both of the openings that he wrote for the film, as the modern Joan declares (anticipating the later scene), "We pronounce you excommunicate! You are heretic damned" (Briley 2, C). By intercutting shots of this confrontation with shots of the peace activists, the opening Briley envisioned would have raised the question: could an undisguised late twentieth-century woman (like the modern Joan) employ moral authority and popular support to confront military and political leaders as effectively as the disguised popess does?[6] Thus, suppressing the modern frame suppresses the film's crucial question about the possibility of contemporary challenges to power.

Like Protestant polemics centuries earlier, the reedited film insistently presents the legend as history rather than fantasy. However, whereas those earlier polemics assert the legend's relevance to controversies of their day (such as papal claims to apostolic succession), the reedited film *distances* the legend from contemporary controversies and effaces the connections that the screenwriter and director had drawn between the ninth and twentieth centuries. The editor's "castrating" cut thus prevents the Pope Joan film from sowing or reproducing in the audience's minds Briley's cultural critique and perhaps from suggesting that the popess narrative might generate still other meanings. In this twentieth-century instance, the constricting of the legend's meaning and resistance to its polemical appropriation owe less to vexed constructions of witchcraft, hermaphroditism, or atheism and more to the mass marketing of commercial entertainment, a primary mechanism by which orthodoxies are constructed and enforced in our own day.

The act of subversion recounted in the popess legend is relatively modest, effected, as it is, through disguise rather than open defiance of patriarchal institutions, and ultimately undone, as Joan's untimely parturition suggests, by a woman's unruly body. In contrast, the history of the legend and its retelling constitutes a tale of more sustained and radical resistance to absorption into master narratives. Even when drafted into Briley and Anderson's cinematic critique of such master narratives as cultural progress and enlightenment, the legend remains resistant.

Notes

Introduction

1. The cardinal and ecclesiastical historian Cesare Baronius (1538–1607) seems to have introduced this conjecture. Eventually, other writers suggested that the weak, "womanish" prelate who inspired the popess legend might have been another pope, namely John VII, John X, John XI, John XII, or John XIII, or even the antipope Anastasius Bibliothecarius (Boureau, *Myth* 306; Patrides 163; Pardoe and Pardoe 54; Thurston 13–14).

2. The *Oxford English Dictionary* traces the term *pornocracy* to a discussion of the Theophylact women in a nineteenth-century church history (*OED* 12: 136). Several more of Marozia's descendents occupied the Holy See: her grandson John XIII (reigning 965–72), her great-grandsons Benedict VIII (reigning 1012–24) and John XIX (reigning 1024–1032), and her great-great-grandson Benedict IX (reigning 1032–48, with breaks) (Pardoe and Pardoe 54). The nineteenth-century scholar Félix Vernet seems to have introduced this theory concerning the legend's origins (Thurston 14–15; Boureau, *Myth* 306). Scholars have also suggested that the popess legend developed as an insult directed against still other women, particularly the ninth-century pseudoprophetess Thiota, or Giovanna, wife of the antipope Nicholas V (reigning 1328–30) (Boureau, *Myth* 306).

3. As Pardoe and Pardoe have noted, Leo IX somewhat misrepresents that first canon of the Council of Nicea, which bars from the clergy those who have castrated themselves but not those who, victimized perhaps by brutal barbarians, suffered castration at the hands of others (Pardoe and Pardoe 57–58).

4. Accounts of the female patriarch appear in the anonymous *Chronicon Salernitanum* (sometimes attributed to Radoald of Salerno) and in Erchempert's *Historia Langobardorum Beneventanorum* (Pardoe and Pardoe 57).

5. Baronius seems to have introduced this hypothesis as well as the one concerning John VIII (Patrides 163). The English Jesuit Robert Persons (or Parsons, 1546–1610) and the Italian cardinal and polemicist Robert Bellarmine (1542–1621) both cited Leo IX's letter to Michael Cerularius not to explain the legend's origins but rather to challenge its veracity. Persons argues, for example, that Leo IX would never have alluded to a female prelate if he had known that, due to Joan's scandalous pontificate, "the Patriarch of Constantinople might have returned the matter back upon him" (qtd. in Thurston 10, 15).

6. Rosemary Pardoe and Darroll Pardoe suggest that because the popess narrative in the *Chronica minor* seems unrelated to the contents of the surrounding paragraphs (which concern the deeds of popes and emperors reigning in the 890s), it is "evidently a slightly more recent addition" inserted "very soon after" the composition of the original text and perhaps "by the initial compiler himself" (18). Neither Boureau nor Patrides, who both have identified interpolations in other medieval texts addressing Pope Joan, has suggested that the popess narrative was absent from the original *Chronica minor* (Boureau, *Myth* 140; Patrides 158). Indeed, since thirteenth-century texts proposed several different dates for the popess's pontificate (855, 1099, 1100), and since the handwriting in the popess narrative evidently resembles that in the rest of the manuscript so closely that, Pardoe and Pardoe believe, it might belong to the original compiler, the evidence of interpolation seems slight. In any case, the *Chronica minor* account had certainly been written and circulated by 1304, when the priest Siegfried of Blahusen (or of Meissen) copied it before adding his own report of a marble statue in Rome that allegedly memorialized Joan (Boureau, *Myth* 140–41).

7. The phrase in the *Chronica minor* begins with "Papa" (O Pope) rather than "Petre" (O Peter). Also, this Franciscan report claims not that the phrase marked the popess's grave but rather that it was pronounced by a demon who exposed her deception and pregnancy even before she gave birth (Pardoe and Pardoe 16–19).

8. By introducing a new imperative, *parce* (forbear), into the phrase, Etienne fashions an exhortation not to publish but rather to suppress the narrative: "Forbear, Father of Fathers, to betray the childbearing of the female pope" (Parce, Pater Patrum, Papisse Prodere Partum) (Pardoe and Pardoe 16–17).

9. I have used Morris's helpfully literal translation of the *Chronicon* account, with a few small changes.

10. Vague references to the popess appear in rhymed chronicles composed in the 1280s (roughly twenty years after Jean de Mailly's account), written not in Latin but in Old High German and Flemish and not by Dominicans or Franciscans but by lay burghers: Jacob van Maerlant's *Spiegel Historiael* and Jansen Enikel's *Weltchronik*. According to Boureau, these references further suggest that popess rumors were circulating in oral culture while the Pope Joan narrative was first entering written culture (*Myth* 116–17).

11. Martinus Polonus composed at least two versions of the *Chronicon*, and although the discussion of the popess does not appear in the earliest of these (written no later than 1268), it does appear in some copies of a later expanded edition, composed around 1277. The entry on Joan, however, fits awkwardly into the carefully structured format of even these later versions. Martinus devotes each fifty-line page to fifty years of imperial or ecclesiastical history, so that each line corresponds to one year. As Pardoe and Pardoe have pointed out, to conform to this structure Joan's pontificate (which according to Martinus lasted fewer than three years) should take up no more than three lines. Martinus's entry on the popess, however, consists of nearly 150 words in the original Latin, dwarfs the entry for her successor Benedict III (whose pontificate reportedly was just four days shorter than hers), and takes up seven lines in most manuscripts (Boureau, *Myth* 123; Pardoe and Pardoe 22; Embree 3).

12. The German chronicle *Flores temporum* (ca. 1290), often attributed to the Franciscan friar Martinus Minorita, cites Martinus Polonus as a principal source and includes an entry on the popess that (although it introduces some new material on Joan's interaction with a demoniac) seems to be based on the *Chronicon* since it echoes several details introduced in that earlier chronicle: the popess's name, her studies in Athens, the ninth-century date of her pontificate, and the precise site of her fateful parturition (Pardoe and Pardoe 19–20, 22; Boureau, *Myth* 141, Patrides 160). Similarly, in his *Chronique de l'Abbaye de Saint-Pierre-Vif de Sens,* Geoffroy de Courlon (Gaufridus de Collone, died ca. 1295) echoes details from the *Chronicon* account (Pardoe and Pardoe 22; Boureau, *Myth* 128–29; Patrides 160). Further, an expanded version of the *Flores historiarum* (originally composed in 1265), produced at a Norfolk monastery around 1304, summarizes the *Chronicon* account and explicitly cites the prominent Dominican as its source with the closing words "Thus Martinus" (Pardoe and Pardoe 19–20, 22; Boureau, *Myth* 128–29, 141; Patrides 160).

13. Drawing upon the work of the twentieth-century historian Giuseppe Billanovich, Joan Morris has sketched the history of the manuscript Vaticanus latinus 3762 from the twelfth to the fourteenth centuries (71–72). Boureau credits Louis Duchesne with demonstrating that the marginal entry on Pope Joan was an interpolation (*Myth* 116).

14. Boureau proposes two additional likely origins for the legend: twelfth- or thirteenth-century Roman parodies of ceremonies celebrating the investiture of new popes and the late thirteenth-century Guglielmite heresy, which prophesied the establishing of a new church ruled by a female pope and female cardinals. Since that heresy was confined to Milan and did not attract the Inquisition's attention until 1300, it seems to have been too local and to have become known too late to have influenced the popess narrative that Jean de Mailly composed around 1250. Boureau speculates, however, that before arriving in Milan the heresy's founder, Guglielma, who reportedly was a Bohemian princess and claimed to be the Holy Spirit incarnate, passed near Metz (Jean's home) and Erfurt (home of the anonymous Franciscan who composed the *Chronica minor*) and through Burgundy (where Etienne de Bourbon worked as a preacher and inquisitor) (Boureau, *Myth* 174; Wessley 289).

15. John Bale, for example, approvingly cites and paraphrases "Funcius" (probably Johann Funk, a sixteenth-century author who composed an ambitious *Chronologia* covering events from the beginning of the world to 1552), who, noting parallels between the popess and the scriptural Whore of Babylon (Rev. 17–18), "sayth boldely that this was suffered by Gods especiall providence, that this woman should be made Pope being also an harlot, . . . whereby Antichrist might be knowen" (Bale, *Pageant* 56v).

16. Evidently, economic pressures contributed to the canons' reluctance to admit women. During the twelfth century four different popes admonished the Premonstratensians to provide adequate maintenance for the order's sisters (Southern 312). However, one abbot, Conrad of Marchtal, argued that the order rejected additional sisters in order to protect the canons' "souls" as well as their "bodies and goods" from the wickedness and anger of women, whom they resolved to avoid, as he put it, "like poisonous animals" (qtd. in Southern 314).

17. In contrast, the Guglielmite heresy, a late thirteenth-century episode cited by both Boureau and Pardoe and Pardoe, reveals that at least for a heterodox minority a female pope constituted a sign of hoped-for ecclesiastical renewal (Boureau, *Myth* 171–75; Pardoe and Pardoe 93–94). In 1300 inquisitors prosecuted a heretical sect whose leader Maifreda (or Manfreda) di Pirovano, a nun of the Umiliata Order, celebrated Easter Mass and was hailed as "Lord Vicar" of the Holy Spirit. The heretics (roughly thirty men and women belonging, in several cases, to wealthy, influential Milanese families) believed that Guglielma, a saintly woman who had died in Milan in 1281, was the incarnation of the Holy Spirit, "true God and true human in the female sex," and they expected her second coming on Pentecost 1300, when the Roman Church, ruled by a false pope, would pass away to be replaced by a new church led by female cardinals and headed by Maifreda as popess (Newman 182, 185–86, 188; Lea 3: 94; Wessley 289).

18. Drawing upon evidence collected by Vittorio Lusini, Joan Morris has cited accounting records documenting the painting of the papal busts between 1490 and 1501 and thus demonstrating that they were fashioned sometime before that. Morris reasons that, since the busts depict popes wearing the papal triple tiara, they must have been sculpted sometime after the tiara's introduction by Pope Benedict XI in 1304 (138–40). Lusini has found documents within the archives of Siena reporting that on August 9, 1600, two days after the governor of Siena delivered an edict commanding, "Remove the popess from the cathedral" (levasse dal duomo la papessa), the bust of the popess (John VII) was altered to depict Pope Zacharias (2: 149–50).

19. As Jewel acknowledges, his Catholic antagonist Thomas Harding (1516–72) dismissed the Roman image and charged that it was as crude and indecipherable as the ruins at Stonehenge (Jewel, *Defence* 644; Harding 167). Boureau warns against assuming that Raemond and Clement VIII were right to believe that the controversial bust "was initially meant to figure Joan." He rightly notes that the "quite undifferentiated" faces on the papal busts suggest that their sculptors were not attempting to portray their subjects' actual appearances. He further asserts, without citing his source, that the labels that now serve to identify the specific subject of each bust were "placed on them at a much later date." In contrast, and again without citing a source, the *Historia de Donne Famose,* written before the bust's removal, reports that it bore "this inscription, *Femina de Anglia*" (*Historia* C4v; Boureau, *Myth* 250).

20. The *OED* cites the use of *embezzle* to mean "tamper with" in the following quotation from Henry More's *An Explanation of the Grand Mystery of Godliness* (1660): "The Writings of the Evangelists . . . were never embeseled" (*OED* 5: 162).

21. Humphrey Shuttleworth, *A Present for a Papist: or The Life and Death of Pope Joan* (London, 1675); *The History of Pope Joan and the Whores of Rome* (London, 1687); R. W., *Pope Joan: or, An Account Collected out of the Romish Authors . . .* (London, 1689); and Elkanah Settle, *The Female Prelate: Being the History of the Life and Death of Pope Joan, A Tragedy* (London, 1680 and 1689). Shuttleworth's text was a monologic adaptation of Alexander Cooke's 1610 *Pope Joane: A Dialogue between a Protestant and a Papist,* and *The History of Pope Joan and the Whores of Rome* was an anonymous publication.

22. Steven M. Taylor has appended the eighteen stanzas concerning Pope Joan to

his article on *Le Champion des dames* (271–76). Here, I have drawn upon translations of particular stanzas by Edelgard E. DuBruck (78) and by Boureau's translator, Lydia G. Cochrane (*Myth* 156).

23. Hemmerli (ca 1388–ca. 1460) was a reformist Swiss churchman, canon lawyer, and provost of the collegiate church of St. Ursus at Solothurn. His *De nobilitate et rusticitate dialogus,* composed around 1450, includes a popess narrative. Drawing upon a reference in the 1671 edition of Johann Wolf's *Lectionum memorabilium et reconditarum,* Pardoe and Pardoe have cited a guidebook to Rome compiled around 1500 by Stephan Blanck that reports the angel's question and the popess's choice in much the same way that Schernberg dramatizes it (28).

24. Donna Spivey Ellington has contrasted the images of the Virgin produced before and after the Catholic Counter-Reformation (248).

25. The title page of *Pope Joan: or, An Account* attributes it to R. W. (possibly Robert Ware, died 1696), and the *Historia* is an anonymous English translation of a German treatise. The *Historia* cites a 1473 German translation of Boccaccio, as well as another edition, most likely a 1539 volume published at Bern in the original Latin and illustrated with such a "picture and spectacle." Boccaccio's text circulated in a large number of sometimes brilliantly illuminated manuscripts, more than a hundred of which still survive. Complete Latin editions were published in 1473, 1474–75, 1487, and 1539. Translations appeared in print in French (1493, 1538, and 1551), Dutch (1525), German (1473, 1479, 1543, and 1576), and Spanish (1494). Unpublished English translations appeared in the fifteenth and sixteenth centuries but contained only some of Boccaccio's 106 chapters (V. Brown xxi, 505–7).

26. The *Historia* mentions nothing about the verbal content of Schedel's entry on the popess, and R. W. notes only that Schedel (1440–1514) "useth the same Words as *Platina* doth." In *Pope Joane: A Dialogue* (1610), Alexander Cooke (1564–1632) cites the Nuremberg illustration and suggests that Schedel included it "to imprint the matter deeper into the reader's memory"; R. W. in turn echoes Cooke (*Historia* D4r; R. W. 15; Cooke, *Pope* 23). Schedel's *Nuremberg Chronicle* appeared in Latin and German editions in 1493 and in pirated editions again in 1497. Today eight hundred Latin and four hundred German copies of that first edition remain extant (Wilson, *Making* 42, 191). The Adrian Wilson (born in 1923) who has studied the *Nuremberg Chronicle* is a different scholar than the social historian Adrian Wilson (born in 1947) whom I cite in chapter 2.

27. Boureau treats one of these manuscripts, Bibliothèque Nationale, Paris, 226, as a translation of *De mulieribus claris;* however, that volume does not appear in Brigitte Buettner's list of fifteenth-century French manuscript translations of *De mulieribus claris,* and the Bibliothèque Nationale catalogs that manuscript as a translation of *De casibus* (Boureau, *Myth* 358 n. 83; Buettner 100–101). Translators appear to have added the *De mulieribus claris* chapter on Pope Joan to editions of *De casibus,* so that the popess, although absent from Boccaccio's original, appears, for example, in John Lydgate's *Fall of Princes* (Lydgate 3: 946–47).

28. Valla and Pecock reached their conclusions independently and presented them in *De falso credita et ementita Constantini donatione declamatio* and *The Repressor of Over Much Blaming of the Clergy,* respectively. Earlier in the fifteenth century,

Nicholas of Cusa challenged the authenticity of the "Donation" in his *De concordantia catholica* (1432–35). In 1443, Enea Silvio Piccolomini, later Pope Pius II, observed that the document's genuineness "was bewildering many minds" and recommended that a church council should settle the matter. After Cardinal Cesare Baronius, writing in his *Annales ecclesiastici* (1588–1607), conceded that the "Donation" was a forgery, Catholic attempts to defend its authenticity ended (Coleman 1–4; Zinkeisen 632; J. Levine 118).

29. One might be tempted to infer from this unconventional image of the popess that those responsible for the *Nuremberg Chronicle* held unconventional religious views. In fact, Raemond dismissed Schedel's account on just such grounds, asserting that Nuremberg was infected with Hussite heresy ("infectee de l'erreur des Hussites") (34). On the contrary, Schedel, who supplemented his personal copy of the *Chronicle* with additional leaves celebrating Mary Magdalene, St. Jerome, and the Blessed Virgin crowned Queen of Heaven, seems to have earned his characterization in the 1914 *Catholic Encyclopedia* as "thoughtful, conservative, and rigidly orthodox" (Wilson, *Making* 210–211; *Catholic* 13: 525). Further, Anton Koberger, the prominent Nuremberg printer who brought out Schedel's chronicle, also published Pope Boniface VIII's decretals, Thomas Aquinas's *Summa theologica,* and Jacopo da Voragine's collection of saints' lives *Legenda aurea.* The emperor Maximilian even sought him out to publish Latin and German editions of St. Bridget. However, when later approached to publish the works of Reformers such as Martin Luther and Philip Melanchthon, Koberger's firm declined (Wilson, *Making* 177–79).

30. As if investing such representations of the Virgin with apostolic authority, another *Nuremberg Chronicle* woodcut depicts St. Luke painting Mary crowned Queen of Heaven and cradling the infant Jesus (fol. CVIII).

31. Eamon Duffy has observed that every parish church in medieval England contained a very different image of Mary and Jesus, since the crucifix appearing across the chancel arch was "invariably flanked by the mourning figures of Mary and the Beloved Disciple" (*Stripping* 260). In fact, the Catholic Floyd answers Crashaw by citing, as a counterexample, paintings of "Christ as a *perfect Man,* redeeming the world vpon the Crosse" (150).

32. The devotion expressed by pious Catholics such as Schedel, who hailed Mary as divine and compared her to Diana, lent credibility to that charge (Wilson, *Making* 211). So too did the fears, expressed by medieval writers such as Peter Abelard, that visual depictions of the Virgin would imply an equivalence between Mary and pagan goddesses. "Can our lady wish to be represented in a sculpted image as Vesta did?" Abelard asked. Further documenting those fears, Michael Camille cites a narrative that appears in the eighth-century *Libri Carolini* and concerns an artist whose pictures of Venus and the Virgin Mary were indistinguishable (Camille 220–22).

Chapter 1

1. Martinus sets the duration of Joan's pontificate at "two years, seven months and four days" (Pardoe and Pardoe 11). Ockham refers to the popess in *Opus nonagnta dierum* (Work of Ninety Days) (1332) and again in *Octo quaestiones de potestate pape* (Eight Questions on the Power of the Pope) (1340–42) (Boureau, *Myth* 154–55).

2. Instead, Hus's accusers charged him with "playing a prophet" by concluding that the popess's "monstrous" rule demonstrated the Church needed no earthly head, since Christ, "through His true disciples scattered over the circumference of the earth, would rule His Church better" (Petr 212).

3. Several factors seem to have contributed to the popularity of this legend concerning an English princess martyred with her companions at Cologne. The twelfth-century excavation of a Roman cemetery in Cologne unearthed what were thought to be relics of the eleven thousand martyred virgins. The mystic Elizabeth of Schönau (ca. 1129–65) reported that the virgins appeared to her in visions, revealing new details about their lives and martyrdom. Relics of the virgins were sent to medieval dignitaries such as the theologian Albertus Magnus (ca. 1206–80), Queen Isabella of England (1296–1358), and her son Edward III (1312–77) (Holladay 72–80). Jacopo de Voragine (ca. 1230–98) included Ursula's life in his influential hagiographic collection *Legenda aurea,* and the accomplished artists Hans Memling (ca. 1430–94) and Vittore Carpaccio (ca. 1450–1522) painted scenes from the legend.

4. Taking a step toward Blondel's later, more systematic skepticism, John Donne observed in passing in a 1626 sermon, "there are some passages in the Legend of Pope *Joan,* which I am not very apt to believe" (7: 153).

5. The Elizabethan *Homilie against Peril of Idolatrie* (1563–71) cites and paraphrases Gregory's letter to the iconoclastic Bishop Serenus of Marseilles, condemning the adoration of images but warning against the destruction of images that might teach believers what they should adore. The fifteenth-century dialogue *Dives and Pauper* echoes Gregory, arguing that images are "ordeynyd to been a tokene and a book to [th]e lewyd [illiterate] peple, [th]at [th]ey moun [may] redyn in imagerye and peynture [th]at clerkys redyn in boke" (*Dives* 82; Phillips 90).

6. Beginning in the sixteenth century, the Via San Giovanni in Laterano cut through the ruins of the Ludus magnus, eliminating the need to veer to one side near San Clemente (Boureau, *Myth* 90).

7. Boureau argues that even the Swedish jurist Lars Banck (Laurentius Gunnari Banck, 1611–62), who presents himself as an eyewitness to the 1644 investiture of Innocent X, reveals in his report that he did not actually see the rite of verification. Banck insists that he has seen the pierced chair "with my own eyes on several occasions" without explicitly claiming that he has seen the ritual itself. For the ritual, he cites the authority of historians such as Platina and Sabellico (Marco Antonio Coccio, 1436–1506). Moreover, he confuses the pierced marble chairs (kept in the chapel of San Silvestro) with the stercory chair or "seat of mire" (kept at the portico of the Basilica of St. John Lateran) and anachronistically describes that chair's use in a humiliation ritual that Pius IV had eliminated decades earlier in 1560 (Boureau, *Myth* 27, 48).

8. The *OED* traces the term *hickscorner* to the title character in an allegorical drama by Wynkyn de Worde. Since that character notably scoffs at religion, the term came to mean a scoffer in general (*OED* 7: 206).

9. In *Institutes of the Christian Religion,* Calvin insists, "there is no true administration of the sacrament without the word," and, critiquing the Catholic Mass, complains, "Nothing more preposterous, therefore, can be done with respect to the

[Lord's] supper, than to convert it into a mute action, as we have seen done under the tyranny of the pope . . . as if it had nothing to do with the people, to whom the mystery ought principally to be explained" (2: 697–98). "What helpeth it," Tyndale asks, "that the priest when he goeth to mass disguiseth himself with a great part of the passion of Christ, and playeth out the rest under silence, with signs and proffers, with nodding, becking and mowing, as it were jackanapes. . . . It bringeth them [the laity] into such superstition, that they think they have done abundantly enough for God . . . if they be present once in a day at such mumming" (qtd. in Barish 160). Here, Tyndale's term *mumming* suggests both inarticulate sound—"mum's the word"—and theatricality—"mummers."

10. The *OED* cites, for example, John Harington's 1591 observation regarding allegorical poetry: "The ancient Poets haue . . . wrapped in their writings divers . . . meanings which they call the senses or mysteries thereof" (*OED* 10: 173).

11. Concerning the materials from which history might be written, Barbara J. Shapiro has identified in early modern England a "cultural preference," reinforced by "ancient models and legal practice," for eyewitness reports or at least documentary evidence (such as treaties, charters, or public records) (47). Those attempting to prove the truth of the popess legend could offer neither.

12. As Rosemary Pardoe and Darroll Pardoe have noted, early modern Protestant polemicists seem to have been unaware that an early manuscript of the *Liber pontificalis* does mention Joan (13–14).

13. Marianus died before the dates that Jean de Mailly and Etienne de Bourbon assign to Joan's pontificate, namely 1099 and 1100. As Pardoe and Pardoe have explained, shortly after Jean and Etienne composed their popess narratives, their texts slipped into obscurity and were not rediscovered until the nineteenth century. After Jacob von Maerlant repeated details from Jean's and Etienne's popess narratives in his *Spiegel Historiael* (ca. 1283), the two French Dominicans' versions of the legend ceased to play a part in Pope Joan discourse. Consequently, 855, the date Martinus Polonus advanced, became widely accepted as the year when Joan's alleged pontificate began (Pardoe and Pardoe 21).

14. Concerning "printed copies" of Marianus's text, Boureau refers to a 1583 edition prepared by Johann Pistorius and based on a fourteenth-century manuscript that includes a reference to Joan; for their part, Cooke's interlocutors discuss "the printed copy, which Heroldus set out," presumably the 1559 *Chronicon* edited by Johannes Herold (Boureau, *Myth* 116; Cooke, *Pope* 42).

15. Cooke implies that these scriptural expurgations occurred at least as early as the fourth and fifth centuries by asserting that one appeared "in a manuscript of" Eusebius of Caesarea (ca. 263–ca. 339) and that St. Jerome (ca. 347–ca. 420) reported the other (*Pope* 42–43).

16. After suggesting that the Bible is self-evidently the word of God, Calvin goes on to articulate what he characterizes as "rational proofs" that confirm scripture's authenticity (*Institutes* 1: 93, 104).

17. Concerning the relationship between the phallus and castration, Gary Taylor takes issue with psychoanalytical discussions that equate castration with the loss of the penis or phallus, since, he insists, castration entails removing the testicles, not the

penis, and, when performed on postpubescent subjects, does not prevent penile erection. He even cites eighteenth- and nineteenth-century reports that women found castrati to be especially attractive sexual partners since they offered an opportunity for pleasure without impregnation (52, 93).

18. As an example of this archaic use of *control,* the *OED* cites the following clause from Sir John Davies's 1612 *A Discoverie of the True Causes Why Ireland Was Neuer Entirely Subdued:* "Which by mine owne search and view of the Records Here I can justly control" (*OED* 3: 851–52).

19. Recognizing perhaps that the Roman Church had survived the invalid election of several antipopes, Cooke contends that in Joan's case the harm was not undone, since there is no record that succeeding popes declared invalid the ordinations that Joan performed (*Pope* 108).

Chapter 2

1. The diary entry implies that this play was performed more than once. Although Henslowe marks another play on the same page as "ne[w]," he assigns no such designation to "poope Jone." The recorded performance brought in fifteen shillings, comparable to the receipts generated that same month by a performance of "fryer bacon" (fifteen shillings and six pence) and double those generated by "the lockinglasse," Robert Greene and Thomas Lodge's *A Looking Glass for London* (seven shillings). Both Walter W. Greg and Alfred W. Pollard exclude the play from their catalogs of early English publications.

2. In a similar vein, Annabel Patterson has cited several notable instances of theatrical noncensorship extending into the Stuart era (*Censorship* 17; *Shakespeare* 78).

3. Perhaps with the original German tract in mind, Rosemary Pardoe and Darroll Pardoe assign the initials "H. S." to *Historia de Donne Famose* (69). The English translation that I have examined, however, includes the initials "T. B." instead.

4. In his bibliography, Boureau cites a third Elizabethan publication: a 1598 text reportedly printed in London under the title *Assertio contra Jesuitas, papam Johannem VIII fuisse mulierem* and attributed with some uncertainty to William Perkins. Boureau does not mention this text in the body of his study, and I have found no other record of it (*Myth* 324). The Stuart Pope Joan publications are as follows: Alexander Cooke, *Pope Joan* (London, 1610); Alexander Cooke, *A Dialogue betweene a Protestant and a Papist, Manifestly Proving That a Woman, Called Joan, Was Pope of Rome* (London, 1625); John Mayo [I. M.], *The Anatomie of Pope Joane* (London, 1624); Humphrey Shuttleworth, *A Present for a Papist: or The Life and Death of Pope Joan* (London, 1675); Elkanah Settle, *The Female Prelate* (London, 1680, 1689); *The History of Pope Joan and the Whores of Rome* (London, 1687); and R. W., *Pope Joan: or, An account collected out of the Romish authors . . .* (London, 1689).

5. Without specifically citing the Pope Joan legend, Persons's fellow Catholic exile William Allen implicitly compared Elizabeth to a popess, as he rebuked those who foolishly chose "to abandon the Pope's authority and to invest a woman (which is against nature) in his supremacy and spiritual charge over all her subjects' souls" (*True* 213). In his 1625 *Dialogue betweene a Protestant and a Papist,* Alexander Cooke closely paraphrases Persons's charge in order to rebut it (106). Although Raemond's

comparison between Pope Joan and Queen Elizabeth first appeared in the 1594 edition of his *Erreur populaire de la papesse Jane,* my quotations and paraphrases refer to a 1595 edition.

6. That same month, the Privy Council was expressing concern about the political and religious content of plays and complaining about impertinent players who "take upon themselves" without "judgement or decorum" to "handle in their plaies certen matters of Divinytie and of State unfitt to be suffred" (E. K. Chambers 4: 306).

7. It would be tempting to speculate about how the Pope Joan play served the interests of the company's patron; however, the notorious inscrutability of Ferdinando Stanley, Lord Strange and later fifth Earl of Derby (1559–94), makes such speculations especially uncertain. The 1594 tract *A Conference about the Next Succession . . . ,* for example, observes that Stanley's religion "is held to be . . . doubtful, so as some do thinke him to be of all three religions [Catholic, Protestant, and Puritan]; and some others of none" (Allen, *Conference* 253). The company's performance of "poope Jone" (as well as other anti-Catholic plays in the Rose Theatre repertoire) implies that the religious loyalties of its patron were decidedly Protestant. Projecting orthodoxy likely enhanced the security of Stanley, whose mother was a practicing Catholic; whose father had been accused of treating recusants far too leniently; and who, as a potential claimant to the English throne (great-grandson of Henry VIII's younger sister Mary), attracted government scrutiny (Honigmann 119; Manley 274). Of course, projecting Protestant sympathies also likely alienated Catholics at home and abroad who had offered to back Stanley's claim as a successor to Queen Elizabeth. However, far from encouraging such Catholic support, in 1593 Stanley turned one recusant plotter, Richard Hesketh, over to government officials for questioning that resulted in Hesketh's execution. At the same time, the company's performance of "poope Jone" may have allowed Stanley subtly to discomfit the queen, who more than a decade earlier had banished his mother (Elizabeth I's second cousin) from the royal court and briefly held her under house arrest, allegedly for hiring a conjurer to divine the length of the queen's reign (Manley 273–76, 279–80). Some confusion surrounds the authorship of *A Conference about the Next Succession . . . ,* which has been attributed to both William Allen and Robert Persons (Parsons); in this study I have followed the Allen attribution that appears in the 1594 edition available through Early English Books Online. I am indebted to John Klause for pointing out the possible significance of Stanley's patronage of the company that performed "poope Jone."

8. G. B. Harrison has cited a 1603 report that links James I's doubts concerning the royal touch to his uneasiness concerning the royal unction (*Jacobean* 30–31).

9. Deborah Willis quotes (but does not cite page numbers for) William Clowes, *A Right Fruitfull and Approved Treatise for the Aritficiall Cure of that Malady called in Latin, Struma, and in English, the Evill Cured by Kynges and Queenes of England* (London, 1602).

10. An account of the 1572–73 Maundy at Greenwich describes "holy water basons . . . being brought into the Hall"; presumably, these were the same "basons of

warm water and sweet flowers" that, according to this account, the queen used when bathing the women's feet (Nichols 1: 345–47).

11. Keith Thomas notes that in 1643 a Royalist addressing Charles I characterized the royal touch as a "supernatural means of cure which is inherent in your sacred majesty" (195). In contrast, Stuart Clark observes, the Jesuit scholar Martin del Rio (1551–1608) suggested the cures Elizabeth achieved through the royal touch might derive "from either a tacit or an express pact with the demon" (665). As note 9, this chapter, indicates, the title of William Clowes's treatise characterizes the royal touch as an "artificaill cure."

12. Leah S. Marcus has detailed parallels between Elizabeth and another demonized popish woman: Joan of Arc as portrayed in William Shakespeare's *I Henry VI*. Concerning Elizabeth and La Pucelle, Marcus argues, "What must remain unspoken is spoken of somebody else who is either an alter ego of the queen or her debased image" (66–83).

13. Robert W. Scribner has suggested that the Pope Joan legend may have inspired the equation between the Whore of Babylon and the papacy. Scribner has also identified a mid-sixteenth-century German illustration that expounds that equation (171).

14. The *National Union Catalogue* indicates that the dating for the two editions of *A Concent of Scripture* is somewhat uncertain and appears variously as 1588 or 1589 and 1590 or 1591 (6: 24–26).

15. One could argue that Rogers's Whore resembles the amazonian Elizabeth wearing armor and a helmet in Thomas Cecil's oft-reproduced engraving *Truth Presents the Queen with a Lance*. However, since Cecil produced his portrait more than thirty years after Rogers's illustration, it does not bear upon the refashioning of illustrations in Broughton's text. Winfried Schleiner simply assigns it to the reign of Charles I (Frye 111; C. Levin, *"Heart"* 124; Schleiner 168–74).

16. Carole Levin cites Broughton's narrative but does not address his identity or career as a Protestant divine. Although, of course, more than one man named Hugh Broughton might have been alive in 1600, details in Knyght's report match what we know about the biblical scholar. Broughton the scholar left England for Germany in 1592 and evidently remained there until 1603, as if, like Knyght's interlocutor, he had resolved "not to come into the realm" until Elizabeth's death. Broughton the scholar may well have felt the professional frustration that Knyght's interlocutor expressed, since in 1595 he had unsuccessfully sought appointment to the archbishopric of Tomon (Tuam), and since during the 1590s he had failed to interest political and ecclesiastical authorities in his plan for a new translation of the Bible. Further, Knyght's Broughton affirmed that "the King of Scots is the right successor to the crown" and boasted that James had promised him "the best office in the Exchequer." In a similar vein, the biblical scholar wrote to King James in 1604 asserting that he had suffered "many years danger for publishing of your right and Gods truth" and requesting (in the third person) "a pension fitt for his age, studye, and travells past." Clearly, then, the man Knyghts met in Frankfurt in 1600 was the embittered author of *A Concent of Scripture*. An engraving of the Whore appeared not only in the two

editions of *A Concent of Scripture* but also in Broughton's *Moses' Sights on Mt. Sinai* (1592) (*Calendar of State Papers* 23–24; *Dictionary* 2: 1368–69; McEachern 54; C. Levin, *"Heart"* 76, 83, 84; C. Levin, " 'We' " 90).

17. Foxe's account was so sensational that it prompted the Catholic polemicist Thomas Harding to respond, primarily by castigating the conduct of the infant's mother. In turn, Foxe answered Harding in later editions of the *Acts and Monuments* (8: 227–41). Carole Levin discusses this case in detail in " 'Murder Not Then the Fruit within my Womb': Shakespeare's Joan, Foxe's Guernsey Martyr, and Women Pleading Pregnancy in Early Modern English History and Culture."

18. Focusing not on Dekker's two antagonistic queens but rather on their subjects and attendants, Jean E. Howard has noted that the play's "implicit debate structure," as well as Dekker's use of antitheatrical rhetoric, destabilizes "the binary oppositions upon which the play's whole polemical strategy rests" (53–56).

19. Valerie Traub has observed that the Anglican practice of "churching" women after childbirth reveals that "women's sexual and reproductive bodies" appeared to pose "a psychic threat to the social order" (464). For instances of Elizabeth's subjects referring to her as their mother, see C. Levin, *"Heart"* 87.

20. The linen sails also suggest extravagance and most likely allude to Spanish Catholic oppression of the textile-producing Netherlands. Dekker addresses the plight of Dutch Protestants earlier in the play, as Titania receives an embassy entreating aid for a neighboring nation:

> With whom our Faries enterchange commerce,
> And by negotiation growne so like vs,
> That halfe of them are Fayries. (2.1.234–36)

Shakespeare's Prince Hal plays upon the conventional association between Holland and linen, as he tells Poins: "But that the tennis-court keeper knows better than I, for it is a low ebb of linen with thee when thou keepest not racket there; as thou hast not a great while, because the rest of thy low countries have made a shift to eat up thy holland" (*2H4* 2.2.18–22).

21. The metaphor of unnatural births befits an assault orchestrated by the Whore of Babylon, since early seventeenth-century medicine attributed congenital deformities to parents' immoderate sexual activities, particularly intercourse during menstruation (Niccoli 15–20). Similarly, the conflation of feminine imagery of childbirth with masculine imagery of a cutting, possibly phallic assault on "soft" shores befits the Empresse, whom Florimell condemns as "that mannish woman-devil" (5.2.4).

22. Dekker announces his debt to Spenser by borrowing the names Florimell and Paridel from *The Faerie Queene*. Of course, the oft-noted appropriation of symbols or images from the cult of the Virgin Mary constitutes a further Elizabethan effort to fill an absence created by the break with Rome (C. Levin, *"Heart"* 26–30).

23. Such wariness also finds expression in the evolution of the term *gossip,* which derives from "god-sib" or "god-sibling," denoting someone who witnesses a birth in order to sponsor the child at baptism. As if expressing suspicions concerning the sorts of conversations that might take place within the private, feminine domain of

the lying-in chamber, *gossip* eventually acquired its more familiar, derogatory meaning as a name for idle or malicious talk (*OED* 6: 699–700). Judith Haber has clarified the context within *The Woman's Advocate* of the reference to women's plans for petty treason (143).

24. Susan E. Krantz quotes Francis Osborne's report about Puritan prophesies concerning Prince Henry (273–76).

25. Leeds Barroll has questioned how much the performance of (presumably William Shakespeare's) *Richard II* on the eve of the Essex rebellion troubled the queen's government. Nonetheless, Barroll has found abundant evidence that, even before the Essex rebellion, royal officials investigated the representation of Richard II's deposition in John Hayward's prose history *The First Part of the Life and Raigne of King Henrie the IIII;* they even imprisoned the author in the Tower. Royal concern over this historical precedent, then, seems clear (444–52).

26. In a similar vein, in 1596 and 1598 other Englishmen asserted that it "would never be a merrye worlde till her majestie was dead or killed" or wished "that Her Majesty had been cut off twenty years since, so that some noble prince might have reigned in her stead." Carole Levin has found these quotations among court records for Essex and Kent ("'We'" 78, 90). Early English texts recounting the popess legend, such as John Lydgate's *Fall of Princes,* drew upon Boccaccio (Lydgate 3: 946).

Chapter 3

1. Although the title page attributes this text to Alan Cope, an English Catholic exile residing in Rome as a canon of St. Peter's, scholars have speculated that a colophon at the end of the book cryptically identifies the true author. The letters printed there, "A. H. L. N. H. E. V. E. A. C," reportedly signify "Auctor hujus libri, Nicholas Harpsfield, eum vero edidit Alanus Copus" (The author of this book is Nicholas Harpsfield, Alan Cope truly published it) (*Dictionary* 4: 1090, 8: 1314). Sixteenth-century writers responded to the dialogues as Cope's work, and my own analysis does not rely upon the biographies of Cope or Harpsfield. Consequently, here I follow the attribution on the title page.

2. Alain Boureau somewhat oversimplifies Huguccio's position by claiming the jurist concluded "that because a hermaphrodite's sexual nature is more hot than cold, his ordination must be accepted" (*Myth* 42).

3. Concerning hermaphrodites' legal status, Jones and Stallybrass note that in seventeenth-century France they enjoyed significant rights: to testify in court; to inherit and bequeath property; and even to marry, provided that their dress and demeanor matched their physiologically dominant gender and that they did not attempt to change their gender identification. In England, Sir Edward Coke contended that a hermaphrodite could exercise property rights "according to that sexe which prevaileth" (Jones and Stallybrass 91, 105).

4. In the sixteenth century Golding's adjective *lither* could convey several different meanings appropriate to this context: "wicked," "impotent," or "sluggish" (*OED* 8: 1031).

5. Drawing upon internal evidence and an eighteenth-century report of a (now lost) manuscript in the poet's own hand, Philip J. Finkelpearl lays out the case for

Beaumont's authorship in an 1969 essay in *Notes and Queries*.

6. Oddly, the serpent simile seems to complicate or even reverse the roles of predator and prey, since the eagle appears to have initiated the encounter by first grasping the serpent. Ovid's Latin clarifies the sequence of events: "ut serpens, quam regia sustinet ales / sublimemque rapit" (as a serpent, whom the kingly flyer seizes and holds aloft) (362–63). Golding's use of "gripes" and "griping" to describe first Salmacis and then the eagle who represents Hermaphroditus further confuses the relation between pursuer and pursued. Perhaps, then, Beaumont's revision builds upon some ambivalence already implicit in his source.

7. Mark Eccles contends that Beaumont wrote this parody of a lecture on orthography, etymology, and syntax as part of the Christmas festivities at the Inner Temple sometime between 1601 and 1605 (Eccles 402–3).

8. Keach notes the contrast between Ovid's "semivir" and Beaumont's "halfe a virgine" and proposes that the Elizabethan poet may have wished to suggest a double meaning for "virgin" referring to both effeminization and "the incomplete spoiling of Hermaphroditus's sexual purity in a union which begins in a lustful embrace but which makes genuine sexual consummation impossible" (217). Keach does not clarify, however, whether Beaumont implies that Hermaphroditus is aware of the double meaning invested in his lines.

9. By 1600 *to infect* had acquired the meaning "to corrupt" (as well as the more neutral "to imbue") and had been used in that sense by George Gascoigne, Thomas Lodge, and Ben Jonson (*OED* 7: 920–21). Concerning *blest,* Keach encourages a cautious, possibly ironic reading of the adjective and points to its use to describe Astræa's sanctioning of Jove's promise to make Salmacis a (literal) star if she gratifies his erotic desires (234, 248). True, Jove's pursuit of Salmacis falls short of consummation; however, the descriptions of the nymph's beauty and her capacity to attract the amorous attention of Jove, Apollo, and Bacchus suggest that such a consummation might aptly be described as a "blessing." Further, a more illuminating use of the term occurs just fifteen lines before the account of the fountain's enchanting. As Beaumont reports the joining of nymph and youth in response to Salmacis's prayer, he employs the adjective *blest* quite straightforwardly to characterize a woman's overpowering ability to arouse reciprocal, invigorating desire:

> She felt his youthful blood in every vaine;
> And he felt hers warme his cold brest againe.
> And ever since was womans love so blest,
> That it will draw bloud from the strongest brest. (903–6)

Perhaps, contrary to Keach's view, Beaumont characterizes the pair as "lucklesse" not because their bodies eventually merge but rather because their desires never do.

10. His family's recusancy, which subjected them to investigation and prosecution, may have fostered Beaumont's skepticism regarding the justice meted out by England's Astræa. Beaumont's mother and uncles were charged with aiding the Jesuit priest and martyr Edmund Campion; even his father was rumored to have supported seminary priests before becoming a justice of the assize. Just a year before

this poem's publication, Beaumont's uncle Gervase Pierrepoint was imprisoned in the Tower and tortured due to his recusant activities. The absence of baptismal records for Beaumont and his brothers in the parish register of Belton has prompted speculation regarding secret Catholic baptisms. After the accession of James I, the recusancy of Beaumont's brother John resulted in the forfeiture of much of the family estate at Grace Dieu. Since Thomas Pestell, a Leicestershire clergyman and Beaumont's contemporary, credited the poet with "confound[ing]" Jesuit debaters, Francis Beaumont himself seems to have been free of overt Catholic loyalties (Finkelpearl, *Court and Country* 11–12).

11. To cite a few prominent examples, upon learning of a romance between Sir Walter Raleigh and Elizabeth Throckmorton, an attendant in the royal privy chamber, the queen ordered the two lovers imprisoned (in separate confinement) in the Tower and, even after their release, banished them from the court (*Dictionary* 16: 634–35). Elizabeth also initially opposed the engagement of Sir Philip Sidney and Frances Walsingham (*Dictionary* 18: 225). Later, when she learned that Sidney's widow had married Robert Devereux, the Earl of Essex, Elizabeth became incensed, ordered the seizure of Essex's papers, and required that the earl's wife live "very retired in her mother's house" (*Dictionary* 5: 877). The secret marriage between Robert Dudley, Earl of Leicester, and Lettice Knollys also enraged the queen, prompting her to confine him for some time in Greenwich (*Dictionary* 6: 117). Drawing upon a report by the queen's godson John Harrington, Louis Adrian Montrose relates an episode in which Elizabeth, provoked by one female attendants' reckless expression of eagerness for marriage, appealed to the young woman's father for authority to determine whether and whom she should wed and then bluntly informed the maid that she intended to use that authority to see that she never married at all. Montrose also reports that the queen used the Court of Wards to exercise the traditional paternal authority to give or withhold marriageable daughters ("Shaping" 49).

12. In a tract composed in 1587, circulated in manuscript in 1589, and published in 1598, Peter Wentworth warns Elizabeth of the catastrophes that might follow if she should die without naming an heir. In the chaos and civil strife that will erupt, he worries that "your noble person [body] shall lie upon the earth unburied, as a doleful spectacle to the world." Moreover, she will "leave behind" her "such a name of infamy throughout the whole world" and will experience "ten thousand Hells in your soul, even such bitter vexation of soul and heart for the periling of the Church of God and of your natural country" (qtd. in Neale 2: 255).

13. "Tree trunk" as the meaning of *stock* seems to befit the lovers' "long embracement" better than other definitions such as "stump" or "block."

14. The popular, early modern belief that hares could change back and forth between male and female, which Sir Thomas Browne addresses in *Pseudodoxia Epidemica* (1646), seems at odds with Paré's assertion. Although, like Paré, Paolo Zacchia focuses on nature's tendency to perfect, in a passing remark in a 1653 treatise, he does provide an anatomical explanation for the impossibility of changing from male to female. Assuming, as Galenic medicine did, that female sexual organs were simply inverted and internal versions of the male organs, he contends that the male body

affords no internal space for the inverted penis of an emasculated man (Laqueur 18, 141–42).

15. Jones and Stallybrass have noted Paré's puzzling use of the term *degenerate* (84).

16. Mark Breitenberg (150–74), Thomas Laqueur (122–28), Laura Levine, and Patricia Parker, among others, offer valuable explorations of that fear.

17. Although Buck cites mostly seventeenth-century documents concerning breeching, sixteenth-century paintings of children, as well as Leontes's nostalgic recollection of himself as an "unbreeched" boy in William Shakespeare's *The Winter's Tale* (1.2.155; ca. 1609–11), suggest that these customs did not differ markedly in the two centuries. Since a prince's childhood was doubtless atypical in many ways, the records of royal households offer limited insight into social history. Nonetheless, at the beginning of the seventeenth century the future Louis XIII of France seems to have recognized and enjoyed the gender indeterminacy afforded an unbreeched boy, reportedly dressing at times as a shepherdess, peasant girl, or chambermaid (Hunt 181). Clearly, class as well as gender crossings are at work here. Although Buck notes some differences in the clothing of unbreeched boys and girls (a front-fastening doublet for the boys and a back-fastening bodice for the girls), the diaries and letters cited in her study confirm that breeching marked a transition to masculine status (Buck 81, 149–51).

18. I am indebted to Cora Fox for drawing my attention to this passage in Knox.

19. If, as Marjorie Garber and Frances E. Dolan have suggested, early modern culture frequently represented priests as particularly womanish, a cleric like Jewel would have had a further reason to fear effeminacy (Dolan, *Whores* 85–86; Garber 218).

Chapter 4

1. Rosemary Pardoe and Darroll Pardoe suggest that the earliest reference to Joan's necromantic writing appeared in *De legibus connubialibus,* written by the French scholar André Tiraqueau (1488–1558) and first published in 1513 (Pardoe and Pardoe 34). However, in their notes they cite a posthumous edition of Tiraqueau's *Opera omnia* (1597). Similarly, Alain Boureau, who includes Tiraqueau in his bibliography, cites a posthumous 1561 edition of *De legibus* (*Myth* 320). The copy of the 1597 *Opera omnia* that I have consulted includes, near the discussion of Joan, a reference to Bale's *Scriptorvm illustrium* as a source for information on Eleanor of Aquitaine (pt. 2, 188). Since editions of Tiraqueau's *De legibus* were published after Bale's 1548 *Summarium* and 1557 *Scriptorvm illustrium,* in 1560, 1561, 1566, 1568, and 1588, Tiraqueau's report may have been added after 1513 and may in fact be indebted to Bale's. In any case, Bale was the first English writer to report Joan's necromantic writing and, I argue, did so for reasons rooted in English religious and political controversies.

2. At the opening of his biographical sketch of Alexander VI (Rodrigo Borgia, ca. 1431–1503), Bale reports that he was "in league with the devil to obtaine the Papacye" (*Pageant* 170r). Similarly, Barnabe Barnes's play *The Devil's Charter: A Tragedy Containing the Life and Death of Pope Alexander the Sixth* (1607) opens with a dumb

show that depicts Borgia conjuring a demon in order to gain the papal triple tiara. Concerning Sylvester II (Gerbert of Aurillac, died 1003), see my discussion of parallels between Sylvester and Joan later in this chapter.

3. Prefaced by a papal bull endorsing the witch-hunting work of its authors, the *Malleus maleficarum* appeared in fourteen editions between 1487 and 1520 and at least sixteen editions between 1574 and 1669 (Summers viii).

4. Available records documenting witchcraft prosecutions do not necessarily support these claims that far more women practiced witchcraft than men. Robin Briggs reports that of thirteen hundred witchcraft cases appealed to the Parlement of Paris during the sixteenth and seventeenth centuries, a little more than half involved male defendants. Briggs cites other studies reporting that men accounted for 25 percent of witchcraft prosecutions in southwest Germany. In Iceland, men made up 90 percent of those accused of witchcraft, 60 percent in Estonia, nearly 50 percent in Finland, but only 10 percent in Hungary (Briggs 441–42). Admittedly, these statistics suggest wide regional variations and may reflect differences in how authorities approached men and women suspected of witchcraft. Nonetheless, they seem to cast doubt on James I's ratio of twenty to one.

5. Oddly, this emphasis on Joan's verbal facility appears in the *Scriptorvm illustrium* entry that focuses on her career as pope rather than in a second entry that addresses her necromantic writing.

6. Peter Happé's annotation identifies the *Officina* (1520) of Joannes Ravisius Textor (ca. 1480–1524) as the source of Bale's list of transvestite men, which also includes the Assyrian emperor Sardanapalus and Euclides of Megara, a student of Socrates mentioned in Aulus Gellius's second-century C.E. *Attic Nights* (*Gellius* 2: 118–19; Happé 163).

7. According to Donald N. Mager, Bale associates Sodomismus with a range of disapproved sexual practices including adultery, promiscuity, onanism, bestiality, and pederasty (150).

8. Scholars have been unable to confirm reports that the first edition of the *Enchiridion* was published in Rome in 1523 and that other editions were published in Parma, Ancona, and Frankfurt before 1660. Based on internal evidence in a letter purportedly from Charlemagne to Pope Leo, reproduced at the opening of the *Enchiridion,* Arthur Edward Waite questions the legend surrounding this text's origins (54–55).

9. E. M. Butler and John Davis report a 1629 publication date, and the 1670 text remains extant. Some confusion between Honorius, the putative author of a fourteenth-century conjuring book entitled *Liber juratus, or The Sworne Booke of Honorius,* and Honorius III may have inspired the authors or editors of the *The Great Grimoire of Pope Honorius* to attribute it to the learned medieval pope (E. M. Butler 89, Davis xxi; Waite 31–33).

10. Alain Boureau cites, for example, a thirteenth-century account of a woman who healed a cyst by touching the affected area with a book on the life and miracles of St. Francis while praying, "By the truth that is inscribed on this page, O St. Francis, deliver me now from this wound by your holy merits" ("Franciscan" 16).

11. Richard Kieckhefer has examined the "fusion of devotion, contemplation and

the occult" in the *Liber juratus, or The Sworne Booke of Honorius,* and another tract, the *Liber visionum,* by the monk John of Morigny (250–65). Similarly, Diane Purkiss has noted "survivals" of Catholic prayers and rituals in the practices reported in sixteenth- and seventeenth-century witchcraft prosecutions (154–59).

12. As the well-documented case of Mary Glover demonstrates, witchcraft and possession intersected when exorcists proposed to relieve the victims of alleged bewitching (Paul 104–5). Complaining that "these popish exorcists doo manie times forget" the rules intended to distinguish them from "old women" whose charms include "unknowne names" and "vaine characters," Reginald Scot declares "I SEE no difference betweene" popish exorcists and other conjurors "but that the papists doo it without shame openlie, the other doo it in hugger mugger secretlie" (252, 256). In *Henry VI, Part 2* Shakespeare's "wizard" Roger Bolingbroke appears to equate conjuring and exorcism as he asks whether the Duchess of Gloucester "will behold and hear our exorcisms" (1.4.4, 16).

13. In a valuable footnote, Joanna Levin has forcefully countered the persistent conviction that James I brought his witch-hunting zeal with him to England. By 1597, the king had revoked all of the Scottish special commissions for the trial of witchcraft, and fewer witchcraft persecutions occurred in England during James's reign than during Elizabeth's (Larner 19). Rather than fanning the 1612 Lancashire witch panic, during a later journey to that county James interrogated a boy who had accused fifteen women of witchcraft, declared him an impostor, and spared the lives of nine remaining defendants who had not yet suffered execution. Indeed, as Levin has observed, the king's ability to expose impostures won him the praise of English prosecutors (J. Levin 54).

14. Bellarmine does not refer to Bale by name; instead he cites the "Magdeburgians," thus alluding to Matthias Illyricus Flacius's 1565 *Magdeburg Centuries,* a text that, as I have noted, repeats Bale's report concerning Joan's necromantic writing and, in fact, specifies Bale as the source (qtd. in Morris 162). The two other details that Bellarmine contends the "Magdeburgians" have added to Martinus Polonus's account—Joan's ties to Fulda and the report that her father was an English priest— appear in both Bale's account and Flacius's. I am not aware of any writer who introduced those details before Bale. Michael Walpole quotes Bellarmine's discussion of the popess legend at length in his 1613 *A Treatise of Antichrist* (418–19).

Chapter 5

1. In their correspondence, members of the Verney family estimated the 1679 crowd variously at twenty thousand and one hundred thousand (Verney 4: 260). A 1679 broadside estimates "not . . . fewer than two hundred thousand spectators" (*Solemn Mock Procession of the POPE . . . 1679*). John Miller and Tim Harris cite the two hundred thousand figure (Miller 183–87; Harris 101–6).

2. Although the 1687 title page of *The History of Pope Joan and The Whores of Rome* designates it as a second edition, I have not been able to locate an extant copy of any first edition.

3. The lost 1592 Pope Joan play mentioned in Philip Henslowe's diary and addressed in chapter 2 may have made the transition to fiction nearly a century ear-

lier (Henslowe 22). As I also note in chapter 2, John Mayo indulged in a different form of open fictionalizing in the 1591 *Popes Parliament,* as he imagined how the sixteenth-century Pope Gregory XIV would react to the popess legend.

4. Although Jean de Mailly and Etienne de Bourbon assign Joan's pontificate to the years 1099–1101, even this later date precedes the development of the rosary devotion. Popular legend attributed the devotion's invention to St. Dominic de Guzman (1170–1210), and more skeptical historians have contended that in its modern form the rosary originated even later, in the fifteenth century (Wilkins 30–31, 37–40).

5. In his *Memoirs of Great Britain,* John Dalrymple presents relevant correspondence from the French ambassador Paul de Barillon to Louis XIV (2: 193–98, 255–64).

6. Semiramis inherited the Assyrian throne from her husband, King Ninus, whom, according to some accounts, she arrested and deposed. Perhaps with such rumors in mind, her military enemy, the Indian King Stabrobates, reportedly denounced her as a strumpet. The androgyny that Semiramis manifested when she donned a unisex costume to lead troops into battle apparently appeals to Joanna, who praises the "Kingly Soul" that this queen's "borrowed manhood wore" (*Female* 5; Diodorus of Sicily 2: 4–20).

7. Although he does not suggest that Donna Olympia's image appeared in the 1673 pope burning, the anonymous author of *The Burning of the Whore of Babylon* mentions this notorious matron and, to characterize her influence, asserts that "the *Pope* formerly kept one" of the keys to Purgatory "and *Donna Olympia* the other" (*Burning* 3).

8. *The Scarlet Beast Stripped Naked* (1680) claims that Cellier has "become a more terrible Champion in the behalf of Roman Catholicks, than . . . all the Sturdy Pillars of their Church, since their Female Prelate dropped her untimely Bastard in Procession to *Angello*" (2, 8 [misnumbered], 4). Anne Barbeau Gardiner has also noted the Pope Joan comparison in a 1680 London broadside entitled *To the Praise of Mrs. Cellier the Popish Midwife; on her incomparable book* (Introduction xi, n. 5).

9. Cellier likely amplified her reputation as an intractable virago when she resisted English men's attempts to secure governance over midwifery (A. Gardiner, "Elizabeth Cellier" 24–26, 30–31).

10. George Saville, Marquis of Halifax (1633–95), for example, observed that though Charles I "gave the most glorious evidence that ever man did of his being a Protestant, yet by the more than ordinary influence the Queen was thought to have over him, and it so happening that the greater part of his anger was directed against the Puritans, . . . men disposed to suspect" could incite rebellion by credibly charging that the king favored papists (78).

11. John Kenyon reports that between 1662 and 1678 the vast majority of the 290 weddings performed in the queen's chapel united English couples—a detail that gains significance in light of the way that intermarriage helped to deplete the Catholic peerage. The Earl of Danby (Thomas Osborne, 1631–1712), for example, the lord chancellor who investigated the Popish Plot, was the Protestant child of such a mixed union (Kenyon 28–31).

12. Hostility toward earlier Catholic queens also buttressed distrust of Restora-

tion consorts. In *The Character of a Popish Successour,* for example, Settle reminds his readers of the Marian persecutions and warns that Protestant martyrs might once again suffer at the stake in Smithfield (3, 7). In a similar vein, another polemicist characterizes the popish heir presumptive James as a rather androgynous "Queen Mary in breeches" (Miller 75).

13. Ros Ballaster cites several texts that illustrate the conventional association between Catholicism and female rebellion at the time of the Popish Plot.

14. John Kenyon's estimate that Catholics constituted 4.7 percent of the population in Restoration England may be rather high. Based on the Compton Census of 1676, Anne Barbeau Gardiner has recently estimated that only 1 percent of the English were Catholic (*Ancient* 131).

15. In *The Popish Successour* Settle suggests that if a papist king should reign in England, his conflicting loyalties to the English Constitution (as well as his Coronation Oath) and to the Catholic Church would foster extraordinary duplicity: "he shall come to the *Protestant* Church, and be a Member of their communion, notwithstanding at the same time his face belies his Heart, and in his Soul he is a *Romanist*. Nay, he shall vary his Disguises as often as an *Algerine* [Algerian] his Colours, and change his Flag to conceal the Pyrate" (5).

16. Unlike many earlier chroniclers, Bale and Foxe specify that a monk from the Benedictine abbey at Fulda accompanied Joan to Athens at the beginning of her transvestite career (Foxe 2:7; Bale, *Pageant* 56r).

17. Saxony's analogy to Antony and Caesar seems misplaced. The duke decries a private rape (as well as murder) rather than a political assassination and reviles a lecherous tyrant rather than self-proclaimed tyrannicides. Surely, then, the more apt comparison is the one that Joanna and the duchess herself have already drawn to Tarquin and Lucrece. As this muddled analogy suggests, Saxony's rhetorical appeal to the masses in this scene does not match the sensational standards of Settle's November 17 pageant. Susan Owen contends that in order to counter the Tory charge that Whigs were rabble-rousing, plays such as *The Female Prelate* depict Catholic mobs run amok. Here, however, the antipapist hero Saxony aspires to rabble-rousing but fails in the attempt (Settle, *Female* 34, 53; Owen 150–51).

18. Writers also posited Germanic roots for English resistance to, as Settle puts it, "the first Foundations of *Popery, (viz. Arbitrary Power)."* Through some imaginative historiography, Coke and Francis Whyte, for example, projected English restraints on royal authority back into the Saxon past and saw the Magna Carta as a confirmation of pre-Norman liberties. For Settle, who in his November 17, 1680, pageant juxtaposed Protestantism and the Magna Carta (on Queen Elizabeth's shield), the younger duke may also represent a political ideal of limited monarchy (Miller 81, 169, 181; MacDougall 56–57, 62).

19. Young Saxony's courageous railing against Joanna—"he stands my Rage like a *Corinthian / Colossus,*" she marvels—first arouses her lust for him; in turn, Angeline's stoic defiance of papal power and her exhortations to Saxony to preserve his "Princely Honour" arouse analogous desires in Joanna's henchman Lorenzo (Settle, *Female* 20, 28). In a similar vein, in *The Popish Successour,* Settle argues that Catholicism would bend all a popish monarch's excellence to En-

gland's ruin: "Nay, grant him to be the most absolute Master of all the *Cardinal Vertues,* there's not one of them that shall not be a particular instrument for our Destruction" (4).

20. According to Ovid, the lovely Trojan boy Ganymede serves as Jove's cup-bearer "invitaque . . . Iunone" (against the will of Juno) (*Metamorphoses* 10: 161). On Ganymede as Jove's homosexual lover, see James M. Saslow's *Ganymede in the Renaissance: Homosexuality in Art and Society.*

21. Settle's stage directions at the opening of act 4 denote that, immediately after her first tryst with Saxony, Joanna appears "in her Womans Habit." The playwright never specifies such a costume change for Amiran, who evidently remains, as the list of dramatis personae reports, "in the Habit of a Page" (38).

22. According to the humors theory, psychological traits like women's weaker intellect resulted from physiological differences, specifically women's colder metabolisms. If, as Ian Maclean reports, early modern physiologists generally agreed that "the hottest male is hotter than the hottest female," the intellect of the most gifted woman should not surpass that of the most gifted man. Maclean characterizes Aristotle's *Historia animalium* (9.1) as a locus classicus for this approach to gender difference (34, 42–43).

23. I cite this parallel process, since in Garber's own illustrative example, David Henry Hwang's *M. Butterfly,* the transvestite, who proves unexpected for the protagonist, seems less "supplementary" and more central than Garber's general remarks might suggest (17).

24. Here, I specify "principled" dissenters, since in private moments Joanna expresses skepticism at least as profound as what the play's accused heretics espouse. She wonders, for example,

. . . if there's any thing in the airy Dreams
of Faith, Religion, Piety,
Things which poor little unambitious Church-men
Have nothing else to do but to believe in,
Whilst we the great and glorious Mitred heads
Have other work and other game to mind. (47)

25. Concern over atheism and impiety exercised clerics and politicians in late seventeenth-century England. At their 1674–75 conference, Anglican bishops cited atheism as a major threat to the Church. Not surprisingly, then, in January 1667 (new style) and again eleven years later, Parliament drafted bills to impose fines or imprisonment for "atheism, profaneness," or "blasphemy" on "any person who denies or derides the essence, persons, or attributes of God . . . or the omnipotency, wisdom, justice, mercy, goodness, or providence of God." Eventually, Parliament passed a 1697 law against "blasphemy and profaneness," which (without mentioning atheism explicitly) made it a crime to "deny any one of the persons in the holy Trinity to be God, or . . . assert or maintain there are more Gods than one, or . . . deny the Christian religion to be true, or the holy Scriptures . . . to be of divine authority" (qtd. in Berman 35, 48–49; Spurr 248).

Afterword

1. Rosemary Pardoe and Darroll Pardoe mention the modern scenes in passing and with little attention to the problematic reediting that Ullman and Briley deplore: "Originally the intention was to intersperse the historical scenes with modern ones, featuring a young woman suffering from the delusion that she is Pope Joan. The extra material was shot but not used in the final film, and it is difficult to say whether it would have made any improvement in practice" (86).

2. If Briley has in mind Bill Lenny, who is credited as the film's editor, then his dismissive characterization of the editor's "previous experience"—limited, it would seem, to a single, low-status genre—is inaccurate. More than a dozen years earlier Lenny had edited the Hammer films *The Abominable Snowman* (1957), *Dracula* (1958), and *The Camp on Blood Island* (1958), but his more recent work included a diverse set of commercial projects: the space-race comedy *The Mouse on the Moon* (1963), the James Bond parody *Casino Royale* (1967), and the historical epic *Cromwell* (1970). I have gained insight into the editing and reediting of this film from letters Briley wrote to me on August 6 and September 5, 1996.

3. The copy of the film held in the Library of Congress, like the one graciously provided to me by the assistant producer Daniel Unger (presumably a relative of the producer Kurt Unger), lacks the modern scenes.

4. Critics who reported viewing a version of the film that interspersed modern and medieval materials still denounced its "ineptitude," contending that "it fails absolutely and on every level" (Schickel 18; Greenspun 29).

5. In Briley's fictionalized version of Carolingian history, after Lothair I, grandson of Charlemagne, succeeds his father, Louis I, as Emperor of the West, Lothair's younger son Charles rebels, sparking a civil war. To secure Saxon support in that conflict, Lothair authorizes a return to "Wotan worship" that prompts a brutal Saxon raid on Joan's nunnery. Later, when Lothair's elder son Louis II is named emperor, Charles again threatens to challenge the succession by force.

6. The answer implied in Briley's screenplay may, in fact, be no. The modern Joan is seduced by a handsome politician (the counterpart of the medieval Louis II), leading to her concealed pregnancy and, in turn, perhaps, to her descent into delusions.

Works Cited

Adam of Usk. *Chronicon Adae de Usk A.D. 1377–1404*. Trans. and ed. Edward Maunde Thompson. London: John Murray, 1876.

Agrippa, Henricus Cornelius. *Declamation on the Nobility and Preeminence of the Female Sex*. Trans. and ed. Albert Rabill Jr. Chicago: U of Chicago P, 1996.

Allen, William. *An Admonition to the Nobility, 1588*. English Recusant Literature 1558–1640. Vol. 74. Ed. D. M. Rogers. Menston: Scolar P, 1971.

———. *A Conference about the Next Succession to the Crowne of Ingland*. London: R. Doleman, 1594.

———. *A True, Sincere, and Modest Defense of English Catholics*. Ed. Richard M. Kingdon. Folger Documents of Tudor and Stuart Civilization. Ithaca: Cornell UP, 1965.

Anson, John. "The Female Transvestite in Early Monasticism: The Origin and Development of a Motif." *Viator: Medieval and Renaissance Studies* 5 (1974): 1–32.

Ardolino, Frank R. "'In Saint *Iagoes* Parke': Iago as Catholic Machiavel in Dekker's *The Whore of Babylon*." *Names* 30.1 (1982): 1–4.

Aristophanes. *Aristophanes*. Ed. and trans. Jeffrey Henderson. 4 vols. Loeb Classical Library. Cambridge: Harvard UP, 1998.

Ausonius, Decimus Magnus. *Works*. Trans. Hugh G. Evelyn White. 2 vols. London: W. Heinemann; New York, G. P. Putnam, 1919–21.

Axton, Marie. *The Queen's Two Bodies: Drama and the Elizabethan Succession*. London: Royal Historical Society, 1977.

Axton, Richard, "Spenser's 'Faire Hermaphrodite': Rewriting *The Faerie Queene*." *A Day Festival: Essays on the Music, Poetry and History of Scotland and England and Poems Previously Unpublished*. Ed. Alisoun Gardiner-Medwin and Janet Hadley Williams. Aberdeen: Aberdeen UP, 1990. 35–47.

Bacon, Francis. *Works*. Ed. James Spedding, Robert Leslie Ellis, and Douglas Denon Heath. 15 vols. Cambridge: Cambridge UP, 1863.

Bainton, Roland H. "The Bible in the Reformation." *The Cambridge History of the Bible: The West from the Reformation to the Present Day*. Ed. S. L. Greenslade. Cambridge: Cambridge UP, 1963. 1–37.

Bale, John. *A Comedy Concernynge Three Lawes of Nature. The Complete Plays*. Vol. 2. Woodbridge, Suffolk, and Dover, N.H.: Boydell and Brewer, 1986.

————. "Conclusion." *The Glass of the Sinful Soul.* By Elizabeth Tudor. *Elizabeth's Glass.* Ed. Marc Shell. Lincoln: U of Nebraska P, 1993.

————, ed. *The Examinations of Anne Askew.* Ed. Elaine V. Beilin. New York: Oxford UP, 1996.

————. *Laboryouse Journey & Serche of Johan Leylande.* London: 1549. Amsterdam: Theatrum Orbis Terrarum, 1975.

————. *The Pageant of Popes.* Trans. John Studley. London, 1574.

————. *Scriptorvm illustrium Maioris Brytannie quam nunc Angliam & Scotiam uocant: Catalogus . . .* 2 vols. Basileae, 1557–59.

Ballaster, Ros. "Fiction Feigning Femininity: False Counts and Pageant Kings in Aphra Behn's Popish Plot Writings." *Aphra Behn Studies.* Ed. Janet Todd. Cambridge: Cambridge UP, 1996. 50–65.

Barasch, Moshe. *Giotto and the Language of Gesture.* Cambridge: Cambridge UP, 1987.

Barish, Jonas. *The Antitheatrical Prejudice.* Berkeley: U of California P, 1981.

Barroll, Leeds. "A New History for Shakespeare and His Time." *Shakespeare Quarterly* 39.4 (1988): 441–64.

Bayle, Pierre. *The Dictionary Historical and Critical.* 2nd ed. 5 vols. London: J. J. and P. Knapton, 1734–38.

Beaumont, Francis. *Salmacis and Hermaphroditus. Elizabethan Narrative Verse.* Ed. Nigel Alexander. Cambridge: Harvard UP, 1968. 168–91.

Becon, Thomas. *A Comparison between the Lord's Supper and the Pope's Mass. Prayers and Other Pieces.* Ed. John Ayre. Cambridge: Cambridge UP, 1844.

Bell, Thomas. *The Survey of Popery.* London: Valentine Sims, 1596.

Benson. George. *A Sermon Preached at Paules Crosse the Seaventh of May M. DC. IX.* London: H. L[ownes] for Richard Moore, 1609.

Berman, David. *A History of Atheism in Britain: From Hobbes to Russell.* London and New York: Croom Helm, 1988.

Berry, Philippa. *Of Chastity and Power: Elizabethan Literature and the Unmarried Queen.* London: Routledge, 1989.

Bloch, Marc. *The Royal Touch: Sacred Monarchy and Scrofula in England and France.* Trans. J. E. Anderson. London: Routledge and Kegan Paul; Montreal: McGill-Queen's UP, 1973.

Boccaccio, Giovanni. *Concerning Famous Women.* Trans. Guido A. Guarino. London: George Allen and Unwin, 1964.

————. *Des cleres et nobles femmes.* Manuscript 12420, Bibliothèque Nationale, Paris.

————. *Ioannis Boccatii de certaldo insigne opvs De claris mulieribus . . .* Berne, 1539.

————. *Libri Johan[n]is Baccaccij de Certaldo De mulieribus claris.* Ulm, 1473.

Book of Common Prayer 1559: The Elizabethan Prayer Book. Ed. John E. Booty. Washington, D.C.: Folger Shakespeare Library, 1976.

Booty, J. W. Introduction. *An Apology of the Church of England.* By John Jewel. Charlottesville: U of Virginia P, 1963. ix–xlvii.

Boughton, Lynne C. "From Pious Legend to Feminist Fantasy: Distinguishing

Hagiographical License from Apostolic Practice in the *Acts of Paul/Acts of Thecla*." *Journal of Religion* 71.3 (1991): 362–83.

Boureau, Alain. "Franciscan Piety and Voracity: Uses and Stratagems in the Hagiographic Pamphlet." *The Culture of Print: Power and the Uses of Print in Early Modern Europe*. Ed. Roger Chartier. Trans. Lydia G. Cochrane. Princeton: Princeton UP, 1989. 15–58.

———. *The Myth of Pope Joan*. Trans. Lydia G. Cochrane. Chicago: U of Chicago P, 2001.

Breitenberg, Mark. *Anxious Masculinity in Early Modern England*. Cambridge: Cambridge UP, 1996.

Briggs, Robin. "Women as Victims? Witches, Judges and the Community." *French History* 5.4 (1991): 438–50.

Briley, John, screenwriter. *Pope Joan*. Dir. Michael Anderson. Perf. Liv Ullmann, Maximillian Schell, Franco Nero, Trevor Howard, Olivia de Havilland. Columbia, 1972.

Broughton, Hugh. *A Concent of Scripture*. London, [1588].

———. *A Concent of Scripture*. London, [1590].

Brown, F. C. *Elkanah Settle: His Life and Works*. Chicago: U of Chicago P, 1910.

Brown, Peter Robert Lamont. *The Body and Society: Men, Women, and Sexual Renunciation in Early Christianity*. New York: Columbia UP, 1988.

Brown, Virginia. Introduction and Bibliography. *Famous Women*. By Giovanni Boccaccio. Ed. and trans. Virginia Brown. Cambridge: Harvard UP, 2001. i–xxiii, 505–10.

Browne, Sir Thomas. *Works*. Ed. Geoffrey Keynes. 4 vols. Chicago: U of Chicago P, 1964.

Buck, Anne. *Clothes and the Child: A Handbook of Children's Dress in England 1500–1900*. New York: Holmes and Meier, 1996.

Buettner, Brigitte. *Boccaccio's* Des cleres et nobles femmes: *Systems of Signification in an Illuminated Manuscript*. Seattle: U of Washington P, 1996.

Burning of the Whore of Babylon, As It Was Acted, with Great Applause . . . London, 1673.

Burton, Robert. *The Anatomy of Melancholy*. Ed. Holbrook Jackson. New York: Vintage, 1977.

Butler, E. M. *Ritual Magic*. Cambridge: Cambridge UP, 1949.

Butler, Judith. *Gender Trouble: Feminism and the Subversion of Identity*. New York: Routledge, 1999.

Bynum, Caroline Walker. *Jesus as Mother: Studies in the Spirituality of the High Middle Ages*. Berkeley: U of California P, 1982.

Calendar of State Papers, Domestic Series, of the Reign of Elizabeth, 1601–1603. Ed. Mary Anne Everett Green. London: Stationery Office, 1870. Nendeln, Liechtenstein: Kraus Reprint, 1967.

Calvin, John. *The Commentaries of M. John Calvin upon the Actes of the Apostles*. Trans. Christopher Fetherstone. London: G. Bishop, 1585.

———. *Institutes of the Christian Religion*. Trans. John Allen. 2 vols. Philadelphia: Presbyterian Board of Christian Education, 1936.

Camden, William. *Annales.* London: Beniamin Fisher, 1625.

Camille, Michael. *The Gothic Idol: Ideology and Image-Making in Medieval Art.* Cambridge: Cambridge UP, 1989.

Catholic Encyclopedia: An International Work of Reference of the Constitution, Doctrine, and History of the Catholic Church. Ed. Charles G. Herbermann, Edward A. Pace, Conde B. Pallen, Thomas J. Shahan, and John J. Wynne. 15 vols. New York: Robert Appleton, 1907–12.

Cavanagh, Sheila. "The Bad Seed: Princess Elizabeth and the Seymour Incident." *Dissing Elizabeth: Negative Representations of Gloriana.* Ed. Julia M. Walker. Durham: Duke UP, 1998. 9–29.

Certaine Sermons or Homilies Appointed to be Read in Churches in the Time of Queen Elizabeth (1547–1571): A Facsimile Reproduction of the Edition of 1623. Ed. Mary Ellen Rickey and Thomas B. Stroup. Gainesville, Fla.: Scholars' Facsimiles and Reprints, 1968.

Certayne Sermons or Homilies, Appointed by the Kynges Majestie . . . London, 1547.

Chambers, E. K. *The Elizabethan Stage.* 4 vols. Oxford: Clarendon P, 1965.

Chambers, Robert. Epistle Dedicatorie. *Miracles Lately Wrought by the Intercession of the Glorious Virgin Marie at Montaigu near unto Siche[m] in Brabant.* By Philippe Numan. Trans. Robert Chambers. Antwerp, 1606.

Cheney, Donald. "Spenser's Hermaphrodite and the 1590 *Faerie Queene.*" *PMLA* 87.2 (1972): 192–200.

Cheney, Patrick. "Jonson's *The New Inn* and Plato's Myth of the Hermaphrodite." *Renaissance Drama* 14 (1983): 173–94.

Clark, Stuart. *Thinking with Demons: The Idea of Witchcraft in Early Modern Europe.* Oxford: Clarendon P; New York: Oxford UP, 1997.

Coleman, Christopher. Introduction. *The Treatise of Lorenzo Valla on the Donation of Constantine.* By Lorenzo Valla. Trans. Christopher Coleman. New Haven: Yale UP, 1922.

Cooke, Alexander. *The Abatement of Popish Brags, Pretending Scripture to Be Theirs.* London: William Jones, 1625.

———. *Johanna papissa toti orbi manifestata . . .* Oppenheim, 1619.

———. *Pope Joan: A Dialogue between a Protestant and Papist. The Harleian Miscellany.* 12 vols. London: Robert Dutton, 1809. 4: 9–109.

Cope, Alan. *Dialogi sex contra summi pontificatus, monasticae vitae, sanctorum, sacrarum imaginum oppugnatores, et pseudomartyres . . .* Antwerp, 1573.

Crashaw, William. *The Iesvites Gospel by W. Crashawe, B. of Diuinity and Preacher at the Temple.* London, 1610.

———. *Romish Forgeries and Falsifications.* London: Matthew Lownes, 1606.

———. *The Sermon Preached at the Cross, Feb. 14, 1607.* New York: Johnson Reprint Corp., 1972.

Crawford, Patricia. *Women and Religion in England 1500–1720.* Christianity and Society in the Modern World. London: Routledge, 1993.

Cressy, David. *Bonfires and Bells: National Memory and the Protestant Calendar in Elizabethan and Stuart England.* London: Weidenfeld and Nicolson, 1989.

Cross, Claire. *The Royal Supremacy in the Elizabethan Church.* London: Allen and Unwin; New York: Barnes and Noble, 1969.

Dalrymple, John. *Memoirs of Great Britain and Ireland from the Dissolution of the Last Parliament of Charles II until the Sea Battle off La Hogue.* 2 vols. 2nd ed. London: W. Strahan and T. Cadell, 1773.

Daston, Lorraine, and Katherine Park, "The Hermaphrodite and the Orders of Nature." *GLQ: A Journal of Lesbian and Gay Studies* 1.4 (1995): 419–38.

Davis, John. Bibliographic Prolegomenon. *The Great Grimoire of Pope Honorius.* Trans. Kineta Ch'ien and Matthew Sullivan. Seattle: Trident, 1999.

Dekker, Thomas. *The Dramatic Works.* Ed. Fredson Bowers. 4 vols. Cambridge: Cambridge UP, 1955.

———. *The Plague Pamphlets.* Ed. F. P. Wilson. Oxford: Clarendon P, 1923.

Delcourt, Marie. *Hermaphrodite: Myths and Rites of the Bisexual Figure in Classical Antiquity.* Trans. Jennifer Nicholson. London: Studio Books, 1961.

Dickinson, J. C. *The Shrine of Our Lady of Walsingham.* Cambridge: Cambridge UP, 1956.

Dictionary of National Biography: From the Earliest Times to 1900. Ed. Sir Leslie Stephen and Sir Sidney Lee. Oxford: Oxford UP, 1959–60.

Diehl, Huston. *Staging Reform, Reforming the Stage: Protestantism and Popular Theater in Early Modern England.* Ithaca: Cornell UP, 1997.

Diodorus of Sicily. *The Library of History.* Trans. C. H. Oldfather. 10 vols. London: William Heinemann; Cambridge: Harvard UP, 1946.

Dives and Pauper. Ed. Priscilla Heath Barnum. London: Oxford UP, 1976.

Dolan, Frances E. *Dangerous Familiars: Representations of Domestic Crime in England 1500–1700.* Ithaca: Cornell UP, 1994.

———, ed. *The Taming of the Shrew: Texts and Contexts.* Boston and New York: St. Martin's, 1996.

———. *Whores of Babylon: Catholicism, Gender, and Seventeenth-Century Print Culture.* Ithaca: Cornell UP, 1999.

Donne, John. *Sermons.* Ed. Evelyn M. Simpson and George R. Potter. 10 vols. Berkeley: U of California P, 1953.

D'Onofrio, Cesare. *La papessa Giovanna: Roma e papato tra storia e leggenda.* Roma: Romana Societa Editrice, 1979.

Dreger, Alice Domurat. *Hermaphrodites and the Medical Invention of Sex.* Cambridge: Harvard UP, 1998.

DuBruck, Edelgard E. "Pope Joan: Another Look upon Martin LeFranc's *Papesse Jeanne* (c. 1440) and Dietrich Schernberg's Play *Frau Jutta* (1480)." *Fifteenth-Century Studies* 26 (2001): 75–85.

Duffy, Eamon. *Saints and Sinners: A History of the Popes.* New Haven: Yale UP, 1997.

———. *The Stripping of the Altars: Traditional Religion in England, c. 1400–c. 1580.* New Haven: Yale UP, 1992.

Eccles, Mark. "Francis Beaumont's *Grammar Lecture.*" *Review of English Studies* 10 (1940): 402–14.

Eliade, Mircea. *The Two and the One.* Trans. J. M. Cohen. Chicago: U of Chicago P, 1979.

Ellington, Donna Spivey. *From Sacred Body to Angelic Soul: Understanding Mary in Late Medieval and Early Modern Europe.* Washington, D.C.: Catholic U of America P, 2001.

Embree, Dan. Introduction. *The Chronicles of Rome: An Edition of the Middle English* Chronicle of Popes and Emperors *and* Lollard Chronicle. Ed. Dan Embree. Rochester: Boydell, 1999.

Empedocles. *The Fragments.* Trans. William Ellery Leonard. LaSalle, Ill.: Open Court, 1908.

Epp, Garret P. J. "'Into a Womannys Lykenes': Bale's Personification of Idolatry, A Response to Alan Stewart." *Medieval English Theatre* 18 (1996): 63–73.

Finkelpearl, Philip J. "The Authorship of 'Salmacis and Hermaphroditus.'" *Notes and Queries* 16 (1969): 367–68.

———. *Court and Country Politics in the Plays of Beaumont and Fletcher.* Princeton: Princeton UP, 1990.

Fletcher, Anthony. *Gender, Sex, and Subordination in England 1500–1800.* New Haven: Yale UP, 1995.

Floyd, John. *Purgatories Triumph over Hell (1613).* English Recusant Literature 1558–1640. Vol. 143. Ed. D. M. Rogers. Menston: Scolar P, 1973.

Foresti, Jacopo Filippo, of Bergamo. *De claris mulieribus.* Ferrera: Laurentius de Rubeis, de Valentia, 1497.

Foucault, Michel. *The History of Sexuality, Volume I: An Introduction.* Trans. Robert Hurley. New York: Vintage, 1980.

Foxe, John. *The Acts and Monuments.* Ed. George Townsend. 8 vols. New York: AMS, 1965.

Frantzen, Allen J. "When Women Aren't Enough." *Speculum: A Journal of Medieval Studies* 68.2 (1993): 445–71.

Frye, Susan. "The Myth of Elizabeth at Tilbury." *Sixteenth-Century Journal* 33.1 (1992): 95–114.

Fulke, William. *Two Treatises Written against the Papistes* . . . London: Thomas Vautrollier, 1577.

Garber, Marjorie. *Vested Interests: Cross-Dressing and Cultural Anxiety.* London: Routledge, 1992; New York: Harper Perennial, 1993.

Gardiner, Anne Barbeau. *Ancient Faith and Modern Freedom in John Dryden's the Hind and the Panther.* Washington, D.C.: Catholic UP, 1998.

———. "Elizabeth Cellier in 1688 on Envious Doctors and Heroic Midwives Ancient and Modern." *Eighteenth-Century Life* ns. 14.1 (1990): 24–54.

———. Introduction. *Malice Defeated and The Matchless Rogue.* By Elizabeth Cellier. Augustan Reprint Society, nos. 249–50. Los Angeles: William William Andrews Clark Memorial Library, 1988. iii–xiv.

Gardiner, Stephen. *The Letters.* Ed. James Arthur Muller. Westport, Conn.: Greenwood P, 1933.

Gasper, Julia. *The Dragon and the Dove: The Plays of Thomas Dekker.* Oxford: Clarendon P, 1990.

Gellius, Aulus. *The Attic Nights.* Trans. John C. Rolfe. 3 vols. Loeb Classical Library. London: W. Heinemann; New York: Putnam, 1927.

Golding, Arthur. *Shakespeare's Ovid, Being Arthur Golding's Translation of the* Metamorphoses. Ed. W. H. D. Rouse. Carbondale: Southern Illinois UP, 1961.

Graef, Hilda C. *Mary: A History of Doctrine and Devotion.* 2 vols. New York: Sheed and Ward, 1964.

Greenblatt, Stephen. *Shakespearean Negotiations: The Circulation of Social Energy in Renaissance England.* Berkeley: U of California P, 1988.

———. "Shakespeare Bewitched." *Shakespeare and Cultural Traditions.* Ed. Tetsuo Kishi, Roger Pringle, and Stanley Wells. Newark: U of Delaware P, 1994. 17–42.

Greenspun, Roger. "In and Out of the Middle Ages with *Pope Joan.*" Rev. of *Pope Joan,* dir. Michael Anderson. *New York Times* August 17, 1972: 29.

Greg, W. W. *A Bibliography of the English Printed Drama to the Restoration.* 4 vols. London: Oxford UP, 1939–59.

———. *A List of English Plays Written before 1643 and Printed before 1700.* New York: Haskell House, 1969.

Haber, Judith. "'My Body Bestow upon My Women': The Space of the Feminine in *The Duchess of Malfi.*" *Renaissance Drama* ns. 28 (1997): 133–59.

Haliczer, Stephen. *Sexuality in the Confessional: A Sacrament Profaned.* Oxford: Oxford UP, 1996.

Hall, James. *Illustrated Dictionary of Symbols in Eastern and Western Art.* New York: Icon Editions, 1994.

Halpern, Richard. *The Poetics of Primitive Accumulation: English Renaissance Culture and the Genealogy of Capital.* Ithaca: Cornell UP, 1991.

Happé, Peter, ed. Notes and Glossary. *The Complete Plays.* Vol. 2. By John Bale. Woodbridge, Suffolk, and Dover, N.H.: Boydell and Brewer, 1986.

Harding, Thomas. *A Confutation of a Booke Intituled* An Apologie of the Chvrch of England. Ed. D. M. Rogers. English Recusant Literature 1558–1640, Vol. 310. New York: Scolar P, 1976.

Harris, Tim. *London Crowds in the Reign of Charles II: Propaganda and Politics from the Restoration until the Exclusion Crisis.* Cambridge: Cambridge UP, 1987.

Harrison, G. B. *A Jacobean Journal.* London: Routledge, 1941.

———. *A Second Jacobean Journal: Being a Record of Those Things Most Talked of during the Years 1607 to 1610.* Ann Arbor: U of Michigan P, 1958.

Harsnett, Samuel. *A Declaration of Egregious Popish Impostures . . .* London: James Roberts, 1603.

Hay, Denys. *The Italian Renaissance in Its Historical Background.* Cambridge: Cambridge UP, 1961.

Henslowe, Philip. *The Diary.* Ed. J. Payne Collier. London: Shakespeare Society, 1845.

Higden, Ranulph. *Polychronicon Ranulph Higden Monachi Cestrensis: Together with the English Translations of John Trevisa and of an Unknown Writer of the Fifteenth Century.* Ed. Joseph Rawson Lumby. 9 vols. London: Longman, 1876.

Hildersam, Arthur. *CVIII Lectvres upon the Fovrth of Iohn: Preached at Ashby-Delazouch in Leicester-shire.* London: George Miller for Edward Brewster, 1632.

Hill, Bridget. "A Refuge from Men: The Idea of a Protestant Nunnery." *Past and Present* 117 (1987): 107–30.

Hill, Christopher. *The Century of Revolution 1603–1714.* New York: Norton, 1980.

Historia de Donne Famose, or The Romaine Iubile which Happened in the Yeare 855. London, 1599.

The History of Pope Joan and the Whores of Rome. 2nd ed. London, 1687.

Holladay, Joan A. "Relics, Reliquaries, and Religious Women: Visualizing the Holy Virgins of Cologne." *Studies in Iconography* 18 (1997): 67–118.

Holy Bible Containing the Old and New Testament, King James Version. Nashville: Thomas Nelson, 1990.

Honigmann, E. A. J. *Shakespeare: The "Lost Years."* Totowa, N.J.: Barnes and Noble Books, 1985.

Hornblower, Simon, and Anthony Spawforth. *The Oxford Classical Dictionary.* Oxford: Oxford UP, 1996.

Hotchkiss, Valerie R. "Dietrich Schernberg's *Ein schön Spiel von Frau Jutten:* The Salvation of the Female Pope." *Canon and Canon Transgression in Medieval German Literature.* Ed. Albrecht Classen. Göppingen: Kümmeree Verlag, 1993. 195–207.

———. "The Legend of the Female Pope in the Reformation." *Acta Conventus Neo-Latini Hafniensis: Proceedings of the Eighth International Congress of Neo-Latin Studies.* Gen. Ed. Rhoda Schur. Ed. Ann Moss, Philip Dust, Paul Gerhard Schmidt, Jacques Chomarat, and Francesco Tateo. Binghamton, N.Y.: Medieval and Renaissance Texts and Studies, 1994. 495–505.

Hotchkiss, Valerie R., and David Price. *The Reformation of the Bible, the Bible of the Reformation.* New Haven and London: Yale UP, 1996.

Howard, Jean. *The Stage and Social Struggle in Early Modern England.* London and New York: Routledge, 1994.

Hult, David. *Self-Fulfilling Prophecies: Readership and Authority in the First* Roman de la Rose. Cambridge and New York: Cambridge UP, 1986.

Hunt, David. *Parents and Children in History: The Psychology of Family Life in Early Modern France.* New York: Basic Books, 1970.

Huss [Hus], John [Jan]. *The Church.* Trans. David S. Schaff. Westport, Conn.: Greenwood P, 1974.

James VI and I. *Minor Prose Works.* Ed. James Craigie. Edinburgh: Scottish Text Society, 1982.

Jenkins, J. S. "The Voice of the Castrato." *Lancet* 351.9119 (1998): 1877–78.

Jewel, John. *An Apology of the Church of England.* Ed. J. E. Booty. Trans. Lady Anne Bacon. Folger Shakespeare Library. Charlottesville: U of Virginia P, 1963.

———. *The Defence of the Apology of the Church of England.* Vol. 4 of *The Works.* Ed. John Ayre. 4 vols. Parker Society. Cambridge: Cambridge UP, 1850.

Jones, Ann Rosalind, and Peter Stallybrass. *Body Guards: the Cultural Politics of Gender Ambiguity.* Ed. Julia Epstein and Kristina Straub. New York: Routledge, 1991.

Jones, J. R. *The First Whigs: The Politics of the Exclusion Crisis 1678–1683.* London: Oxford UP, 1961.

Jordan, Constance. *Renaissance Feminism: Literary Texts and Political Models.* Ithaca and London: Cornell, UP, 1990.

Kaminsky, Howard. *A History of the Hussite Revolution.* Berkeley: U of California P, 1967.

Keach, William. *Elizabethan Erotic Narratives: Irony and Pathos in the Ovidian Poetry of Shakespeare, Marlowe, and Their Contemporaries.* New Brunswick: Rutgers UP, 1977.

Kelly, J. N. D. *The Oxford Dictionary of Popes.* Oxford: Oxford UP, 1986.

Kenyon, John. *The Popish Plot.* New York: St. Martin's, 1972.

Kieckhefer, Richard. "The Devil's Contemplatives: The *Liber juratus,* the *Liber visonum* and Christian Appropriation of Jewish Occultism." *Conjuring Spirits: Texts and Traditions of Medieval Ritual Magic.* Ed. Claire Fanger. Stroud, U.K.: Sutton Publishing; University Park: Pennsylvania State UP, 1998. 250–65.

King, John N. *English Reformation Literature: The Tudor Origins of the Protestant Tradition.* Princeton: Princeton UP, 1982.

———. "John Bale." *Sixteenth-Century British Nondramatic Writers.* Ed. David A. Richardson. *Dictionary of Literary Biography* 132. Detroit: Gale, 1993.

———. *Tudor Royal Iconography: Literature and Art in an Age of Religious Crisis.* Princeton: Princeton UP, 1989.

Knox, John. *The Political Writings.* Ed. Marvin A. Breslow. Washington, D.C.: Folger and Associated University Presses, 1985.

Kramer, Heinrich, and James Sprenger. *The Malleus maleficarum.* Trans. and Ed. Montague Summers. London: John Rodker, 1948; New York: Dover, 1971.

Krantz, Susan. "Thomas Dekker's Political Commentary in *The Whore of Babylon.*" *Studies in English Literature 1500–1900* 55.2 (1995): 271–91.

Krier, Theresa M. "Sappho's Apples: The Allusiveness of Blushes in Ovid and Beaumont." *Comparative Literature Studies* 25.1 (1988): 1–21.

Kristof, Jane. "Michelangelo as Nicodemus: The Florence Pieta." *Sixteenth-Century Journal* 20.2 (1989): 163–82.

Lacan, Jacques. *Feminine Sexuality.* Ed. Juliet Mitchell and Jacqueline Rose. Trans. Jacqueline Rose. New York: Norton, 1982.

Laqueur, Thomas. *Making Sex: Body and Gender from the Greeks to Freud.* Cambridge: Harvard UP, 1990.

Larner, Christina. *Witchcraft and Religion: The Politics of Popular Belief.* New York: Blackwell, 1984.

Lea, Henry Charles. *A History of the Inquisition of the Middle Ages.* 3 vols. New York: Russell and Russell, 1955.

Leti, Gregorio. *The Life of Donna Olimpia Maldachini . . .* Trans. Henry Compton. London, 1667.

Levin, Carole. *"The Heart and Stomach of a King": Elizabeth I and the Politics of Sex and Power.* Philadelphia: U of Pennsylvania P, 1994.

———. " 'Murder Not Then the Fruit within My Womb': Shakespeare's Joan, Foxe's Guernsey Martyr, and Women Pleading Pregnancy in Early Modern English History and Culture." *Quidditas: Journal of the Rocky Mountain Medieval and Renaissance Association* 20 (1999): 75–93.

———. " 'We Shall Never Have a Merry World while the Queene Lyveth': Gender,

Monarchy, and the Power of Seditious Words." *Dissing Elizabeth: Negative Representations of Gloriana.* Ed. Julia M. Walker. Durham: Duke UP, 1998. 77–95.

Levin, Joanna. "Lady Macbeth and the Daemonologie of Hysteria." *ELH* 69.1 (2002): 21–55.

Levine, Joseph M. "Reginald Pecock and Lorenzo Valla on the Donation of Constantine." *Studies in the Renaissance* 20 (1973): 118–43.

Levine, Laura. "Men in Women's Clothing: Anti-theatricality and Effeminization from 1579–1642." *Criticism* 28.2 (1986): 121–43.

Lewalski, Barbara Kiefer. *Writing Women in Jacobean England.* Cambridge: Harvard UP, 1993.

Liber juratus Honorii: A Critical Edition of the Latin Version of the Sworn Book of Honorius. Ed. Gosta Hedegard. Stockholm: Almqvist and Wiksell, 2002.

Lichtmann, Maria. "Marguerite Porete and Meister Eckhart: *The Mirror for Simple Souls* Mirrored." *Meister Eckhart and the Beguine Mystics: Hadewijch of Brabant, Mechthild of Magdeburg, and Marguerite Porete.* Ed. Bernard McGinn. New York: Continuum, 1994. 65–86.

Lipsius, Justus. *Miracles of the B. Virgin. Or, An Historical Account of the Original, and Stupendious Performances of the Image, Entituled, Our Blessed Lady of Halle.* London, 1688.

Londons Defiance to Rome. London, 1679.

Lusini, Vittorio. *Il duomo di Siena.* 2 vols. Siena: S. Bernardino, 1911–39.

Luther, Martin. *Luther's Works.* Ed. Jaroslav Pelikan and Helmut T. Lehman. 55 vols. St. Louis and Philadelphia: Concordia Fortress P, 1955–76.

Lydgate, John. *Lydgate's Fall of Princes.* Ed. Henry Bergen. 4 vols. London: Oxford UP, 1924–27.

Lynne, Walter. *The Beginning and Endynge of All Popery, or Popishe Kyngedome.* London: Iohn Herforde, 1548.

MacDougall, Hugh A. *Racial Myth in English History: Trojans, Teutons, and Anglo-Saxons.* Hanover and London: UP of New England, 1982.

Maclean, Ian. *The Renaissance Notion of Woman: A Study in the Fortunes of Scholasticism and Medical Science in European Intellectual Life.* Cambridge: Cambridge UP, 1980.

Mager, Donald N. "John Bale and Early Tudor Sodomy Discourse." *Queering the Renaissance.* Ed. Jonathan Goldberg. Durham: Duke UP, 1994. 141–61.

Malpezzi, Frances M. "Adam, Christ, and Mr. Tilman: God's Blest Hermaphrodites." *American Benedictine Review* 40.3 (1989): 250–60.

Manley, Lawrence. "From Strange's Men to Pembroke's Men: *2 Henry VI* and *The First Part of the Contention.*" *Shakespeare Quarterly* 54.3 (2003): 253–87.

Marcus, Leah S. *Puzzling Shakespeare: Local Reading and Its Discontents.* Berkeley: U of California P, 1988,

Marlowe, Christopher. *Doctor Faustus. Drama of the English Renaissance I; The Tudor Period.* Ed. Russell A. Fraser and Norman Rabkin. New York: Macmillan, 1976.

———. *The Jew of Malta. Drama of the English Renaissance I; The Tudor Period.* Ed. Russell A. Fraser and Norman Rabkin. New York: Macmillan, 1976.

Marvell, Andrew. *The Complete Works.* Ed. Alexander B. Grosart. 4 vols. London, 1872–75. New York: AMS, 1966.

Mathiesen, Robert. "A 13th-Century Ritual to Attain the Beatific Vision from the *Sworn Book* of Honorius of Thebes." *Conjuring Spirits: Texts and Traditions of Medieval Ritual Magic.* Ed. Claire Fanger. Stroud, U.K.: Sutton Publishing; University Park: Pennsylvania State UP, 1998. 143–62.

Mayo, John [I. M.]. *The Anatomie of Pope Joane.* London: Richard Field, 1624.

———. *The Popes Parliament . . . Whereunto Is Annexed an Anatomie of Pope Joane.* London: Richard Field, 1591.

McEachern, Claire. *The Poetics of English Nationhood, 1590–1612.* Cambridge and New York: Cambridge UP, 1996.

McGinn, Bernard. "Introduction: Meister Eckhart and the Beguines in the Context of Vernacular Theology." *Meister Eckhart and the Beguine Mystics: Hadewijch of Brabant, Mechthild of Magdeburg, and Marguerite Porete.* Ed. Bernard McGinn. New York: Continuum, 1994. 1–14.

"Medieval Sermon Stories." *Translations and Reprints from the Original Sources of European History* 2.4 (1971): 1–20.

Miller, John. *Popery and Politics in England 1660–1688.* Cambridge: Cambridge UP, 1973.

Minnis, A. J. *Medieval Theory of Authorship: Scholastic Literary Attitudes in the Later Middle Ages.* Philadelphia: U of Pennsylvania P, 1988.

Mitchell, Juliet. *Psychoanalysis and Feminism: Freud, Reich, Laing, and Women.* New York: Vintage, 1975.

Moakley, Gertrude. *The Tarot Cards Painted by Bonifacio Bembo for the Visconti-Sforza Family: An Iconographic and Historical Study.* New York: New York Public Library, 1966.

Montrose, Louis Adrian. "The Elizabethan Subject and the Spenserian Text." *Literary Theory / Renaissance Texts.* Ed. Patricia Parker, and David Quint. Baltimore: Johns Hopkins, 1986. 303–40.

———. "'Shaping Fantasies': Figurations of Gender and Power in Elizabethan Culture." *Representing the English Renaissance.* Ed. Stephen Greenblatt. Berkeley: U of California P, 1988. 31–64.

Moorman, John. *A History of the Franciscan Order from Its Origins to the Year 1517.* Oxford: Clarendon P, 1968.

More, Sir Thomas. *Dialogue Concerning Heresies.* Volume 6 of *The Yale Edition of the Complete Works of St. Thomas More.* Ed. Thomas M. C. Lawler, Germain Marc'Hadour, and Richard C. Marius. New Haven: Yale UP, 1981.

Morley, James Fredric. *John Foxe and His Book.* New York: Octagon, 1970.

Morris, Joan. *Pope John VIII: An English Woman: Alias Pope Joan.* London: Vrai, 1985.

Mowat, Barbara A. "Prospero's Book." *Shakespeare Quarterly* 52.1 (2001): 1–33.

National Union Catalog, Pre-1956 Imprints. 753 vols. London: Mansell, 1968.

Neale, J. E. *Elizabeth I and Her Parliaments: 1584–1601.* New York: St. Martin's, 1958.

New, Maria I., and Elizabeth S. Kitzinger, "Pope Joan: A Recognizable Syndrome." *Journal of Clinical Endrocrinology and Metabolism* 76.1 (1993): 3–13.

New, Maria I., and Robert C. Wilson. "Steroid Disorders in Children: Congenital Adrenal Hyperplasia and Apparent Mineralocorticoid Excess." *Proceedings of the National Academy of Sciences of the United States of America* 96.22 (1999): 12790–97.

Newman, Barbara. *From Virile Women to WomanChrist: Studies in Medieval Religion and Literature.* Middle Ages Series. Philadelphia: U of Pennsylvania P, 1995.

Niccoli, Ottavia. "'Menstruum Quasi Monstruum': Monstrous Births and Menstrual Taboo in the Sixteenth Century." *Sex and Gender in Historical Perspective.* Ed. Edward Muir and Guido Ruggiero. Trans. Margaret A. Gallucci, Mary M. Gallucci, and Carole C. Gallucci. Baltimore and London: Johns Hopkins UP, 1990. 1–25.

Nichols, John. *The Progresses and Public Processions of Queen Elizabeth.* 3 vols. New York: AMS, 1969.

O'Meara, Thomas A. *Mary in Protestant and Catholic Theology.* New York: Sheed and Ward, 1966.

Orgel, Stephen. *Impersonations: The Performance of Gender in Shakespeare's England.* Cambridge: Cambridge UP, 1996.

Ovid. *Metamorphoses.* Trans. Frank Justus Miller. Rev. G. P. Gould. 2nd ed. 2 vols. London: William Heinemann; Cambridge: Harvard UP, 1984.

Owen, Susan J. *Restoration Theatre and Crisis.* Oxford: Clarendon P; New York: Oxford UP, 1996.

Oxford English Dictionary. Ed. J. A. Simpson and E. S. C. Weiner. 20 vols. Oxford: Clarendon P; New York: Oxford UP, 1989.

Pardoe, Rosemary, and Darroll Pardoe. *The Female Pope: The Mystery of Pope Joan.* Wellingborough, England: Crucible, 1988.

Paré, Ambroise. *Des monstres et prodiges.* Ed. Jean Céard. Geneva: Librairie Droz, 1971.

———. *On Monsters and Marvels.* Trans. Janis L. Pallister. Chicago: U of Chicago P, 1982.

Parker, Patricia. "Gender Ideology, Gender Change: The Case of Marie Germain." *Critical Inquiry* 19.2 (1993): 337–64.

Patrides, C. A. *Premises and Motifs in Renaissance Thought and Literature.* Princeton: Princeton UP, 1982.

Patterson, Annabel. *Censorship and Interpretation: The Conditions of Writing and Reading in Early Modern England.* Madison: U of Wisconsin P, 1984.

———. *Shakespeare and the Popular Voice.* Oxford: Blackwell, 1989.

Paul, Henry Neill. *The Royal Play of Macbeth: When, Why, and How It was Written by Shakespeare.* New York: Macmillan, 1950.

Pavlovskis, Zoja. "The Life of St. Pelagia the Harlot: Hagiographic Adaptation of Pagan Romance." *Classical Folia: Studies in the Christian Perpetuation of the Classics* 30 (1976): 138–49.

Pelikan, Jaroslav. *Mary through the Centuries: Her Place in the History of Culture.* New Haven: Yale UP, 1996.

Perreiah, Alan. "Humanistic Critiques of Scholastic Dialectic." *Sixteenth-Century Journal* 13.3 (1982): 3–22.

Persons, Robert. *A Treatise of Three Conversions (Volume One) 1603.* London: Scolar P, 1976.

Petr z. Mladenovic. *John Hus at the Council of Constance.* Trans. and Ed. Matthew Spinka. New York: Columbia UP, 1966.

Phillips, John. *The Reformation of Images: Destruction of Art in England, 1535–1660.* Berkeley: U of California P, 1973.

Platina. *Lives of the Popes.* Ed. W. Benham. 2 vols. London: Griffith, Farran, Okeden, and Welsh, 1888.

Pollard, Alfred W. *A Short Title Catalogue of Books Printed in England, Scotland, and Ireland and of English Books Printed Abroad, 1475–1640.* London: Bibliographical Society, 1926.

Purkiss, Diane. *The Witch in History: Early Modern and Twentieth-Century Representations.* London and New York: Routledge, 1996.

Rabelais, François. *The Five Books of Gargantua and Pantagruel.* Trans. Jacques Le Clercq. New York: Random House, 1936.

Raemond, Florimond de. *Erreur populaire de la papesse Jane.* Lyon, 1595.

Raming, Ida. *The Exclusion of Women from the Priesthood: Divine Law or Sex Discrimination.* Trans. Norman R. Adams. Metuchen, N.J.: Scarecrow, 1976.

Ross, Trevor. "Dissolution and the Making of the English Literary Canon: The Catalogues of Leland and Bale." *Renaissance and Reformation / Renaissance et Réforme* 26.1 (1991): 57–80.

Rummel, Erika. *The Humanist-Scholastic Debate in the Renaissance and Reformation.* Cambridge: Harvard UP, 1995.

R. W. *Pope Joan: or, An Account Collected out of the Romish Authors . . .* London, 1689.

Sandys, George. *Ovid's Metamorphosis Englished: Oxford, 1632.* New York: Garland, 1976.

Saslow, James M. *Ganymede in the Renaissance: Homosexuality in Art and Society.* New Haven: Yale UP, 1986.

Saville, George, Marquis of Halifax. *Complete Works.* Ed. John Kenyon. Baltimore: Penguin, 1969.

Scarlet Beast Stripped Naked . . . Or a Brief Answer to the Popish Midwives scandalous Narrative, Intituled Mallice defeated. London, 1680.

Schaff, Philip. *The Creeds of Christendom.* 3 vols. New York: Harper, 1877.

Schedel, Hartmann. *Liber chronicarum.* Nuremberg, 1493.

Schernberg, Dietrich. *Play of Lady Jutta. Medieval German Drama: Four Plays in Translation.* Ed. and trans. Stephen K. Wright. Fairview, N.C.: Pegasus P, 2002. 159–219.

Schickel, Richard. "Two More-or-Less Liberated Ladies." Rev. of *Pope Joan,* dir. Michael Anderson. *Life* September 8, 1972: 18.

Schleiner, Winfried. "Divine Virago: Queen Elizabeth as an Amazon." *Studies in Philology* 75 (1978): 163–80.

Scholz, Piotr O. *Eunuchs and Castrati: A Cultural History.* Princeton: Markus Wiener, 2001.

Schwartz, Jerome. "Scatology and Eschatology in Gargantua's Androgyne Device." *Etudes Rabelaisiennes* 14 (1977): 265–75.

Scot, Reginald. *The Discoverie of Witchcraft.* Ed. Montague Summers. London: John Rodker, 1930; New York: Dover, 1972.

Scott, Jonathan. "England's Troubles: Exhuming the Popish Plot." *The Politics of Religion in Restoration England.* Ed. Tim Harris, Paul Seaward, and Mark Goldie. Oxford: Basil Blackwell, 1990. 107–31.

Scribner, Robert W. *For the Sake of Simple Folk: Popular Propaganda for the German Reformation.* Cambridge: Cambridge UP, 1981,

Settle, Elkanah. *The Character of a Popish Successour, and What* England *May Expect from Such a One.* London, 1681.

———. *The Female Prelate: Being the History of the Life and Death of Pope Joan, A Tragedy.* London, 1689.

Shakespeare, William. *The Complete Works.* Ed. David Bevington. 4th ed. New York: Harper Collins, 1992.

Shapiro, Barbara J. *A Culture of Fact: England 1550–1720.* Ithaca: Cornell UP, 1999.

Shapiro, James. "*The Scot's Tragedy* and the Politics of Popular Drama." *English Literary Renaissance* 23.3 (1993): 428–49.

Shorter, Edward. *A History of Women's Bodies.* New York: Basic Books, 1982.

Shuttleworth, Humphrey. *A Present for a Papist: or The Life and Death of Pope Joan.* London, 1675.

Siebert, Frederick Seaton. *Freedom of the Press in England 1476–1777: The Rise and Decline of Government Controls.* Urbana: U of Illinois P, 1952.

Silberman, Lauren. "Mythographic Interpretations of Ovid's Hermaphrodite." *Sixteenth-Century Journal* 19.4 (1988): 643–52.

Simpson, James. "Ageism: Leland, Bale, and the Laborious Start of English Literary History." *New Medieval Literatures.* Ed. Wendy Scase, Rita Copeland, and David Lawton. Oxford: Clarendon P, 1997. 213–35.

Solemn Mock Procession of the Pope Cardinalls Jesuits Fryers, &c. London 1680. London, 1680.

Solemn Mock Procession of the POPE, Cardinalls, Iesuits, Fryers, etc.; through the City of London, November 17, 1679. London, 1679.

Solemn Mock Procession of the Pope, Cardinals, Jesuits, Friars, Etc. through the City of London, November 17 1679. The Works of John Dryden, Illustrated with Notes Historical, Critical, and Explanatory. Ed. Sir Walter Scott. Rev. George Saintsbury. 18 vols. Edinburgh: William Paterson, 1883. 6: 238–40.

Southern, R. W. *Western Society and the Church in the Middle Ages.* Harmondsworth: Penguin, 1970.

Spenser, Edmund. *The Faerie Queene.* Ed. Thomas P. Roche, Jr. Harmondsworth: Penguin, 1978.

Spurr, John. *The Restoration Church of England, 1646–89.* New Haven: Yale UP, 1991.

Stewart, Alan. "'Ydolatricall Sodometrye': John Bale's Allegory." *Medieval English Theatre* 15 (1993): 3–20.

Stow, John. *A Survey of London.* Ed. Charles Lethbridge Kingsford. 2 vols. Oxford: Clarendon P, 1971.

Strick, Philip. "Harold Becker's Dream Worth Sharing." Rev. of *Pope Joan,* dir. Michael Anderson. *Times* [London] October 27, 1972: 9.

Strype, John. *Annals of the Reformation.* 4 vols. Oxford: Clarendon P, 1821.

Summers, Montague, ed. Introduction. *The Malleus maleficarum.* By Heinrich Kramer and James Sprenger. London: John Rodker, 1948; New York: Dover, 1971.

Summit, Jennifer. *Lost Property: The Woman Writer and English Literary History, 1380–1589.* Chicago: U of Chicago P, 2000.

Taylor, Gary. *Castration: An Abbreviated History of Western Manhood.* New York and London: Routledge, 2002.

Taylor, Steven M. "Martin Le Franc's Rehabilitation of Notorious Women: The Case of Pope Joan." *Fifteenth-Century Studies* 19 (1992): 261–78.

Thomas, Keith. *Religion and the Decline of Magic.* New York: Scribner, 1971.

Thompson, Ann. "Death by Water: The Originality of *Salmacis and Hermaphroditus.*" *Modern Language Quarterly* 40.2 (1979): 90–114.

Thurston, Herbert. *Pope Joan.* London: Catholic Truth Society, 1946.

Tinsley, Barbara Sher. *History and Polemics in the French Reformation: Florimond de Raemond, Defender of the Church.* Selinsgrove: Susquehanna UP, 1992.

———. "Pope Joan Polemic in Early Modern France: The Use and Disabuse of Myth." *Sixteenth-Century Journal* 18.3 (1987): 381–98.

———. "Sozzini's Ghost: Pierre Bayle and Socinian Toleration." *Journal of the History of Ideas* 57.4 (1996): 609–24.

Tiraqueau, Andre. *Opera omnia.* Francofurth, Moenum: S. Feyrabendij, 1597.

Torjesen, Karen Jo. "Martyrs, Ascetics, and Gnostics: Gender Crossing in Early Christianity." *Gender Reversals and Gender Cultures: Anthropological and Historical Perspectives.* Ed. Sabrina Petra Ramet. London: Routledge, 1996. 79–91.

Tout, Mary. "The Legend of St. Ursula and the Eleven Thousand Virgins." *Historical Essays by Members of the Owens College, Manchester, Published in Commemoration of its Jubilee (1851–1901).* Ed. T. F. Tout and James Tait. London: Longmans, 1902.

Traub, Valerie. "Prince Hal's Falstaff: Positioning Psychoanalysis and the Female Reproductive Body." *Shakespeare Quarterly* 40.1 (1989): 456–74.

Tumbleson, Raymond D. *Catholicism in the English Protestant Imagination: Nationalism, Religion, and Literature, 1660–1745.* Cambridge: Cambridge UP, 1998.

Ullmann, Liv. *Without Makeup, Liv Ullmann: A Photo-Biography.* New York: Morrow, 1979.

Vavneh, Naomi. "The Spiritual Eroticism of Leone's Hermaphrodite." *Playing with Gender: A Renaissance Pursuit.* Ed. Joan R. Brink, Maryanne C. Horowitz, and Allison P. Coudert. Urbana: U of Illinois P, 1991. 85–98.

Veith, Ilza. *Hysteria: The History of a Disease.* Chicago: U of Chicago P, 1965.

Verney, Margaret M. *Memoirs of the Verney Family.* 4 vols. London: Longmans, Green, 1892–99.

Waite, Arthur Edward. *The Book of Black Magic.* Bronx, N.Y.: Jamil Products, 1993.

Walpole, Michael. *A Treatise of Antichrist.* English Recusant Literature 1558–1640.

vol. 220. Ed. D. M. Rogers. Saint-Omer: English College P, 1613; Ilkley: Scolar P, 1974.

Walsham, Alexandra. *Church Papists: Catholicism, Conformity and Confessional Polemic in Early Modern England.* Woodbridge and Rochester: Toydell, 1993.

Warner, Marina. *Alone of All Her Sex: The Myth and the Cult of the Virgin Mary.* New York: Knopf, 1976.

———. *Joan of Arc: The Image of Female Heroism.* New York: Knopf, 1981.

Welch, J. L. "Cross-Dressing and Cross-Purposes: Gender Possibilities in the Acts of Thecla." *Gender Reversals and Gender Cultures: Anthropological and Historical Perspectives.* Ed. Sabrina Petra Ramet. London: Routledge, 1996. 66–78.

Wessley, Stephen. "The Thirteenth-Century Guglielmites: Salvation through Women." *Medieval Women.* Ed. Derek Baker. Oxford: Blackwell, 1978. 289–303.

Weyer, Johann. *Witches, Devils, and Doctors in the Renaissance: Johann Weyer,* De praestigiis daemonum. Ed. George Mora and Benjamin Kohl. Trans. John Shea. Binghamton, N.Y.: Medieval and Renaissance Texts and Studies, 1991.

White, Paul Whitfield. *Theatre and Reformation: Protestantism, Patronage, and Playing in Tudor England.* Cambridge: Cambridge UP, 1993.

Widdowes Mite, Cast into the Treasure-House of the Prerogtivues, and Prayses of our B. Lady, . . . (1619). English Recusant Literature 1558–1640. Vol. 143. Ed. D. M. Rogers. Ilkley: Scolar P, 1976.

Wilkins, Eithne. *The Rose-Garden Game: A Tradition of Beads and Flowers.* New York: Herder and Herder, 1969.

Willet, Andrew. *Synopsis Papismi, That Is, A General View of Papistrie.* London, 1614.

William of Malmesbury. *De gestus regum Anglorum.* Ed. William Stubbs. 2 vols. London: H. M. Stationary Office, 1887–89.

Williamson, J. W. *The Myth of the Conqueror: Prince Henry Stuart, a Study in 17th Century Personation.* New York: AMS, 1978.

Willis, Deborah. "The Monarch and the Sacred: Shakespeare and the Ceremony of the Healing of the King's Evil." *True Rites and Maimed Rites: Ritual and Anti-Ritual in Shakespeare and His Age.* Ed. Linda Woodbridge and Edward Berry. Urbana: U of Illinois P, 1992. 147–68.

Wilson, Adrian. "The Ceremony of Childbirth and Its Interpretation." *Women as Mothers in Pre-Industrial England: Essays in Memory of Dorothy McLaren.* Ed. Valerie Fildes. London and New York: Routledge, 1990. 68–107.

Wilson, Adrian. *The Making of the* Nuremberg Chronicle. Amsterdam: Nico Israel, 1976.

Wogan-Browne, Jocelyn, and Glyn S. Burgess. *Virgin Lives and Holy Deaths: Two Exemplary Biographies for Anglo-Norman Women.* London: J. M. Dent; Rutland, Vt.: C. E. Tuttle, 1996.

Wolf, Johann. *Lectionum memorabilium et reconditarium centenarii XVI.* 2 vols. Lavingae, 1600.

Woodbridge, Linda. *Women and the English Renaissance: Literature and the Nature of Womankind, 1540 to 1620.* Urbana: U of Illinois P, 1984.

Wright, Stephen K. "Joseph as Mother, Jutta as Pope: Gender and Transgression in Medieval German Drama." *Theatre Journal* 51.2 (1999): 149–66.

———, ed. *Medieval German Drama: Four Plays in Translation.* Fairview, N.C.: Pegasus P, 2002.

Yates, Frances A. *Astræa: The Imperial Theme in the Sixteenth Century.* London: Pimlico, 1993.

Yost, John K. "The Reformation Defense of Clerical Marriage in the Reigns of Henry VIII and Edward VI." *Church History* 50 (1981): 152–65.

Zinkeisen, F. "The Donation of Constantine as Applied by the Roman Church." *English Historical Review* 9.36 (1894): 625–32.

Index